NO SUCH THING
AS FAILURE

David Hempleman-Adams

Constable • London

CONSTABLE

First published in Great Britain in 2014 by Constable,
an imprint of Constable & Robinson

This paperback edition published in 2015 by Constable

A CIP catalogue record for this book
is available from the British Library.

ISBN 978-1-47211-304-7 (paperback)
ISBN: 978-1-47212-305-4 (ebook)

Typeset in Palatino Linotype by
TW Typesetting, Plymouth, Devon

Printed and bound in Great Britain by CPI Group (UK) Ltd,
Croydon CR0 4YY

Papers used by Constable are from well-managed forests and other responsible
sources

MIX
Paper from
responsible sources
FSC® C104740

Constable
is an imprint of
Little, Brown Book Group
Carmelite House
50 Victoria Embankment
London EC4Y 0DZ

An Hachette UK Company
www.hachette.co.uk

www.littlebrown.co.uk

'All men dream, but not equally. Those who dream by night in the dusty recesses of their minds, wake in the day to find that it was vanity: but the dreamers of the day are dangerous men, for they may act on their dreams with open eyes, to make them possible.'

– T. E. Lawrence

To the ladies of my life, Claire, Alicia, Camilla and Amelia.

Always loved and never forgotten from the four corners of the world.

Acknowledgements

I have to thank many people who have helped with making this book possible.

Andreas Campomar, who has given encouragement and direction, along with Florence Partridge, Dominic Wakeford, Charlotte Macdonald and everyone else at Constable Little Brown. My great thanks also to David Marshall, my literary agent, who took my ramblings and put them in some semblance of order and has become an expert on all things polar, mountaineering and aviation, and I gained a new friend.

Louise Johncox, who conducted some initial research and made transcripts.

To the people who wash-up behind my work to allow me to go off and do these mad adventures; in particular Nicky and Sue.

The people who have backed me in one way or another, without whose help there wouldn't be any expeditions.

Paul Strasburger, Nigel Hunton, David Newman, Bill Haynes, John Pontin, Frederik Paulsen, Larry and Lynne Tracey, Ashok Rabheru, Malcolm Walker, Bob Holt, Peter Cruddas, Stanley Fink, Peter McPhillips, Colin Fuller, Richard Matthewman, Normon Stoller, Lord Kirkham, Sir Tom Farmer, William Brake, Peter Buckley, Alan Thompson and Mike Edge.

And to all my friends and colleagues who have sweated, shivered, pulled, pushed and lost sleep on so many trips; too many to name. You know who you are. Thank you.

Preface

I'm edging my way slowly down the rock face. I can barely see with the powdered snow blowing in my eyes, and I'm continually being pelted with small bits of ice and rock falling from above. My climbing partner Steve Vincent is somewhere above me, but I can hardly see or hear him in the dark and the screaming wind. Every now and then I sense something much larger come hurtling past from the cliff above, and I know if one of those catches either of us that will be curtains, Christ help us. Suddenly there's a shout, and the next moment Steve pendulums across the face of the rock, the spikes on his crampons throwing sparks from the surface, having lost a hand or foot hold. I know his full falling weight is on the rope fastened to one piton, and if that goes he will take me with him. I hold my breath, and after what seems an age he manages to stop swinging, grasp a crack and hug himself to the bare mountainside. We're still alive, for now.

It was 1976 and we were on our third trip to the Alps. We were still really no more than boys, but we could hitchhike out there in a couple of days and spend a whole summer climbing. We were bloody fit though, and having so little money we couldn't afford cable cars so had to lug all our gear wherever we went. We'd been in the Zermatt Valley for a couple of months, doing some pretty good routes, but we'd decided we wanted to try the north face of the Weisshorn.

We weren't stupid, and obviously checked the weather forecast before we left Zermatt, but a lot can change in twenty-four hours. We'd walked up to the top hut with all our kit, ate, slept, then got up at 1:00 a.m. and trooped off along the normal path until we found the turning for a different and rarer one we'd agreed we wanted to try. Of course, in the dark we could not see any clouds that might be forming. When dawn broke we were high up, but you wouldn't have known it as a fierce electric storm came from nowhere and enveloped the mountain. With the strength of the wind and the snow being driven into our faces we knew in minutes that we must abandon any hope of reaching the summit, and our lives depended on getting down as quickly as possible. We could hear the thunder and see the lightning, which seemed incredibly close and all around us, and all our gear was buzzing from the electricity in the air.

Chunks of rock and ice were falling on us as we retreated, and pretty soon we had used up most of the kit we were carrying trying to abseil down off the mountain. Like Steve, I slipped on a couple of occasions, only to feel my fall saved by the supporting rope. We gradually inched our way down throughout the day, and by about 4:00 a.m. the next morning we finally managed to find our way off the main mountain and onto the snowy path that led back to our hut, situated on a ledge some distance away. But we were utterly done for, exhausted – we could barely stand – cold and totally dehydrated having not eaten or drunk anything in more than 27 hours. The weather was still horrendous.

Steve said he'd had enough, told me just to cut the rope that still joined us together and make my own way back if I could. 'Let me be and leave me here,' he said. For some reason I wasn't having that and began to pull on the rope, which only made him shout out that he'd fucking kill me if he could catch me, which was perhaps what I intended him to try. 'You cut the rope,' I retorted, but flicked it around to make it dance so he couldn't reach it, which only made him angrier. We staggered on another 50 yards, and suddenly saw the silhouette of our hut appear through the snowstorm. At that we both broke down in tears and hugged each other, perhaps the only time I have ever cried at the release from sheer terror as opposed to the emotional elation of achievement. Young and fit as we were, I don't think we would have survived another hour without shelter, *and I still believe that day on the Weisshorn is the closest I have ever come to dying on a mountain. At that very time the same storm was claiming the life of my friend Dave Allcock on a neighbouring peak.*

ROCK

I was born David Kim Hempleman, in Swindon, in October 1956. A rather sickly baby, I was only 2lbs at birth and am told I almost died, being given a tracheotomy in my cot and the last rites by the Catholic priest. My parents married young and I was brought up in a council house initially, until my grandfather helped us out, and I was sent to the local comprehensive school. One of my early childhood memories is of a near-miss drowning accident when I fell into a river, and I vividly recall that I kept sinking, going down and down, which terrified me. I've always been convinced that my fear of water stems from this time, and I only really learned to swim properly when I was sixteen. I am actually still not a terribly strong swimmer and my three daughters, who are all far better than me, often tease me about it.

When I was nine my parents split-up and subsequently divorced, a horribly messy business and something which in the mid-60s was still very rare and retained an element of taboo. This left me with a very stark choice for a young boy to be forced into making: should I choose to live with my father or mother? I'm frankly not now really sure how I made the decision, but partly because my father was often away on business I plumped for the latter, handing the same choice to my five-year-old brother Mark into the bargain.

* * *

We moved to a small village outside Bath and my mother soon remarried, assuming her new husband's name of Adams which of course also passed to me. It must have been around this time that people started calling me by my second Christian name, Kim, rather than my first which I shared with my father, something that a lot of my closest friends from my schooldays still do. I don't think it was a very happy time for me, and for the first year or so I deeply resented my new stepfather, for his supplanting presence rather than that I blamed him at all for my parents' divorce. This didn't last, and over time I came to respect him deeply for the way he had looked after us all, without this in any way altering my affection for my father. When I became an adult I came to the conclusion that my name should reflect both, and adopted Hempleman-Adams. This has had the unintended consequence, over the years, that many people assume I come from a rather more privileged or even aristocratic background than is actually the case, which I certainly don't.

It felt to me as if we lived in the middle of nowhere, and by the age of eleven I had already formed a deep love of the surrounding countryside where we lived and the outdoors. It was a mile's walk just to where I would catch the bus for school, and during the holidays I was allowed to work on the local farm earning extra pocket money. Not only gathering vegetables in the fields, illegal as it would no doubt be now I also drove tractors and combine harvesters. Working in all seasons, shirtsleeves during the summer or pulling sheep from snowdrifts in the raw cold of winter, wrapped up in every sweater that I owned. In the course of just a few years I had been transformed from a boy born in a railway town to a country lad, and even then I knew I would never want to live or work in the smog of a big city.

I went to Writhlington Comprehensive School just outside Bath, and it was there that my actual love affair with adventure was first kindled. There was a PE teacher called Mansel James (naturally nicknamed Jesse by us all). He was in his late thirties and he spoke with a deep Welsh accent. If for any reason you were unable actually to play sport he would still make sure you rolled the cricket pitch or whitened the batting pads, never letting you off scot-free. He was universally feared, but for some reason seemed to take an early shine to me and would sit down to chat in a way that he did with no one else. Perhaps it had something to do with my being the only kid in the school with divorced parents, which despite my mother's best attempts to hide the fact everyone naturally knew about. Anyway, it was through his guidance and encouragement that I first became involved in the Duke of Edinburgh's Award scheme, which the school eagerly offered to its pupils.

I was thirteen when I started, and a group of us were bussed out to camp in a big, old army tent in the Brecon Beacons of Wales. I'd never been on a mountain before – it was even my first time away from home by myself – and I'd never seen skies so clear, stars so apparently near and bright. I loved the untarnished beauty of the rugged terrain and I think I felt an immediate affinity with the wilderness and one's own sense of solitude when set against it. Although at the time I didn't feel that affected by my parents' divorce, I think it was probably the sense of inner tranquillity I experienced in the mountains, the stark contrast with home, that drew me so strongly. On that trip I tried my first bit of rock climbing, and loved it instantly. When the week came to an end I didn't want to go home.

By the time I was sixteen I'd been through the three levels of the Award scheme, bronze, silver and gold, which involved acquiring basic skills such as first aid, physical fitness, a hobby (I chose badminton, for some reason) and progressively tougher field expeditions, the part I enjoyed most. The first level of these saw me back in the Brecon Beacons, setting out with four companions to reach a checkpoint 30 miles away using maps and compasses. Jesse was waiting for us at the other end, but as the day wore on it became increasingly obvious that we weren't going to make the 6.00 p.m. deadline. I was determined not to fail and I must have been the strongest as well as the cockiest of our group, as I said I would go on ahead and find Jesse, and tell him the others were just a short way behind coming over the hill. I reached him in time and assumed I'd get a pat on the head for being the only one to do so, but was rapidly disabused of this idea with a clip round the ear and a strict dressing down for leaving the rest of the group behind. Either you get there as a team, he told me, or you don't get there at all. This was my first serious lesson about teamwork and it is one I have never forgotten to this day. I was a very impressionable young man and Jesse's words stuck with me, 'always bring back your dead.'

By this time I'd also been on my first school skiing trip, an activity I seemed to pick up pretty well, and had hitched my way to north Wales with a few mates in the Easter holidays, scrambling up Snowdon and some other mountains. In a short space of time mountaineering was becoming my life, and I very soon realized that I was at my happiest half-way up a mountain, something that has never changed. I also felt compelled to prove myself against increasingly stiffer climbing challenges, to show that I was as good as, if not better than, everyone else.

I lived and breathed mountaineering, devouring everything I could read on the subject. I remember going to a lecture in Bristol in 1972 delivered by members of Chris Bonington's team, who had just returned from Everest having narrowly failed to reach the summit by the difficult South-West Face. Bonington was the only really professional mountaineer around in Britain at the time, his expeditions being run in an entirely different way to those of the 1920s and 1950s that were sponsored by the Royal Geographical Society, Alpine Club and the armed services.

He certainly paved the way for the financial rewards that some mountaineers can obtain today. These were my heroes! Dougal Haston reminded me of my uncle Peter, my father's brother, and Doug Scott, with his John Lennon-style National Health glasses, his bandanna and his long hair wasn't very different to the poster of Che Guevara which, like most teenagers at the time, adorned my bedroom wall. I wanted to ask them loads of questions, but when the opportunity arose I just froze and simply thanked them for signing my poster.

One thing I remembered from the lecture, and indeed must already have known, was how the expedition used a huge number of porters to reach Base Camp, which is already higher than anywhere in the Alps. Men, women and (it seemed to me) kids, not to mention yaks and dogs, were all involved. I decided that I would write to Bonington, telling him that I was sixteen and midway through my gold Duke of Edinburgh's Award, and ask if there was any chance I could be a porter on his next expedition to the mountain, scheduled for the following year, if I paid my own way out there. I'd willingly have left home and school if it got me to Everest. He replied within a week, and although he told me that I was too young he congratulated me on what I was doing and felt sure I should hang on to my dreams. Everyone, he said, should have the equivalent of their own Everest, whatever it might be, and even in turning me down his letter gave me an incredible boost – he didn't tell me to get lost or simply ignore me. But of course it was Everest in particular that obsessed me. I knew every route on the mountain, the details of every expedition that had been made there and the name of every person who had reached the summit.

I got a place at college in Manchester to read business studies and almost at once was selected for a student exchange programme, heading off via New York City to Camp Ranger near Swan Lake in upper New York State. It hosted kids between the ages of six and seventeen, and was a school of excellence light years ahead of anything Britain could offer at the time. I was a pretty accomplished climber by now, or so I felt, and I had been chosen as the rock climbing specialist. Only seventeen myself, technically I shouldn't have been there, and was only picked when someone else dropped out and the organizers were able to sort out the insurance issues my age caused. An eighteen-year-old, and there to teach sub-aqua diving, was a guy called Steve Vincent. We hit it off almost at once, and over a burger one night we discovered we were actually both from Swindon. We spent more and more time together, driving the kids out to the Catskill mountains to learn hill and rock climbing, and when the eight-week camp was over Steve and I decided to set out for a further five weeks climbing by ourselves, first in New Paltz nearby and then further afield in Wyoming and California.

After that we were climbing partners, and the next Easter we made our first trip to the Alps. I managed to raise the £250 I needed, which seemed a lot at the time, through a rudimentary form of sponsorship. I took one of my mother's sheets and painted a red lion on it, then found ten pubs with that name in the Bath area and phoned them up, offering to give them a photograph of me holding up the sheet with their name on at the top of Mount Rosa, which at 15,000 feet is the highest in Switzerland. Each one obviously thought they were the only Red Lion referred to.

Steve and I soon found we had a deep rapport on a mountain, which meant we could understand each other even without speaking. Perhaps I had the better technical knowledge, but I think that Steve was undoubtedly the bolder climber. By the time we were twenty-two we'd climbed the Matterhorn, Mont Blanc and the Eiger, amongst many, many others. I discovered in the Alps that I had found my vocation in life, and how many people can honestly say the same thing, at that or any other age? Their sheer size, grandeur and beauty convinced me that a whole host of wonderful challenges lay ahead, and I owed it to myself to grasp this opportunity with both hands.

By 1980 I was studying in Bristol, doing an MBA at what would become Bristol Polytechnic. The academic work was hard, but it still left plenty of time for Steve and me to spend months in the Alps, to which we'd made numerous trips. I'd also been out to the Himalayas once by myself, without Steve as he'd broken his leg in an accident earning some extra cash as a dispatch rider. We'd decided we wanted a different level of challenge for that summer, and as we both loved America had set our eyes on Mount McKinley in Alaska, at 20,320 feet the highest mountain on the North American continent. I had no idea at the time, of course, that McKinley would turn out to be the first of my seven such summits.

I'd managed to scrape together £1,000 in sponsorship, and having flown to New York we then hitch-hiked from the George Washington Bridge. We were carrying a Union Jack flag and people would cross four lanes and reverse back to pick us up, and truckers would arrange lifts for 'these two Limeys' over their CB radios. All the way across the Mid-West, past Chicago and into Canada, crossing to the west coast and all the way up to Anchorage and then on to a tiny hicksville town called Talkeetna. Quite incredibly the whole journey only took us about four days. From there we flew in a Cessna light aircraft up to the McKinley base camp on the Kahiltna Glacier. There isn't much there, to be honest, apart from a shack christened the Talkeetna Hilton by the climbing fraternity, from where a meteorologist issues weather reports, but we stayed there for a week climbing around the foot of the mountain and acclimatizing until we felt we were ready. By now we were into August, which is pretty late in the season to be climbing McKinley, and apart from us there was just a Japanese team there that would be aiming at the summit.

McKinley is a beast of a mountain. Some people view it as the highest of all in some ways, since the base rises from not much more than a couple of thousand feet above sea level, whereas Everest for instance begins from the already very much higher Tibetan plateau. More importantly it is very near to the Arctic Circle, so it is a bloody cold mountain, one of the coldest on earth. It's also dangerous due to the mixture of snow and rock, with many crevasses and the constant possibility of avalanches. For both of us it was our first really big mountain, and we were obviously incredibly naïve. I thought I could recognize an avalanche path when I saw one, but the truth was that once out on the slopes we crossed several, any one of which could have swept us to our deaths. Just as with motorbike accidents, a lot of young men die because they are so inexperienced. If I was climbing McKinley again I would do things very differently. To be honest, how we got away with it is astonishing. Sometimes we were roped together, but at other times we would cross crevasses without doing this. We were very, very lucky boys to get off that mountain alive.

One night while we were in our tent we felt the ground start to shake. Steve and I sat there absolutely petrified for several minutes as this went on, trying to keep still, but as soon as the actual shaking ceased the rumbling began. Even we knew what was happening: a minor earthquake, not an infrequent event in Alaska, had set off a number of avalanches and what we could hear was the ice and snow cascading down the mountain towards us. I plucked up the courage to stick my head out of the tent, but a combination of the weather and probably the earthquake itself had brought an almost total white-out, with nothing visible more than 5 yards away. All we could do was sit there staring at each other, scared witless and mute, waiting to see if we would be eaten up by an avalanche.

The rumblings slowly seemed to die away, and through a

combination of fear and our exhaustion after our climbing efforts that day we must both have fallen asleep. When we woke in the morning and nervously crawled from our tent immensely relieved to be alive, we saw just how close we had come. An avalanche had ground to a halt no more than 50 yards away, for no reason that we could see, and had it not done so we'd have been buried with absolutely no chance of rescue, if not killed outright by being swept on down the mountainside.

After that dreadful scare we flew up the mountain, following the cane-marked route as we neared the summit, but perhaps because we were so extremely fit we were also arrogant, assuming we knew everything when we really knew very little, particularly about the dangers of altitude sickness. We'd climbed very fast, reaching the summit in only just over four days, an incredibly quick time for what we mistakenly believed was a previously unclimbed new route up the mountain, but neither of us could understand why we kept throwing up. On reaching the top we didn't feel it was a time for hanging around or emotion, so we just shook hands, took a couple of photographs and got the hell out of there. We were both scared, homesick and very tired, and the only thing on our minds was setting off back to base camp. The weather was frankly atrocious, and to be honest we shouldn't really even have been on the mountain in the first place.

It was a long way down, over several days. The closest we came to not making it was when I was out leading, trying to retrace our steps and find our tent. The weather remained ghastly and it was another white-out. The wind was howling around us and my eyelids were starting to freeze up, whilst the thick Mexican moustache that Steve had grown was crusted with ice. We wouldn't survive much longer out in the open. I was sure I knew the right way, but Steve had other ideas and told me I was wrong. 'Fucking bollocks,' I hurled back over my shoulder, probably the only angry words I've ever used to him. And since we could hardly see anything what the hell made him feel so sure? It was just his gut feeling, he couldn't explain it any more than that, but he was certain we were going in completely the wrong direction. I stared at him for some time, but he was clearly so full of conviction that I eventually decided to do it his way and we turned round and set off in the other direction. We'd only been walking a couple of minutes before we found our tent, and in my sleeping bag that night I decided that probably made us quits for our time on the Weisshorn.

Neither of us knew it at the time, but we were about to enter our last year as climbing partners before our lives went different ways. After Alaska we made our way down through the United States, climbing in the Yosemite National Park, and then on to Mexico and Central America where we scaled 19,000 foot volcanoes. We'd both now finished our studies and had little to do, wanting nothing more than to climb in the moment. Neither of us really thought much about our futures then to be honest. We kept going into South America towards the Andes, bumming our way through Ecuador, Peru, Chile and Argentina, before finally ending up in Rio de Janeiro where all our gear was promptly stolen. After managing to obtain a loan of some emergency cash from the British Consulate we learned that Ronnie Biggs could usually be found in a nearby bar, so with little better to do before our flight home we went to seek him out. The former great train robber listened stoically to our sob story, bought us a drink and sent us on our way, probably none of us appreciating the irony of our complaining bitterly about some bastard who had pinched our stuff to a far greater criminal.

We'd been away six months, and almost at once got student railcards and then managed to visit twenty-one European countries inside a week. It almost seemed as if we could have gone on in this way forever, but we were both starting to get the suspicion that we might need to start thinking about how we could earn a living. Before we considered settling down, however, we wanted one last binge, and settled on Mount Kilimanjaro in Tanzania, the highest peak in Africa. Prior to our departure though we both met the women we would end up marrying: Steve a young doctor and myself Claire, who was a first year law student at the time. I think I felt at first sight that she would be the one for me, and although I'm told she took rather more convincing we met a few more times before I left, and Claire rashly agreed to write to me at my base in Nairobi.

Perhaps getting to Kilimanjaro was harder than actually climbing the mountain itself. In August 1981 we weaved our way on various buses through Europe to Greece, Turkey, Israel and down into Egypt. At the border with north-west Sudan we found it was closed due to civil war, so had to retrace our steps to Cairo and then catch a cheap flight for Nairobi. After a simple climb up Mount Kenya we headed off towards the Tanzanian border, only to be picked up by the Tanzanian police at the foot of the mountain. We were thrown into their pretty grotty cells and not even allowed to phone the British Consulate. We had some back issues of *Playboy* which we gave them in return for some beers. I had started to have visions of them taking us round the back of the police station and blowing our heads off, but eventually they decided that the simpler course of action was just to kick us back across the border into Kenya.

Seeking a different route to our destination we took a local flight to Entebbe in Uganda, still riddled with bullets from the time in 1976 when Israeli commandos had rescued the passengers of a French airliner from hijackers belonging to the Palestinian Liberation Organization. Amazingly there was a flight leaving for Tanzania, and we could secure seats for the equivalent of about £5 each, but since the airline cashiers had no change we each accepted a bunch of bananas instead.

Kilimanjaro is a relatively straightforward and safe mountain to climb, the only real difficulty being the volcanic ash under your feet that turns it into a hard slog. You start off climbing through lush jungle with monkeys swinging from the trees above you, and as the sun rises each morning across the Masai Mara and National Park you instantly recognize that you are in the very heart of Africa. Once past 10,000 feet you rise above the tree line and enter a landscape of volcanic rock across a plateau, and it is only as you near the summit at 19,341 feet that the ice begins to appear. The main trick we found, at least so far as we were concerned, was to climb the mountain as quickly as possible, since for every day you spend on Kilimanjaro there's a fee to be paid to the Tanzanian National Park. Having next to no money, we were likely to see the inside of a police cell again unless we got up and down sharpish.

The final route to the top is marked with bamboo wands and is more of a hike than a climb. Once there we back-slapped and took more pictures, but we'd been away again the best part of two months and were desperate to get back. I think we were also both missing our new-found loves, and once home my thoughts would pretty soon be turning in an entirely new direction, one that would become a parallel obsession and dominate my life from then on.

Everest is special. Ever since June 1921, when the first British Reconnaissance Expedition approached the mountain through southern Tibet, it has become an obsession for so many people, myself included. Indeed, even before then it was so, from the mid-nineteenth century when it was established with certainty as the highest peak in the world and then given the name that has endured to this day, although many people prefer the local Tibetan Chomolungma, or 'Holy Mother'. That year men first climbed high onto its slopes, and they really were the first, since the Tibetans considered the British slightly quaint and dangerously mad. They simply could not understand why anyone would wish to risk their lives so pointlessly as they saw it, venturing into the home of a goddess and demons.

The following year, in May 1922, George Finch, while testing the use of supplementary oxygen on a mountain for the first time, attained the height of 27,300 feet, becoming the first man in history to climb above 8,000 metres into what is truly considered to be the 'Death Zone'. At the end of the next expedition, on 8 June 1924, it is quite possible – in my perhaps romantic view very likely – that George Mallory and Alexander 'Sandy' Irvine reached the summit, but they never returned and we will probably never know for certain. Finally, following the hiatus of the Second World War, having approached the mountain from the south through the now open Nepal, after the closure of Tibet in 1950 due to Chinese annexation, at 11.30 a.m. on 29 May 1953 Edmund Hillary and Tenzing Norgay achieved the summit at 29,029 feet.

I first went to Everest as a relative youngster in 1979, going out under my own steam. I had a trekking permit but couldn't afford one to climb, so was unable to join either the German or Yugoslav teams on the mountain, the only two there at the time. Things have changed so much since then. Unable to do anything else I went climbing by myself around the 18,000 foot Base Camp, heading off towards the gateway between Nepal and Tibet. Although it did not seem it I was higher than I'd ever been before and I had my first serious experience of altitude sickness, only just managing to stumble back disorientated and nauseous. I'd been very stupid going out alone and not appreciating the physical challenges at such height even just trekking, and that could easily have been the end of me then and there.

But I've reached the summit of Everest twice, in October 1993 by the now more frequently climbed southern route, the one taken by Hillary and Tenzing, and in May 2011 by the northern route followed by Mallory and Irvine. Between them, those two trips show what has changed over even such a relatively short passage of time (and what has stayed the same), as well as how very different roles and responsibilities alter how you feel and behave.

The story of my first proper expedition to the Himalayas and attempt to scale Everest began in September 1992. I was reading an article in the *Daily Telegraph* about a Venezuelan climber who had just returned from Broad Peak, an 8,000 metre mountain in the Karakorams of Pakistan. That expedition had been organised by a company called Himalayan Kingdoms, and at the bottom of the page I noticed a small advert which said they were planning to take a small group of climbers to Everest next year. I stared at this for quite some time. It was years since I'd been on a serious climbing expedition, but this was my childhood dream come back to me. The more I thought about it, the more excited I became. This might be my one and only chance to take on the world's highest mountain. I knew that to arrange my own expedition could cost up to £250,000, even assuming I could get the permits to do so. Here was the chance to do it for a tenth of the price, certainly still a lot of money but I could probably scrape it together.

For the next hour I sat in a company board meeting, but I've absolutely no idea what it was about and I know I was in a complete daze. All I could think about was Everest, and the moment the meeting was over I shot out and called the number for a Steve Bell in Bristol, who apparently ran Himalayan Kingdoms. The news was heart-breaking. Not only had all the places on the trip already been taken, but so had all the reserve slots. Maybe I'm just not very good at taking no for an answer, but in desperation I asked if I could drive over some time and buy him lunch to talk about it face to face. I know that turned out to be one of the most important lunches I've ever bought anyone in my life.

Steve couldn't offer much encouragement. Even if I could get on the trip, which as far as he could see there was no way of doing, I would certainly need to reacquaint myself with high-altitude climbing beforehand. He suggested I make a trip to the Pamirs in Russia and climb the 23,400 foot Lenin Peak. I didn't need any convincing that he was right about this, after my experiences at Everest Base Camp in 1979 and on Mount McKinley the year after. I didn't yet really understand in detail the effects of altitude sickness, or hypoxia (deficiency of oxygen reaching the body tissues), and what can be done to cope with them, and knew that if I was to have any chance of success on Everest this would be essential.

My trip to Lenin Peak never happened, as the demands of everyday life intervened. My father had been suffering from leukaemia and we all hoped that he was in remission, but suddenly the illness returned with a vengeance. On 22 October my second daughter, Camilla, was born, but later that same day my father's doctor phoned me to say his condition had deteriorated so sharply that they estimated he had only four days to live. I certainly can't imagine being confronted with more cruelly conflicting emotions in the space of barely a few hours. As soon as Claire came home with our new baby my father insisted on coming round to see his granddaughter, and that evening he somehow took my brother and me out to the pub for what would obviously be our last drink together. The talk was all of company business, pensions, wills and probate, and even if I hadn't known how near the end he was it would have been pretty obvious from the fact that he couldn't touch his beer. Two days later he was dead.

The next six months were all about family and work. Even the thought of Everest was pushed aside by the combination of grieving and giving some order to the family business, imposing a structure that would work in the years ahead after my father's death. Then in June 1993 Steve Bell phoned me out of the blue: someone had been injured and suddenly there was a vacancy on the expedition. Did I still want it? Did I hell! The only question was whether I could afford the time away. I discussed it with my brother and a fellow director, and asked them if they could cope without me if I was gone for nearly three months. As it turned out they seemed remarkably complacent about the prospect, being so kind as to add that they'd positively welcome getting rid of me for a while, so I got right back to Steve and told him I was coming before anyone changed their mind. 'Right,' he answered, 'you've got two months.'

I knew exactly what he meant by that. I reached the conclusion that with my lack of experience in recent years I should put any thought of the summit out of my mind and just treat the expedition as a training exercise, but I still had to throw myself into a concerted fitness programme, running and rowing to build my upper body strength and work on my cardiovascular system, to ensure that my heart and lungs could cope with the Himalayas. I hoped I was ready when on 8 August I drove to Heathrow to meet some of the rest of the team and catch our flight out to Nepal. I knew that at that time, by the end of 1992, only 485 climbers had reached the summit, although ten times that number had tried, and the mountain had claimed the lives of 115 of the very best in the world, including Britain's Pete Boardman and Joe Tasker. And there are so many ways to die; avalanches, crevasses, exposure, frostbite, even drowning in rivers, the dangers always increased by extreme altitude. I think any climber who looks at Everest knows that although their fate will partly depend on their skills and experience, every bit as much remains in the lap of the gods.

The whole group only came together when we arrived in Kathmandu. I soon knew that I was entirely comfortable with Steve, a former marine officer, as a superb leader with supreme organizational abilities, which is always vastly important. Not just that: unlike many in such positions on previous expeditions, he was not only a competent climber but one of the very best in the world. I won't list everyone else on the team, but they included the actor Brian Blessed, a great bear of a man (as I am sure he would be the first to admit), and Graham Hoyland (who became my close friend), a film cameraman and sound recordist who was on the trip both to climb himself and film Blessed for the BBC. The only woman there was Ginette Harrison, a doctor, who later became involved in a battle with Rebecca Stephens, the first British woman to climb Everest, as to which of them would be the first British woman to reach the summits of the highest mountains on the world's seven continents. Apart from that we had a computer operator, accountant, banker, lawyer and a professor of physics. One had been running 30 miles a day to get fit, and I suddenly felt a bit of a fraud, seeing this as a training exercise whereas for the others it was their big and possibly only chance.

The first couple of days in Kathmandu were spent sightseeing and talking incessantly about Everest as we got to know each other. Then one night as we sat in the lounge of the Summit Hotel drinking beer Steve came in looking like a ghost. Our original permit for fourteen people to reach the summit had suddenly been reduced to seven. The only solution to the problem was for half of us to claim we would in fact be climbing Lhotse, the peak adjoining Everest and at 27,940 feet the fourth highest mountain in the world, for which you take exactly the same route only diverging to the right rather than left on the South Col at 26,200 feet. Steve assured us the Nepalese had agreed that any of the Lhotse party who ended up climbing Everest could pay their peak fee retrospectively, but I think we were all still desperate to be part of the group that would be openly aiming for Everest from the outset, and by now I'd completely forgotten

19

any thoughts I might have had about my own limitations. We had to draw lots.

Some things were already determined. Steve as team leader had to be there, as must Roger Mear and Martin Barnicott, who as the most experienced climbers would act as guides. Brian also had to go, because of the BBC interest, so that only left three certain places. Ten pieces of paper went into a hat, just three of them with the capital letter 'E' scrawled on them. Two people drew blanks, then it was my turn. I thought I'd seen Steve screw one of the 'E' pieces up more tightly than the others, and when I looked into the hat there it was slightly smaller than the rest. I grabbed it and held it up, my breath in my mouth, and from the look on everyone's faces I knew I'd come up trumps. I've always been somewhat superstitious, and I started to see this as a good omen.

From Kathmandu we flew to a small village called Lukla where we met up with our Sherpas, cooks and porters, to begin the trek on foot to Base Camp nearly 100 miles away. The reason for this long trek is that first of all there is no other way of getting there, although it is now possible from the south to fly in and out by helicopter, mostly just done to evacuate casualties in medical emergencies, something the Chinese will not allow from northern Base Camp on the other side of the mountain. But the main reason is to start the process of acclimatization to the altitude, as even Base Camp at 18,000 feet is significantly higher than anywhere in the Alps. Much of the journey is through vegetation, so in that respect you might not realize how high you actually are, but you certainly feel it. If you flew straight into Base Camp you'd probably be dead within a matter of hours.

Acclimatization is a life or death necessity, because if you travel too high too fast you are bound to get altitude sickness: dizziness, headaches, exhaustion and weight loss, in the worst cases total disorientation, unconsciousness and ultimately death. The most immediate danger is the collection of fluid on the brain or in the lungs, which can kill you very quickly, but the disorientation you experience can be more than enough to do so by precipitating fatal mistakes. I'd experienced that very clearly myself just at Base Camp back in 1979, and almost as seriously on Mount McKinley. You need to climb higher slowly, allowing your body the chance to adapt itself to the decreasing levels of oxygen in the air. At Base Camp there is one third less oxygen than down in Kathmandu, so a slow trek is absolutely essential. On the summit the air only carries a third of the oxygen you would receive at sea level. How well you cope is partly down to fitness, although also dictated by the natural physiological differences between people, but with acclimatisation your blood thickens enabling it to carry more oxygen. The countervailing danger is that this thickening of the blood also means a much greater risk of heart attacks and strokes at very high altitude. Many very fit and well-acclimatized people never manage to make it beyond Base Camp, and although I had been higher I had no real idea how well I would cope.

Another advantage of the long trek to Base Camp is that you have plenty of time for getting to know your fellow climbers, and naturally start to form judgements concerning who you might want to climb with, who you would want with you in a crisis, and equally who you would not. It was already clear that some of the party were struggling, often coming in up to four hours after the rest of us, although at the time I wondered if they were simply trying to preserve their energy. In Brian Blessed we were obviously blessed with a natural raconteur who provided plenty of entertainment.

After walking through the Nepalese national park we reached Namche Bazaar, the capital of the Khumbu region. It was in the local market there that I met a former Sherpa who ran a tea shop, and also had for sale what is called a 'Z' stone, said to provide exceptional good fortune and protection to the person who carries it. I decided I wanted to buy it from him to bring me luck on the climb ahead, but not at the price he quoted of $200, then about half the average Nepalese annual wage. I don't really like haggling, particularly with someone for whom the money obviously means vastly more than it would to me, but at the same time I was unwilling to spend so much on what at the time I considered to be no more than a good luck charm. Eventually we managed to strike a deal. I would pay $50 now, and then the balance if I returned safely from the summit of Everest. We shook hands on that, and under the circumstances he wanted to wish me well. I've carried the stone with me ever since, wherever I have gone on a trip, and I think I have come genuinely to believe in its powers. If I ever lost it I would probably be seriously worried and when at home I put it away somewhere safe, just in case its luck runs out.

It was at the Thyangboche Monastery that I first caught sight of Everest's summit through the clouds. However much you have seen of the mountain on film or in photos, I don't think anything can prepare you for the reality of glimpsing it for the first time. It's an exhilarating and frightening feeling, and it makes you seem very small and insignificant in comparison. It spurs you on, but it also makes you realize what you will have to go through if you are to have any chance of getting to the top. The local lama gave us each a blessing and presented us with a piece of red string to wear around our necks, which I used to convert my 'Z' stone into a necklace.

At Pheriche it had been planned that we would stay for ten days, now at an altitude of 14,000 feet. From there the idea was that we could carry out some climbing higher up, but always returning to sleep at a lower level. You continue a similar process all the time as you move higher up the mountain. I was frankly rather surprised at how fit and strong I felt, and was even going out for morning runs, until Steve took me aside and with an arm around my shoulder advised me that I should slow down a bit, make sure I did not burn myself out before the really hard work that lay ahead.

From Pheriche we climbed to Lobuje, taking in Island Peak at 17,000 feet or so, and at something like 14,000 feet came to Gorak Shep, a handful of small huts where a few local people still live and the last inhabited area before Everest itself. Then we struck out across the Khumbu Glacier, where the terrain changes dramatically from vegetation to ice, and we left a trail of rocks behind us to mark the route should we need to retrace our steps to Gorak Shep. The fourteen of us, plus all our Sherpas who would accompany us up the mountain, our porters and a fleet of large woolly yaks carried all our equipment up across the glacier to Base Camp. It was 1 September when I reached there again for the first time in fourteen years. It seemed almost like a bustling village when we arrived, although with hindsight nothing like it would be today, since apart from us there were only two other groups on the mountain at the time, a small group of Spanish climbers from the Basque region and a military team from France.

It is here at Base Camp, 11,000 feet below the summit, that the full extent of what you are about to try and do finally strikes home. You can actually hear the mountain groaning at night, the sound of rocks and ice creaking and cracking in the wind. One of our party had to drop out at this point, and having been initially diagnosed with a virus by Ginette was picked-up by helicopter and taken to hospital, although it later transpired that he had a heart complaint. I started to share a tent with a droll New Yorker called Dave Callaway, who was a similar age to me and had been on the mountain twice before. He did have the rather disconcerting habit of suddenly shouting out 'we're all going to die!'. It was the sort of dark joke that climbers often revel in, but I did manage to convince him to stop before someone actually did kill him.

It was only now that I really began to understand the reverence with which the Sherpas regard the mountain, which even if it appears superstitious to us no sensible climber would do anything other than treat with the utmost respect. Another lama and a small entourage of monks made the climb up to Base Camp to conduct a simple but vitally important ceremony called a 'Pujah'. A wooden altar was constructed and a pole fixed in the centre, with scarves tied to the top serving as prayer flags. As the flags flap in the wind it is believed that they release prayers towards the mountain, and juniper is burnt as incense, a smell that always pervades your whole stay there. Rice is thrown in the air, and gifts are laid on the altar. It doesn't seem to matter what they are, but the intention should be that they are significant to the giver, which in our case apparently meant Marmite and a bottle of Jack Daniels.

As I've said, I do have a tendency towards superstition, but this was clearly a step further than wearing my lucky pair of socks. No Sherpa, however, would ever dream of setting foot on the mountain without first going through this ceremony, and when I saw hardened and more experienced climbers than myself throw themselves into the service, I was quick to follow. I don't know whether there are gods living above Everest, or whether the mountain is a god itself as some locals clearly believe. What I do know is that climbing Everest is a humbling experience, one that leaves you in no doubt that your fate lies in the hands of the mountain itself.

We then started to climb. The process was simple and the same as before: climb a little before returning to base, then venture a little further up before returning once more. In this way we would eventually climb to a height of just over 20,000 feet, the site of the first camp, and stay. This would then be repeated, until we felt confident that we could set out for the summit from camp four. It meant that in total we would probably climb the height of Everest three times, but it was an essential part of preparing us for the challenges of altitude and weather that we might otherwise be climbing blind. Every step from now on would be dangerous. Even tackling the Khumbu Icefall, a massive river of constantly moving ice between Base Camp and camp one, is riddled with pitfalls. The Sherpas kept constructing ladders, bridges and laying lots of ropes across a series of wide crevasses, we would follow, clipped on at all times. That way, if you fell into a crevasse, there was a chance you could be hauled out. Otherwise you and your body would disappear entirely.

Still back at Base Camp the process of bonding between us continued, although I am not entirely sure how much our probable altitude world record games of Monopoly actually helped. We also became friendlier with the Spanish team, who always welcomed us with open arms and invited us to join them for dinner. They were still enjoying meals of mussels and prawns with wine, whereas our diet of rice, pasta and chips always tasted slightly of kerosene. I'd also developed a hacking cough, especially at night, which became progressively worse even though I was plying myself with Lemsip and Tunes. Following advice on how to rid myself of a cold at 18,000 feet I was spending much of my time with my head a few inches over a steaming bowl of hot water.

On 6 September we achieved our first carry to camp one, a non-stop climb heaving around 50lbs of weight on our backs, then back again to Base Camp. We set off at 7.00 a.m. and it was imperative to return by 3.00 p.m. before the heat of the sun could vastly increase the risk of avalanches. Despite my cough I seemed to reach camp one with ease. My confidence was growing, and staring around at the inspirational scenery I felt that even getting this far was a bonus for someone who had started out initially just set on a training exercise. Three days later we moved up from Base Camp to stay at camp one.

On 12 September, after a further return to Base Camp to relax, we climbed up into the Western Cwm and carried up to camp two. Dave Callaway and myself, the two biggest men on the trip, were now beginning to understand each other as climbers. Roped together and climbing at a distance between us of about fifty feet, we were very much out there alone by ourselves in the Western Cwm, with other pairs as much as a couple of hours ahead or behind us. The entire South-West Face of Everest loomed to the side and above us, vast and foreboding. My cough now really hurt, and back down at Base Camp I was checked over by Ginette and a Spanish doctor. My chest seemed to be in constant niggling pain, which became excruciating when I actually coughed. Their joint diagnosis was that my coughing itself had led me to crack a rib, which ultimately proved to be correct. The only cure is rest, but Steve told me the choice was mine and by now the Everest bug had well and truly bitten me, so hard that I felt despite the pain only death would stop me.

On 17 September we made the big climb all the way from Base Camp up to camp two, which proved a long and hard day. On the way down we were fortunate that a couple of avalanches decided to miss us out, one party having to run like hell to avoid what Brian Blessed described as a 'white rhinoceros'. A couple of minutes later an even larger one obliterated their tracks and enveloped camp one in a heap of snow crystals.

Back at Base Camp during breakfast the next morning, a Sherpa reported that a body had just emerged from the icefall, the first we would see on this trip. It was soon clear that it was that of the Australian climber Tony Tighe, who had been killed at the top of the icefall by boulders of falling ice, or 'seracs', on Chris

Bonington's unsuccessful 1972 expedition. The corpse was still well-preserved, his clothes and parts of his equipment clearly distinguishable, and it had taken more than twenty years for the body to move down from the top of the icefall to Base Camp. It was a sobering thought that this experienced climber had died on the icefall that we were crossing every day to reach camp one and beyond, a reminder (if that was necessary) that Everest can strike at any time and takes no prisoners. This at least was a case where the remains of someone previously believed lost on the mountain forever could be returned to their family.

We carried up to camp three on 19 September. Now at nearly 24,000 feet and much of the way up the Lhotse Face, we really were climbing at high altitude. We had to use a fixed rope to negotiate an almost vertical wall of ice, but even with thick rope and crampons you are only using your front points and I could feel my calves almost bursting from the back of my legs. It was tough going, but we all wanted to prove we were up for it and would be capable of climbing all the way to the summit, and although I was still coughing I refused to allow the pain to prevent me from matching everyone else's efforts. On reaching camp three we dropped a load of oxygen bottles and made a swift return to camp two, then the next day downwards again to camp one.

Until my great hero Reinhold Messner, together with Peter Habeler, climbed Everest without supplementary oxygen in 1978 it was a huge psychological barrier, very much like the four-minute mile. People doubted their achievement, so a couple of years later Messner just went back and did it again, solo, in winter, by the harder northwest route. There will probably always be arguments about the use of oxygen and some of them are circular. In 1922, when George Finch absolutely proved the advantages it provided with his immensely faster rate of ascent compared to those climbing without its benefit, many still considered it 'unsporting', and you even see that attitude today. It almost makes you wish the mountain was five thousand feet higher, if only because then there would be no chance of reaching the top unaided. I think anyone should get there however they can, with oxygen or pulled up on fixed ropes by a guide. Each to their own.

On our climb we all planned to use oxygen. Our plan now was actually to descend all the way back to Pheriche for a few days of relaxation, as Steve felt it was crucial for us to have rest and keep our spirits up. Most of us felt ready for that, and were starting to imagine the taste of the beers that would be awaiting us. We were getting ready to leave, when two Sherpas radioed our camp to say that a huge avalanche had just wiped out camp three, sweeping away everything including all the oxygen we'd carried up there. Our relief was palpable that we had no longer been on the ice face, as it was patently clear that none of us would have survived, yet now the whole expedition seemed in jeopardy unless we wanted to attempt the summit without oxygen, which none of us considered to be an option. Steve sent a couple of Sherpas back up the mountain to try and recover any oxygen bottles they could find, and Roger Mear agreed to trek all the way back to Namche Bazaar to buy as much oxygen as he could lay his hands on.

The rest of us made our way back to Pheriche. It was good to be able to enjoy a decent meal and a hot shower, but we were all despondent and concerned that our chances of climbing Everest had been taken away from us, swept away with camp three. Roger returned a couple of days later with some more oxygen, but not quite enough for the whole party. Our original intention had been to use oxygen as we climbed from camp three to camp four, at 26,200 feet on the South Col. We would sleep, there that night using oxygen, then push for the summit and back down again to camp three the following day. At a meeting it was agreed that we would split into two teams, but none of us would be able to use oxygen until we reached camp four, except for a small amount at camp three only to sleep on.

The big question for me, and for each of us individually, was which team I would be a part of. I sought the advice of the head Sherpa, Ngatemba, who had more experience on Everest than the rest of us all put together. It all boiled down to a balance of advantages in my view. If you went in the leading team you had first use of the oxygen, which seemed a big plus. Also the Sherpas would be pushing very hard, as they'd all receive a bonus if they managed to help just one person reach the summit. After that, the number of complete ascents made no financial difference to them. The disadvantages of going first were that the lead group had to erect the tents for both teams at camp four, and set up a fixed rope from the South Summit at 28,750 feet to the Hillary Step 150 feet further up. There might also be deep snow, which would mean hard going for those leaving first but easier for others following with a track already laid. If some of the first team failed to reach the summit it could also leave additional oxygen for those coming after, which would allow them to climb at a faster rate. What swung it for me in the end was that Ngatemba said he would be going with the second team. In my view it made sense sticking close to a man who had already reached the summit once before.

There were seven climbers in the lead team, six of us in the second, plus Sherpas of course. My team included Dave Callaway, Roger Mear and Martin Barnicott. I felt the balance of strength and experience was with us, except perhaps for Brian Blessed who was also included. Our group was completed by Lee Nobmann, a Californian timber tradesman. As we made our way back up to Base Camp, excited yet fearful, we all knew that this was finally it. From now on there would be no stopping en route to the summit, if we were going to get there. I was slightly concerned about losing strength, having already dropped 20lbs in weight. Brian on the other hand had very deliberately arrived in Nepal clearly overweight, and as a result was now down to his optimum size and 'fighting weight'.

The first group departed Base Camp on 3 October, with pretty emotional farewells. None of us knew if we would ever see them again, and there were bear hugs and much back-slapping as they went on their way. More rice was thrown and we watched them into the distance until the tiny specks disappeared from view. It was eerie being left behind for the first time, and all we could talk about over dinner that night was how we felt they might be faring. We heard over the radio that they made it safely to camp two without mishap and the weather forecast looked good. All we could do was keep our fingers crossed. Our turn to move would come on 6 October.

The night before we left I walked over to say goodbye to the Spaniards, who strapped up my chest with bandaging and wished me luck. I then went and knelt down alone by the Sherpas' altar. I don't consider myself religious in any traditional sense, but I felt I was going to need a lot of help and guidance over the coming days, so I placed some rice on the altar and said a prayer. I also wrote a letter to Claire, which I'd told Steve I'd do and leave on my sleeping bag in my tent. I remember he just looked me and said, 'Ok Dave, I understand.' I didn't say much, there wasn't much to say, just that if she received this letter it meant I wasn't coming back, that I loved her and knew she would continue to look after our children. I wasn't being morbid or negative, I know other people who do the same thing, and it was something that many men did before going over the top in the Great War. It's the only time I have ever done this, but I suppose it is an indication of just how dangerous I knew the next few days would be, and maybe the pain from my ribs made me reflect even more on my actual prospects of surviving. I had every intention of returning but, as any mountaineer will tell you, each climb could be your last, particularly on Mount Everest. I was now ready to go, filled with trepidation and excitement.

Our team split into two groups, myself with Mear and Callaway. It was a long, hard day to climb from Base Camp, over the Khumbu Icefall, past the site of camp one and up the Western Cwm, finally to overnight at camp two. We woke the next morning brimming with excitement, as whilst we would be climbing to camp three we knew this was summit day for the first party. We set off early before dawn, the lights on our helmets shining brightly like miners down a coal shaft. After a couple of hours I noticed Callaway was struggling, stopping frequently and clearly suffering very badly with diarrhoea, which is something pretty vile to try and put up with on a mountainside. Dave had become a part of me over the last two months, but I was becoming frustrated with our slow going and kept thinking to myself 'Please don't fail again, Dave.'

He stopped a couple more times, then eventually untied himself from the rope, turned round, and began to walk back. I was further up the mountain and started screaming at him: 'Callaway, just make it to camp three. Callaway. Come back!' He didn't even turn his head. 'You poor bastard,' I said out loud to no one in particular. Mear, who had watched the whole episode in silence, pulled the team together and told us to carry on. In moments I was back in climbing mode again.

As we drew closer to camp three one of the first summit group suddenly descended from the heights. We all asked him if he'd reached the top, but he shook his head sadly. He'd reached the South Col before suffering from oedema – a condition characterized by an excess of watery fluid collecting in bodily tissues – which had forced him to turn back. He could see the South Summit from the South Col, but knew he couldn't carry on. It must have been a desperately difficult decision for him to make, a terribly brave one under the circumstances, but undoubtedly the right choice in the position he found himself. Climbing even a few feet higher could very easily have resulted in his death. As I watched him disappear downwards I contemplated the fact that I was hoping to reach the summit with a broken rib, whilst two of the strongest guys on the whole trip were already out of the running.

Twenty minutes later Roger Mear suddenly stopped climbing, moved to one side and sat down. At first I thought he just needed a pee, but he unclipped himself and since I was in the middle of the group came over and handed me the rope. 'I don't feel at all right. I'm having problems and I'm going down,' he said. Barnicott and Blessed were way behind us further down the mountain, which meant just myself and Nobmann were left. We were both shocked by Mear's sudden and totally unexpected departure, but felt relatively strong ourselves as we clambered into camp three late that evening.

The next morning we set off to climb up to camp four on the South Col. We were aware the first group must have reached the summit by now, or failed to do so, but we had no way of knowing which until we hopefully met them on the way down. Blessed set off like an express train this time, seemingly brimming with confidence and strength. He shot across the Lhotse Face and then the Geneva Spur towards the South Col like a man possessed. None of us could keep up with him. Midway through the day the other members of the first group started to appear. Ginette was in the pair who emerged first, jubilant at having succeeded, and I am sure we all felt the same mixture of elation and envy on their behalf. Then came Steve Bell and Graham Hoyland, who had also made it to the top, along with the Venezuelan Ramon Blanco, who at sixty had just become the oldest man thus far to do so, a record he held for a long time. They all looked pretty rough with sunken eyes, but Ramon had suffered the most and was totally shot away. He'd left us at Base Camp fighting fit, but now he looked far older than his years, dehydrated and devoid of any strength.

The final man now arrived, also having reached the summit, but for him the achievement would always be tarnished. Apparently he'd experienced problems with his oxygen and one of the Spanish climbers who was nearby had come over to help out. Just before reaching his camp that evening the Spaniard had failed to clip himself in correctly, and had fallen 4,000 feet to his death. For the man he'd assisted all the exaltation of reaching the summit had been erased by this tragedy and he was in tears. We all chatted for a few minutes but both groups were anxious to go their separate ways. It seemed now as if Everest was posting new danger signals at every turn. At 6.00 p.m. that evening we finally crawled into camp four at the South Col, a flat plateau littered with debris from previous expeditions. On the far side I could clearly see the final inhospitable slopes of the mountain, looking so close but still nearly 3,000 feet away.

As I made my way over to a tent I noticed one more body, frozen in death. He was the corpse of an Indian climber, apparently fully-preserved and half hidden behind a boulder. This and all the other bodies on the mountain will remain there for eternity, although some are subsumed within the body of its ice and snow, sometimes to be spat out many years later as with that of Tony Tighe at the bottom of the icefall. Nobody can ever bring them back down, at that altitude the task would simply be too difficult and dangerous for anyone attempting to do so. I studied them for a while, as it is almost impossible not to do, and reflected that they were probably better climbers than me. The South Col is a windy, desolate place to lie at rest, and it reminded me once again that above all I needed to remain lucky.

I did indeed feel fortunate and reassured to be sharing a tent with Ngatemba that night. The wind was whipping up and I was finding it difficult to breathe. We were aiming to set off for the summit in the early hours of the morning, but with the wind whistling louder and louder around our tents I feared that we would never be able to make the attempt. You don't sleep much at that altitude, if only from the excitement of what you are about to try and do, and it would take us a couple of hours to get ready for the final climb, so I asked Ngatemba what we should do, just as Barnicott's voice echoed across from his tent asking the same question. His view was that we should all be prepared to set off, and reassess the situation when the time came.

At 1.30 a.m. impatient with the wait and almost bursting with adrenalin, I asked whether we were going or not. Quite frankly I'd probably have stupidly headed for the summit by myself if I'd had to, but Ngatemba felt we should all go. From then on we would not be roped together but out there on our own, the four of us remaining in the group – myself, Barnicott, Nobmann and Blessed – plus Ngatemba and two other Sherpas. We were about to leave, when Blessed suddenly piped up. 'I've got a problem,' he announced. 'I've got frostbite.' We all looked and saw some on his fingers, but it's my opinion that it was his decision not to use oxygen that finished him off at this late stage. He wanted to attempt a 'pure' climb, and at that altitude had suddenly tired and burnt himself out. Barnicott offered to remain with him, but Blessed and the rest of us told him to go for the summit. Brian wished us good luck and we disappeared into the night.

The climbing became tough as it got steeper and the snow became deeper. I remembered how I'd read that Chris Bonington had struggled at this stage of the ascent, through to the South Summit. Three hours into the climb, before dawn had begun to break, something made me raise my head and my torch shone directly into the face of yet another frozen body just a couple of yards away. I will never forget it as long as I live, and this time it was very obviously a woman. Her body was upright in a sitting position leaning against her pack. Her eyes were open and her long, blonde hair was flowing out behind her. She looked almost peaceful. I later learned that this was the German climber Hannelore Schmatz who had died on the mountain in 1979, fourteen years previously. Exhausted by her climb to the summit she had stopped to bivouac as night approached, despite her Sherpa guides urging her not to do so. One of them remained with her until after she died, and as a result lost most of his fingers and toes.

As I rose higher and higher part of me was expecting to experience something almost spiritual, as Bonington described when he finally made it to the summit in 1985. I can't say I did. I didn't meet my father or see any angels, and I'm probably glad I didn't as it would have been the surest possible sign of oxygen deprivation. I saw nothing but the sun slowly appearing over Lhotse behind me. But a hundred yards from a ridge where we knew we would be picking up more oxygen I suddenly felt disorientated. I hadn't a clue what was happening to me, but Ngatemba was close by and I told him I didn't think I could make it that far. He checked the valve on my apparatus and quickly discovered that I'd been climbing for the last half hour without receiving any oxygen, because the cylinder I'd been using was only part full. I dragged my confused body up to the ridge, and my senses were soon restored when I could help myself to some much needed oxygen. We'd had so little available that throughout the climb I know I was moving on no more than one litre a minute, less than you should have, and using a much more rudimentary oxygen system than one would have today. Frankly I probably climbed virtually without oxygen, but having a mask does give you a sense of reassurance which seems to make it easier psychologically.

It was from here that Hillary and Tenzing made their final attack. The sun was now beating down, and as I climbed up a gradual ridge to the South Summit I became so unbearably hot that I tore off my fleece and left it on the ice to collect on my return. I decided to stay close by Ngatemba. Barnicott had pressed on ahead and Nobmann was not far behind us. Each step had to be taken with care. I knew climbers had died at this late stage, and when peering through the holes in the cornice, or staring at the deep, deep drop straight down the South-West Face, I could see how easily that might happen.

Looking up I saw Barney on top of Hillary's Step, beckoning me to join him. 'Come on Dave,' he shouted, 'you're nearly there!' The step is only 30 feet or so high but almost vertical, and as I reached the top he helped to haul me up. I fell to my knees and hugged him, partly because he had already reached the top but mostly because I realized that after Hillary's Step there was nothing now between myself and achieving my childhood dream. Barney said he would see me back at the South Col and shot off down the mountain, leaving me to stare up at the final hundred feet to the summit.

However long I live, whatever I do, I'll never forget that moment. At precisely 11.38 a.m. on 9 October 1993, I stood there in disbelief on the peak of Mount Everest. I'm not sure I'd ever really believed this would happen, and now here I was gazing out over the Himalayas, down to China on one side, and in the other direction way, way down south to the plains of India. I took a few deep breaths and tried to comprehend what I'd done. Bending down I dug a small hole and stuck a Twix in it for the gods, for surely they had helped me reach this point. I hope they have a sweet tooth. I also picked up an ice screw, discarded by another climber, which I thought might be a gift my old teacher Mansell James would appreciate.

I had three minutes or so there by myself before Ngatemba appeared, smiling as he reached the summit for his own second time, and moments later we were joined by an ecstatic Lee Nobmann. I had half an hour up there, and we took photos, hugged each other, fought to hold back the tears. Then it was a matter of trying to regain concentration for the descent, as I knew the lives of more climbers were claimed on the way down the mountain than going up, a mixture of exhaustion, dehydration and carelessness taking their inevitable toll. But the weather held for us and we shot down to the South Col, to be greeted by Brian Blessed who gave me a huge bear hug, which this time really did prompt the tears to flow down my cheeks. We were quick off the mark next morning, having no intention of hanging around on the mountain any longer than necessary, dashing down to camp two in a day, despite the fact that I discovered a touch of frostbite myself on my left big toe.

Back at Base Camp, into which we finally crawled at 5.00 p.m., they'd received news of our success and everyone had remained except for a couple who needed to go on to Pheriche to have their own frostbite treated. Even as we clambered down through the icefall for the last time a Sherpa tripped on a ladder, and was left hanging from a fixed rope in mid-air over a deep crevasse. It was a reminder, as we hauled him to safety, that it was never too late for the mountain to claim another victim, but also a clear example of the Sherpas' apparent frequent disregard for safety which I have never been able to understand. They would often laugh at us Westerners for always clipping-on when we crossed crevasses, even though it was clearly the only sensible thing to do. Perhaps it is just the result of their belief in Karma, if it is written that you will die on the mountain then that will happen, but it still strikes me as utterly mad. Some Sherpas can also be relatively inexperienced, since due to the financial rewards on the mountain many actually start their training there. It is also felt that Miyolangsangma, the goddess that supposedly dwells on Everest, only occasionally seeks retribution from those who trespass.

Steve Bell was there to greet us, and just kept saying 'that's brilliant'. In return I told him that, having taken sixteen people to the summit, nine of us and seven Sherpas, he'd just become one of the most successful Everest team leaders of all time. I found myself crying again, now not only because I had reached the summit but because I had also lived to tell the tale. Slipping away for a quiet moment by myself I made my way to the Pujah to express my gratitude to whoever, or whatever, had been watching over me. Then I went over to the tent where I had left my letter to Claire, and ripped the piece of paper up into tiny shreds. She wouldn't need to read it now. I'd be coming home to tell her everything myself.

It was only a week after we had both just summited the mountain from the southern route, that over a cup of tea on our way home back in Pheriche, Graham Hoyland first asked me, smiling, 'Shall we try an Everest expedition from the north side? Shall we go back to Everest one day?'

Everest has always held a magnetic pull over me. I was thirty-eight back then in 1993 and at the height of my fitness, when I was physically ambitious and my aim would always be to reach the top whatever happened. Since then Graham had returned to the mountain on nine occasions but I'd never been able to do so, since I was always working full-time or on other expeditions so could only climb in holidays when I could organize time off.

But over that cup of tea he'd planted the seed in my mind. There were several motivating forces that I found compelling. I had often wondered if I could climb the mountain from the northern and notoriously far harder side, which has all the romance of the great between the wars expeditions, when Nepal was closed and the only approach was from the north through Tibet. I'd also always had ambitions to lead a Himalayan expedition myself, such as Hunt did with Hillary and Tenzing in 1953. Now, at the age of fifty-four, I suppose perhaps I also wanted to see if I could recapture my youth. Were my climbing days over or was I still in the game? The simple fact was that I'd never climbed the North Face before and it appealed, captured my imagination more than anything else ever has, before or since.

So I was desperate to return, but this time I wouldn't be going solo. I wanted to lead a small group, including Graham who'd agreed to manage the expedition and remain at Base Camp and Advanced Base Camp in charge of the logistics. We had been firm friends ever since that expedition back in 1993 and he is one of the men I admire most in the whole world. I trusted him completely. An incredibly well-read individual who can recite long passages of poetry, he is a genuinely sensitive soul (unlike me, you might say). Everest has been a life-long obsession for Graham, throughout the many years he has worked at the BBC, and he actually played a major part in the discovery of George Mallory's body in 1999. His passion for a return to the mountain had ignited my own desire to lead such an expedition to Everest.

Over the year everything took to arrange I pulled together a diverse team of what I suppose you might call typically Alpha males, with a wide mix of experience and skills and a range of ages from thirty to sixty-five. I'm an unusual adventurer in the sense that I make my real living out of the family chemicals firm, which means I don't have to take a salary or expenses out of Cold Climates, the company through which I run these expeditions. The advantage for me is that I get a free trip through organizing it. Apart from climbing the mountain there would also be two other key objectives: to raise £1 million for Alzheimer's charities and to conduct research on the effects of altitude on the body, in order to help British and American soldiers operating in war zones at high altitudes. Because of this the Duke of Edinburgh agreed to be our patron.

I'd first met Malcolm Walker, the CEO of Iceland Foods, the

year before on a helicopter fly-in to the North Pole. After that experience he'd admitted to me his own ambition from an early age had always been to climb Everest. I said I'd be willing to take him there in 2011 and we shook hands on it on the spot. His company also ended up sponsoring the expedition. Malcolm is short and slim, and has a tendency to strut around like Napoleon. He can be a bit of a bruiser but charm the pants off you the next moment, both tight as a duck's arse and yet extraordinarily generous. I think he probably wouldn't disagree with much of this assessment of him. Malcolm's son Richard also decided to come along with his father, but although he'd achieved the Gold medal for the Duke of Edinburgh's Award neither of them had any relevant climbing experience, so we agreed that we should climb Mount Kilimanjaro as a training exercise for Everest.

Justin Packshaw, a former British army officer and businessman, had escorted my daughter Camilla on a trip to the North Pole, when she became the youngest woman ever to ski the last degree to get there. Justin was very supportive and caring towards Camilla, and I had no qualms whatsoever about adding him to the party when he agreed to come along. Graham Duff, otherwise known as Duffy, a former Red Arrows pilot, jumped at the chance as he'd missed out on the opportunity to take part in a previous Everest expedition with an RAF team. I'd first met Duffy at RAF Valley after I had helped a group from there reach the South Pole. The quid pro quo for this had been that I'd get a ride in a fast jet, and Duffy was the pilot who flew me over my house in the village of Box in Wiltshire, at such breakneck speed my eyeballs nearly popped out and my stomach did a loop the loop. Later on I was told that down below the windows shook in their frames.

Sir Charles Hobhouse, a farmer based near where I live, was up for the challenge too. He had a lot of mountaineering experience, having climbed around the world including mountains in North and South America and in the Alps. Then there was Rodney Hogg, an experienced climber who also worked at the BBC, a veteran of the South African Defence Force elite Parachute Regiment and the kind of man who actually claims to enjoy triathlons.

Rikki Hunt, an entrepreneur from the Swindon area who I have known for years, signed up to achieve a lifelong ambition; although he goes by the name of Rikki Hunt, his full name is John Richard Hunt, named after the John Hunt of Everest fame. He already had four of the seven continental summits under his belt. There was to be just one woman in the party, Gina Waggott, whose role was to look after communications at Base Camp and Advanced Base Camp. Gina also worked at the BBC and was Graham's recent and rather younger girlfriend. I called her Ginger Spice (because of her dramatic red hair naturally) and she, only half-jokingly I think, named me Old Spice in return.

Then there was Dr George Rodway who joined the trip with two aims: both to climb the mountain himself and to conduct the medical research we planned, on which he was a leading American authority. Finally there was Yorkshireman Al Hinkes, well known in British mountaineering circles as being the first British man to climb all fourteen 8,000 metre peaks in the world; he joined late in the day specifically to look after Malcolm and Richard Walker. George and Al effectively lifted a great deal of the responsibility off me from both the medical and climbing points of view, which left me free to concentrate more on the organization and planning. That made twelve of us in all.

Each member of the team had their own personal goal. Some were aiming very clearly for the summit, others targeted the North Col, some simply wanted to reach Base Camp. In many ways I felt the pressure was off me as I had reached the top before, but this time I would be leading a group and my personal aim and responsibility was to get each and everyone up (to where they wanted) and back down again safely to as close as you get to sea level in Nepal. Everyone was having to fork out about £28,000, which is a lot of money in anyone's book, more than on the average trip. Partly as a result of my previous experience on the mountain, we had made a number of decisions that made our venture more expensive. We would be employing a greater number of Sherpas than usual and would also take a lot more oxygen. After losing most of our supply in the avalanche in 1993, I'd been forced to make my ascent on little more than the equivalent of a single bottle, an experience I was determined not to repeat if I could possibly help it. Malcolm and Richard contributed considerably more as they were also paying for Al Hinkes and a dedicated Sherpa for each of them. This is extreme adventure, which people are prepared to buy; I don't feel at all uncomfortable about that. It certainly doesn't mean for a moment that it is without danger.

The men who attempted to climb Everest in the 1920s had mostly been through the experience of the Great War, which few if any of us can properly fully comprehend. In many cases they had lost almost all their friends in the trenches, and often they felt a sense of bewilderment at how they were still alive themselves. This did not mean life was cheap for them, but rather ineffably precious, yet they were prepared to sacrifice themselves for something that seemed genuinely worthwhile. Almost certainly the motives for climbing Everest from a sense of duty and nationalistic pride have diminished, but in other respects I honestly don't believe they have changed.

If you spoke to virtually any climber, when they were on the South Summit or just coming up to the top of the Third Step on the North Ridge, and said, 'look, if you carry on, there is a 50 per cent chance you won't come back', I suspect most would continue. At this point on the South Summit you can see the Hillary Step and the final summit beyond, and it's here traditionally that people have to make the decision. Am I strong enough, do I have enough oxygen, is the weather going to hold? Up to this point there has been relatively little exposure and descending should be straightforward, but after this it is different. Many decide that the answer is no and turn back, they know clearly that they should, as did Bourdillon and Evans climbing two days before Hillary and Tenzing on their same expedition in 1953. Others decide to go forward. I think I would always do so having reached this far, and that would remain the same on my second attempt, even when I had already reached the top before, and also if I try to do it again as I definitely shall. It's purely a personal achievement. I've never really done anything for a record, I've always found the record comes after. You are pushing yourself, pushing your knowledge and your equipment. The record is a secondary thing. Many people will never break a record because they don't want to push themselves, others will on a regular basis because their bottom line is further than a record. Perhaps I'll just push myself a bit further than other people when that final point to make a decision becomes clear.

Most trips have one truck up to Base Camp whereas we had four. Most expeditions take about twenty yaks to Advanced Base Camp, we had a hundred and fifty! Usually a team has just the one toilet; Malcolm wanted a toilet and shower of his own, having made it perfectly clear he didn't want to rough it any more than was strictly necessary. Some exceptionally experienced teams don't use oxygen at all, but we had so much we could have used it from take off from Heathrow.

We also had the best quality food, wines and beer, along with the most magnificent mess tent with our own chef, and Malcolm Walker had masterminded specially prepared meals with researchers at Loxton Foods. I'd found it a bit of a problem back in 1993, when I took nothing with me from the UK and ate only local food, which seemed to consist mainly of eggs

– fried, scrambled or boiled – together with the usual rice and pasta everyone ate. Perhaps it hardly mattered that much as everything tasted of the kerosene fuel used for cooking anyway. This time, thanks to Malcolm, the menu at Base Camp included wild Scottish salmon and Catalan chicken. Although this might sound decadent the aim of having genuinely appetizing meals did serve the very serious purpose of helping to stave off the weight loss that can so easily set in at extreme altitude – in 1993 I lost nearly 30lbs in total. I think it is pretty certain that no other Everest expedition has ever eaten as well as we did that time. However, I know for a fact that just because we had fantastic food and some home comforts at Base Camp, it didn't make climbing Everest any easier. When I was trying to force oxygen into my lungs as I climbed up the mountain I didn't for a moment give any thought to all that fine food. We were also all given special food bars impregnated with leucine, an amino acid that helps provide protection from the effects of altitude sickness.

Apart from good food, I knew from direct experience that the other key ingredient for a successful trip was the inclusion of experienced Sherpas. We decided to take with us ten Sherpas this time, who between them had summited a total of thirty-four times. I was delighted and thrilled that my good friend Ngatemba, with whom I had reached the top back in 1993, agreed to join us as Sirdar, the title given to the one amongst them who takes overall charge of the Sherpas. Over the years we have become solid friends, sharing a deep bond thanks to our time spent on the mountain together. Ngatemba's son, Rinchen, was responsible for overall logistics.

Technology had of course undergone a radical transformation since 1993, when we actually needed a runner to go up and down the mountain with messages. This time we had laptops and satellite phones. Such access to outside information also brings with it the ability to use much more sophisticated weather forecasting, which genuinely does mean a reduced chance of disaster. Previously climbers might be acclimatized, see no winds on top and think 'let's have a go'. But you need five reasonably clear days to reach the summit and get safely back, and people would set off and then the weather close in, which happened in 1996 as Jon Krakauer relates in his book *Into Thin Air*. Fifteen climbers died. Now there are meteorologists who will give you forecasts specifically for Everest. They know the mountain very well, have huge amounts of data for the different heights, can see in real-time what is coming in, and say if you leave at a given time you'll have no wind on the summit and reasonable weather to get down again in one piece. We also had all the high-tech clothing you can imagine, which was lighter as well as being much warmer than it used to be.

Despite all these modern innovations the one unchanging and essential item for me was my 'Z' stone, the lucky bead that I'd bought in Namche Bazaar and worn round my neck ever since. I'm genuinely convinced my lucky bead helped me reach the summit that first time. I may seem like a tough nut on the exterior, but deep down I do have an unwavering faith in something far bigger than myself, even if I'm not entirely sure what that is. I certainly wasn't going anywhere near Everest again without my lucky bead.

For any expedition it's essential if possible that the members of the team get to know one another properly before departure, and Malcolm Walker had hosted a dinner for us in London which was a good way initially to break the ice. It wasn't long before there was a real feeling of camaraderie and excitement amongst us about our forthcoming big adventure. When we flew into Kathmandu it was wonderful to see the faces of the first-timers as they absorbed the new culture, met the locals and tasted the food. The place had changed so dramatically since my first expedition there in 1979: there were far more cars on the roads and I could see a cloud of grey pollution hanging over the city. It took us over an hour to travel the one mile in from the airport. The Bagmati River was dirty. Kathmandu had become a seething, squalid mass of humanity.

We had decided to overnight in the same hotel I had stayed in for my 1993 expedition. The next morning, bags unpacked and repacked, we prepared for the first part of our journey. The porters, as usual, took our loads. What struck me at once this time was the fact that most of them carried mobile phones, which seemed an incongruous sight to me. We drove out of the city, now on paved roads that ran all the way to the Chinese border and Tibet. We set off for the village of Nyapul situated alongside the Bhotekhosi River, where we were greeted by our Sherpas for the acclimatization trek, and crossed the river via a 160-foot-high suspension footbridge. We then trekked up a trail path that led us through farms and fields of crop plantations to the village of Pangla at an altitude of 4,725 feet. In the afternoon it started to rain steadily so we hastily put up the tents.

At the end of the acclimatization trek, while waiting to go into Tibet the next day, a Sherpa rushed in to give us the terrible news that one of the trucks carrying our equipment to Base Camp had crashed, gone off the road and down a steep bank where it landed in a ravine. The truck was a complete write-off and the driver and co-driver needed to be rushed to hospital in Kathmandu. We'd been due to meet our trucks here at the border into Tibet and my immediate thought was 'This expedition is over'. Luckily, everyone pulled together and we managed to get all the equipment into another truck we were able to hire. We were in a terrible rush, as it was essential we cross the border on time since our group entry visa was only valid for one day, our entry having already been delayed whilst the Chinese kept the Tibetan border closed during a celebration of the Dalai Lama. We finally did it, but it was an utter nightmare: twelve people, ten Sherpas, unloading trucks, four lots of checks. That night I was deeply relieved that no one had been seriously injured or even killed. I began to feel it was maybe a good omen for the expedition as a whole.

If the border town of Zhang Mu was like something out of *Blade Runner*, then Nyalam was similar to *Seven Years in Tibet*. It seemed to me the big difference yet again was the sight of so many Tibetan people walking about with mobile phones. When we reached Tingri, a village 45 miles north of Everest at 14,500 feet, most of the party were given their first real taste of the dangers faced on an expedition to the mountain. A Swedish climber told us he'd been forced to retreat there after suffering from altitude sickness at Base Camp. Tingri itself is just a tiny village, with hundreds of dogs and desiccated goats hanging outside shops. We stayed in the only 'modern' hotel, which means that they had a plank and a hole for a toilet. The interior of the building was also rather interesting, the walls consisting of yak dung covered by whitewash. Malcolm Walker was none too happy: 'What have you got me into?' he complained.

Unlike Base Camp on the southern side of the mountain, where you have no alternative other than to trek in, approaching from the north a truck can take you and your equipment all the way to Base Camp just before the Rongbuk Glacier. Arriving there things got a lot worse when we met a group who'd just had the sad job of burying one of their Sherpas. Graham, our ever-practical expedition manager, decided now was the time to pose this essential question to the team: 'What shall we do with your body if you die?' I looked around at all these macho men whose faces had suddenly turned varying shades of white and ashen grey. In my own case I knew exactly what I wanted to happen in the event of my death: if possible my body should be transported home to England and buried in a box in Box, my village. My last wish: to be laid to rest in the church's graveyard.

Sadly, Everest is littered with so many corpses because of the often sheer impossibility of transporting bodies back down the mountain. Also, of course, at such altitude there is very little decay, and bodies that have been there decades look virtually as they did in life. If so inclined you can find plenty of photos that people have taken and posted online, but it is certainly not something I would ever do and most climbers strongly disapprove of this, finding it deeply repugnant. You needn't spend very long considering the feelings of those who have lost someone they knew and loved to realize how wrong this is. Everest is truly a place where people can't but help reflect on the meaning of life and death, but this macabre voyeurism just isn't necessary or right.

At Base Camp, we took part in the traditional Pujah ceremony with our Sherpas, which for me will always be an essential part of any Everest expedition and which gives me an added inner strength. The essential key to success when climbing on a mountain like Everest is to stay both mentally strong and bodily healthy, and in my view the spiritual dimension always goes hand in hand with the physical. When you climb in any developing country such as Tibet there is an ever-present range of illnesses, such as respiratory infections or stomach upsets, that can totally sideline your plans, but I felt as a team we'd had a good acclimatization trek which greatly reduced the chances of altitude sickness, and when we arrived in Base Camp at over 17,000 feet everyone felt well. We then took day trips, 1,000 to 2,000 feet higher each time, and returned to Base Camp. Over the course of the next two weeks we started moving the 18 miles up to Advanced Base Camp, at almost 21,000 feet and as far as the yaks could carry our equipment, where we spent three days and did some ladder work on the ice. From there the process was repeated, climbing up to our camp one on the North Col in increasingly lengthened stages, then always back down to Advanced Base Camp.

Early on during our planning it was decided that Al Hinkes would lead Malcolm and Richard Walker only as far as the North Col at 23,000 feet. The Walkers did incredibly well for people with so little experience, and once they had achieved this goal the three of them decided it was right to stick with their initial decision to turn back and head for home. I actually think that Richard was the fittest person in our entire party and I'm certain he would have made it all the way to the top. I even sat down with him and made a serious attempt at convincing him to stick around and have a go. The deciding factor against that in his case was probably his wife's announcement, the night before he flew out to Nepal, that she was expecting another baby, their second child. For him, in his circumstances at that time, it was the right decision and everyone ultimately has to make that for themselves.

It was around this time that we heard some American climbers had put up 'Free Tibet' flags near Rongbuk Monastery, so the Chinese immediately stopped anyone from travelling to and from Base Camp. The Walkers managed to get out just in the nick of time before this happened, but the artist Alan Cotton who I had invited along as the expedition painter was stopped and sent back to the Chinese border. I was extremely disappointed about this, but as I was up on the mountain there was absolutely nothing I could do, other than pass on the message that I hoped I would return with him again one day, which happily I have since done on a brief non-summit attempt trip.

At the North Col the whole team shared our big Marmot tent and everyone was doing well it seemed. It is amazing, though, how swiftly a situation can change on Everest depending on the weather, health and fitness. Amusingly, Dr Rodway had brought along a supply of Viagra with him, which mountaineers quite often now take at very great heights. He told us, 'Some people at altitude simply run out of juice: they have no energy and Viagra can help dilate blood vessels in the lungs, improve blood flow and expose the body to more oxygen.' I won't share with you who agreed to take the Viagra but, suffice to say, we all needed a bit of an energy boost. I didn't myself, however, since when George explained the other side effects (some of them obvious I suppose, like having to force down a raging erection when you are trying to climb, others less so such as an increased risk of heart attack and stroke), I decided on balance to do without.

Having pushed further up, we then returned back down to the North Col and the Advanced Base Camp for a rest. At Advanced Base Camp we waited patiently for the weather men to give us the go ahead to start the climb to the summit proper. This time was interspersed with celebrating the marriage of William and Catherine with good old Sherpa tea. The weather slot came, we all said our goodbyes and steadily trudged off towards the North Col again. We set up camp two, situated in a precarious position high on a steep ridge. Our three tents were roped together into the rock face and the noise of the wind was truly deafening. My biggest fear was that if one person rolled over in the night they could take all the rest of us with them.

En route to camp three Charlie, Rikki and George all suffered from various illnesses forcing them to descend. Charlie had heatstroke (yes, that can happen too on a mountain!), exhaustion and a bad stomach which left him bent double in agony. He was gutted, but there was absolutely no alternative. George felt unwell with bronchitis and a bad cough. Rikki also suffered from bronchitis and had altitude sickness. It was very sad to see them go but it was the only sensible thing to do. I was responsible for getting them down alive and wasn't prepared to take any unnecessary risks. But even if the final say would have been mine, in my experience people always know when they have pushed themselves as far as they can and should go no further, you never have to tell them, so in each case it was their own decision. This left just four of us, along with our loyal Sherpas.

We continued up to camp three where we set up our tents at 3.00 p.m., as the sun goes down there at about 6.00 p.m. I sipped on a small cup of tea and had some noodles. It's very difficult to eat at such a time, as you almost invariably tend to lose your appetite at such altitude and with the inevitable nerves you feel, but more importantly I had started to realize a very serious mistake I had made in our planning, as we didn't really have anything like enough liquid with us to prevent dehydration. We were going to keep going however. At 8.00 p.m. that night we started getting ready for the final summit push. With our head torches radiating before us and oxygen masks on our faces we set off at about 9.00 p.m. We were lucky that there was barely any wind and in the distance I could just make out a line of lights. There was a full moon shining down on us highlighting the contours of the mountain.

We made our way up the North Ridge, which has spectacular drops on either side. Our journey to the First Step was very slow. There was a man from another party who couldn't use crampons properly, which held everyone up. Duffy clipped himself off the rope and trudged slowly past him. I then asked the man if he'd mind and I did the same. On the ridge we saw two dead bodies, always a sobering sight. Duffy powered ahead up the mountain with Justin and Rod, whilst I was at the back with Ngatemba going at our own slower pace. I actually thought I felt better than I'd done on my first summit attempt, maybe partly because psychologically in a sense this time around I didn't give a monkeys as I'd already reached the summit before, but also because I was obviously now climbing on a far greater flow of oxygen than I had done back then.

We slowly arrived at the infamous Second Step, vertical with a 4,000 foot fall straight down the North Face. This may sound terrifying, and I suppose it is, but in truth you don't actually notice the drop because you are so focused on just putting one foot laboriously in front of the other. The notorious aluminium ladder was bolted here in 1975 and looks like it could easily have been bought from B & Q. The ladder transforms this part of the climb from a desperately scary challenge into something that is achievable for most serious climbers. At the ladder I took a little time to look around me to the left.

People will probably always wonder if Mallory and Irvine reached the summit, but most likely we will never know for certain. It has been proven that the Second Step is possible without the ladder fixed there now, but could they have overcome that obstacle? They were going strong, young and fit, certainly determined, and Noel Odell honestly believed he saw them from the North Col, through the clouds and pushing on above the second step. Beyond there it is really just a plod with no further serious problems for experienced climbers. I personally think they could have done it. Mallory had said that he would leave a photo of his wife he had brought with him on the summit, but that was not on his body when it was finally found in 1999, and nor was his camera. We know how stupendously forgetful he could be, and perhaps he lost or left behind either or both, as almost incredibly he did his torch in their final bivouac. Maybe only if we found that pocket camera, as people are trying to do, and any picture they might have taken at the summit could be developed, as we are assured it still possibly could be, will we ever know for sure. As I approached the ladder myself I thought that it was certainly conceivable they could have achieved this feat.

When we reached the Third Step there were three more dead bodies. I blanched at the sight of two booted feet sticking out of a snow-filled crack. People often ask me, perhaps more frequently than about anything else, how I feel when walking past dead bodies on Everest, and each one reminds me of the grim dangers of the mountain. At that height and altitude it's impossible to carry the bodies down without risking your own life. Since the first recorded deaths on Everest in 1922, about 260 people have now died on the mountain and about 150 bodies still remain there in a shockingly preserved state. From time to time the Chinese push some of the bodies over the precipice. My personal feeling is simply that each body is someone's relative. I'm sure their loved ones take solace from the thought that they died in a beautiful place doing what they desired most. Yes, I keep telling myself that.

Rod had known one of the English climbers who'd died there the year before and was pretty certain his was one of the bodies, so he left a letter from the man's relatives with the corpse. Whenever I came to a body I always stopped and bowed my head for a minute out of respect, and not just to get my breath back. This time, as leader of the expedition, I was acutely conscious that the safety of my team was my absolute priority. If I had noticed anyone struggling I wouldn't have hesitated for a moment in helping them and if necessary turning back myself to do so, and I dearly hope I'd do just the same to assist someone I didn't know. I don't frankly know how anyone could come across a stricken climber and just walk past. I'm 'old school', and in such a situation I'd call up all my Sherpas, offer them my oxygen, and do all I could to try and help them down. I for one would never be able to live with myself otherwise. Each of us needs to try and remember 'there, but for the grace of God, go I.' Even if we all should know the dangers and accept the risks, accidents can happen to anyone and you always hope one of your mates would help you down.

The debate surrounding the ethics of climbing has raged for many years, and probably always will, with the Alpine Club even attempting to codify it through their 'Spirit of Mountaineering' initiative. As their former president Doug Scott argued, there can be no 'morality-free zone' in climbing. Inevitably the issues may seem more complex on the highest and most remote mountains, particularly on Everest where there are so many part-time climbers who have saved for years to be there. It can be easy to lose patience with or lack sympathy for those apparently too inexperienced or ill-equipped to be there, perhaps putting other people at risk. None of this should make any difference, but there are too many well-documented cases of climbers walking past others struggling or dying, caught up in their own 'summit fever' and tunnel vision fixation to reach the top. It can be all too possible to tell yourself I'll try and offer assistance on the way down, when it might be far too late. Climbing Everest has become a form of extreme tourism for people with a lot of money and sometimes rather less care for human life.

At 5.00 a.m. the first small glimmers of sunrise appeared and, despite the exhaustion, I felt my spirits lift as the sun slowly rose above the horizon. At this point, the climb got steep again and I had to call on all my reserves of energy. There was one remaining shelf to ascend, which is just rock without snow. It is hard enough technically and I felt drained with each step. After a right turn I saw the summit ahead of me, a sight which took my breath away even more than last time, if that is possible. My next view was of Duffy, Justin and Rod coming down, having successfully reached the top. I felt great relief and excitement for them and then slowly trudged on up with Ngatemba. I had one more hour of gasping on a steep slope ahead of me before I could hope to be there myself.

On that perfect day we were by no means the only party on the mountain, and just before the top I held back to allow a couple of climbers already there time to enjoy their moment of silent privacy. After a while though, since they showed no inclination to get a move on and offer us our own turn, I thought 'bugger that' and climbed the last few steps. Reaching the summit of

Everest for the second time at about 8.00 a.m. on 21 May 2011, I felt utterly elated. It was a crisp, still morning and the sun was shining. Ngatemba and I took our photograph together as we clung on to each other, and I thanked him for helping me reach the top again. I even managed to take off my oxygen mask for the photograph this time, something I hadn't felt able to do back in 1993. Ha! Standing there holding the Explorers' Club flag, the wrong way around as I was later embarrassed to see in the pictures when I got home, I felt the whole gamut of emotions: relief, happiness, exhaustion. I gazed around at the vast expanse of sky and mountaintops. The top of the world!

That feeling of elation on reaching the top didn't last long. I knew I was dangerously dehydrated, as I'd had nothing to drink since that small cup of tea nearly twenty-four hours earlier. As we turned to descend I gasped for water, yet we had absolutely nothing to drink. My legs felt heavy, I struggled to breathe and it was now bitterly cold. The surge of adrenaline you feel on reaching the summit had already worn off. Heading back down, oxygen mask firmly in place, I had to face looking over the 4,000 foot vertical cliff at the second step. I knew that most accidents and deaths occur on the way down the mountain. I had told the team to be even more careful on the descent and now I heard my own words ringing in my ears.

After a painfully slow trek we reached camp three, where we discovered that the Sherpas had taken down our tents. Duffy, Justin and Rod had already descended, but I was certain that without any liquid it would be dangerous for me to keep going. I spotted a tent owned by Seven Summits, so I asked someone if I could take shelter in there. I crawled inside and sat there in a passive state, almost semi-comatose. There were no thermarests and I had no sleeping bag with me, I was exhausted, desperately thirsty and entirely fit for nothing. I tried to massage my foot as I had a little frostbite on one of my toes. The wind was back with a vengeance and I knew that a major storm must be on its way. I had never experienced such strong winds on Everest and I began to wonder whether this time I might have pushed myself too far. I was stuck at 27,000 feet in the 'Death Zone', which refers to altitudes above a certain point where there is insufficient oxygen to sustain human life for any length of time, even without the rigours of climbing. This height is tagged at 8,000 metres or 26,000 feet. At this level the body deteriorates fast, leading to loss of awareness and, ultimately, death.

I slipped in and out of sleep and consciousness, shivering in the freezing −40°C temperature. In the middle of this dreamlike state a man with a beard opened the zip and asked if he could come inside. 'You can come in so long as you keep the fire going,' I said. 'Of course, I can help keep the fire going', he replied with a French accent. He seemed to talk a lot whilst all I wanted to do was sleep, but I knew I must stay awake and keep moving my fingers and toes. My body was weak and fast deteriorating. The Frenchman had a Thuraya satellite phone, and I know I vividly remember that the blue screensaver light kept coming on. The fire wasn't very good, so I said to my new companion, who I called Mr Thuraya: 'If you don't put wood on that fire you will have to leave.' Shortly afterwards the fire went out and I said to Mr Thuraya, 'I'm afraid you are going to have to leave the tent.' He didn't make any fuss, simply nodded and walked out. I assumed he'd gone to one of the other tents nearby.

In the morning I found I was still alive, and began making ready to leave at first light. I felt horribly guilty that I had kicked someone out in the middle of the night into the freezing cold, so I went from tent to tent in search of Mr Thuraya to offer my apologies. I tried in three tents but could not find him anywhere. Ngatemba had slept in a tent nearby. When I mentioned my French visitor to him he smiled and shook his head, looking at me as if I was mad. There had been no one else in the tent, he told me, and no Frenchman nearby. I was too exhausted to understand then that I had just suffered from a classic case of 'The Third Man' syndrome in the 'Death Zone'. The mountain had come very close to claiming me. It was time to descend into the unknown, hoping to escape beyond that.

When I reached the North Col I finally got something to drink, brought up by the Sherpas, and guzzled down as much as I could giving strength to my parched body. Realizing everyone was there in one piece I felt a huge sense of pride that I had managed to bring everyone up and down safely; we'd got four group members and seven Sherpas onto the summit, a fantastic achievement. When we finally reached the bottom of the North Col we arrived at a place called Crampon Point, where you take your crampons off. Charlie turned up with juice and chocolate, gave me a great big hug, then took my rucksack and helped Ngatemba and me back down. This was the most considerate and gentlemanly act, and my god I needed it!

On finally reaching Base Camp I explained the incident with Mr Thuraya to Dr George Rodway, who said I'd clearly been hallucinating. People under immense stress often experience 'The Third Man' syndrome, he told me. I was deeply embarrassed but now accepted that this was what must have happened. There had been no Mr Thuraya in my tent, just as there had been no fire and certainly no wood to put on it high up on Everest. Despite all the restaurant grade food still available all I wanted to eat was egg and chips, which the Sherpas made for us. A glass of beer sealed the celebration. More soberingly I also learned at Base Camp that, at the same time as we'd been on the mountain, an Irishman struggling to descend became a fifth body on the ridge. We had met him a couple of times. The press reported that he'd died alone without anyone to help him down, which is incredibly sad. This was yet another reminder, if one was needed, of how close to death I had come.

My most emotional experience of the expedition came when I returned to the Rombuk Monastery, which is the highest in the world. I had been there on 11 September 2001, when I was planning to fly a balloon over Everest. However, this expedition ended abruptly when those two planes flew into the Twin Towers. All air space over Everest was closed immediately and the expedition cancelled. Returning to the monastery in 2011 brought back memories of unfinished business, as well as deep sadness over so many deaths. That remains the only expedition on which I've failed where I haven't attempted to repeat it. Normally I am determined to go back and try once more, but I made a decision never again to attempt that flight over Everest, as the omens were so bad and there was so much death and sorrow.

We got a lift back to Kathmandu in a van, but were held up overnight at the Chinese border when we missed its closing by just a few minutes. The only rooms we could get in the tiny town there were so vile I slept the night in my clothes, and twelve of our poor Sherpas were crammed into one room. On crossing the border we stopped for a beer at the Eco Lodge before making our way straight to the Hyatt Hotel, the epitome of luxury in the relative terms of Kathmandu. It felt like a strange juxtaposition. We'd been used to sleeping in tents, now we were in a five star hotel. Those of us who had successfully gained the summit shared an inner warmth, but I felt dreadfully sorry for the others who hadn't made it to the top. Everyone copes differently with failure, and they all failed for different reasons, mostly medical. For most people though, Everest is all about either success or failure. Although I've now succeeded twice, Everest will always retain its magnetic hold over me. It's still the highest mountain in the world and I'd love the chance to go back for a third time.

No one 'owns' Everest. Access to the mountain must be democratic and you can't close it, although of course in terms of physical access the Chinese can and sometimes do. It would be deeply hypocritical for me to suggest you should, having climbed it twice myself, been thrilled by the experience, encouraged others to do the same and, indeed, taken them there on trips when they have paid a great deal of money to have that opportunity. For any experienced climber or thrill-seeker it will always be the one thing they want to do. Even the veteran and professional mountaineer Chris Bonington returned and did it by the 'tourist' route, finally to make it to the top. You have to do it by any means.

All the same, there clearly does come a point where you saturate the mountain, as we all saw with pictures in 2013 of bottlenecks on the fixed ropes with climbers waiting to go up and down, the additional time spent only adding to the existing dangers. And the numbers have changed dramatically. Before I went to Everest in 1993, only 485 had reached the summit and 115 of those had died, the number today is more than 4,000 with somewhat more than twice the number of deaths, a tenfold increase in twenty years on the number that achieved the summit in the forty years after it was first climbed. As I write, the number of successful summit attempts actually stands at 6,854, so quite a few of those will be people like me who have been there more than once, and in some cases Sherpas who have done so multiple times. But the Sherpas themselves can be most at risk, as we saw in April 2014 with the death of 16 of their number in a massive avalanche, leading to all climbing being halted for the season from the Nepalese side of the mountain, although the usual fewer climbers will be attempting to do so from the harder Tibetan side.

When we were there in 1993 there were only three teams on the mountain, ourselves, the Spanish and French teams, and not many fixed ropes at all; we only had them going up through the Khumbu and on the Lhotse face. Things are very different now, and Base Camp can seem like a sprawling village. And with a hundred people climbing the mountain you get a huge amount of human waste since people are inevitably forced to stop and defecate where they are, often suffering from bad diarrhoea, not to mention all the other rubbish, although people are now getting much better at bringing the latter down. On my 2011 expedition I paid the Sherpas to collect and bring down any of our gear that they could, part of the deal being that they would keep anything that they found.

There must ultimately be something done to limit the quantity of people on the mountain and a ballot of some sort might be the answer. If the numbers were limited to, say, a hundred on each of the two main routes, but very experienced climbers were allowed to climb other non-standard routes or outside the optimal weather window in May, that could be the way forward. You only get between two and four perfect weather days a year, which is when the real problems occur. Post-monsoon, in August and September, it is colder and there's more snow, and there is less chance of an open weather window. I would never denigrate anyone who is prepared to face the huge challenges involved in reaching the summit, but a way must be found to protect the mountain, whilst also allowing 'ordinary' climbers a chance to climb it. At the same time, there will always be those that have honed their skills over many years who are prepared to face the greater risks involved in tackling more extreme routes, in harsher conditions, to test themselves in one of the world's ultimate challenges.

When I returned home in late October 1993 it was back into the daily grind of the office, not the easiest of changes after what I'd just experienced. My brother and fellow directors might have been happy to see me disappear for three months, but now it was my turn to pick up some of that load and give them a bit of a breather. I hadn't any real idea what I wanted to do next, and having reached the summit of Everest it's easy to feel that there's not much left to do in mountaineering. I'd missed my normal climbing sorties away with my friends, due to Everest and then my commitments at work, but it was them who dragged me back to the mountains with my success only having whetted their own appetites. For August the following year they suggested another trip, and my ears pricked up.

We'd picked Mount Elbrus in southern Russia, in the Caucasus Mountains between the Black and Caspian seas, the very south-eastern corner of Europe, if only because at 18,510 feet it is the highest mountain in Europe. It is nearly 3,000 feet higher than Mont Blanc, the European peak most climbers had to consider the highest challenge in practical terms so long as Elbrus remained inaccessible before the fall of the Berlin Wall. But Russia was changing fast after the collapse of the former Soviet Union, and the private hotel we stayed in at the foot of Elbrus's twin extinct volcanic peaks had once been Leonid Brezhnev's dacha. Elbrus is not tall in absolute terms but you still need acclimatization, and I couldn't suppress a surge of pride when our Russian guide asked us how high we'd actually been before. 14,000 feet, 18,000, 16,000, 10,000 came the answers, before it was my turn and I was able to claim 29,029 feet. Our guide, who bore a remarkable resemblance to Sylvester Stallone, just looked me in the eye for a few moments then shook my hand vigorously, but his attitude towards us as a party noticeably changed from then on. If I'd done what I claimed – and I think most climbers acquire an uncanny sixth sense of knowing immediately if people are fibbing – and I was happy to be climbing with these guys, then he knew we'd be all right.

Six days after leaving Heathrow we were up in the Pruitt Refuge on the side of the mountain, a large aluminium hut that stank of vomit and petrol fumes. The former could have been down to people suffering from nausea due to altitude sickness, but we'd seen so much vodka drunk in the previous few days that there was perhaps a different explanation. It wasn't easy sleeping there overnight, so we were more than happy to get outside the next day for a further acclimatization climb and then early the next morning set off for the summit. It was a truly beautiful night, and the stars that brightly lit the sky seemed close enough to touch. There was no need for us to be roped together as it was a fairly straight climb with crampons, but reaching any snowcapped peak is always special and I knew just how it felt for my friends, who I'd brought higher than they'd ever been in their lives without being buckled into a seat on an aeroplane.

By this time I was already planning a trip to the Antarctic on which Roger Mear had asked me to join him, so just a few months later in December 1994 we decided to head down there and test out our gear, taking in the highest peak on the continent, Mount Vinson, in the process. Towards the South American side of Antarctica in the Ellesworth Mountains and rising to 16,050 feet, Vinson is probably the coldest mountain on earth with many crevasses, and due to the extreme conditions and cost of mounting an expedition there it had been climbed by fewer than a hundred people at the time. A Twin Otter plane landed us on a glacier at base camp, and at 10,000 feet the temperature was already –20°C.

We had a horrible time initially heading up the mountain. Wearing skis and roped up ahead of Roger, I kept finding myself sinking three inches into the ice as the whole area around me seemed to be imploding. These were new conditions for me and I was continuously convinced I was about to fall into a crevasse, until I eventually became a bit more used to the going. We then had to sit out a storm for forty-eight hours, the total white-out leaving us imprisoned in our tent, an experimental one designed by Reinhold Messner. The black lining in theory made the inside warmer and helped with sleeping in the twenty-four hour sunshine of the polar summer, but conversely the total darkness over several days was claustrophobic. At that altitude and temperature you also lose liquid simply by breathing, and I was becoming terribly dehydrated.

On the night of 21 December we noticed that the barometer was finally changing for the better, so we packed up our gear and burst out of our tent, walking straight into the mouth of a still raging storm. Visibility was no more than 20 metres and the wind-chill factor must have reduced the temperature to −70°C, but we were there specifically to test ourselves in such conditions, so whereas most climbers would probably have stayed put it seemed appropriate to sample some of it now. I was suffering from terrible stomach cramps and in my dehydrated condition found the going very tough, but I was determined I would crawl to the top if necessary as there was no way I was ever coming back down to Vinson to attempt it again. It was now or never. Climbing over a cornice I suddenly saw a ski pole sticking out of the ice, and realised this marked the summit. We both felt this seemed to desecrate a totally unspoilt and secluded part of the world, but when we tried to pull it from the ice, Excalibur-like, neither of us had the strength to do so. It is probably still there.

Before then I'd really had no thought of attempting to climb all seven continental summits, but on our way down Roger and I had stopped off in Argentina and decided we'd have a crack at Aconcagua in the Andes (as you do!), the highest mountain in South America. That part of our trip was a bit of a disaster, a dreadful failure of preparation, since even a few days before we left for Santiago in Chile I found that some of my clothes (which had just turned up) were so small I couldn't even pull up the zip. When we got to the mountain the weather was ghastly, but we were pushing on about 4,000 feet below the 22,837 foot summit because we felt we had little choice. Our food supplies were all but gone, it was bitterly cold and our equipment was inadequate, yet I still felt we had a good chance of reaching the top and was willing to give it a good go. All of a sudden Roger announced, 'well, I don't know about you, but I think we should go down.'

It was on this trip before Aconcagua however, on the border between Chile and Argentina, that I first met Rebecca Stephens, there on a top-secret climb as part of her seven-summits race with Ginette Harrison. She asked me if I was setting out to do the same, and when I replied that the idea had really never crossed my mind her response was, 'well, you've done the hardest, Everest, so you might as well finish them off.' She was right of course, and her words started the old heart thumping again.

With five summits now notched on my bedpost Aconcagua still had to be next and I turned to my old friend Neill Williams, with whom I'd previously been to the Arctic and Elbrus. I took him out for dinner on a Tuesday night in February 1995, and four beers later he'd agreed to leave with me that same Friday, our plan being to complete the whole trip in a fortnight before the southern hemisphere summer came to an end and it began getting a little cold. With our job commitments and the season we intended to be up and down the mountain as quickly as possible, and back behind our desks within twelve days.

Arriving in Santiago on the Saturday morning we stocked up with decent food and fuel then made the three-hour bus journey to Punta de l'Inca on the Argentinian border. Four months earlier this area had been covered with snow, but now it was green, lush and beautifully warm. Over the next two days we trekked the 40 miles to Aconcagua base camp at 10,000 feet, the walk serving as our acclimatization process, local gauchos carrying our kit on their mules. Here we found ourselves mingling with climbers from all over the world, and met a couple of young Americans who reminded me vividly of Steve and myself back on McKinley. Like us then they were raring to go and blissfully unaware of the dangers in haste and altitude, leaving Neill and me feeling like old men as we explained how we'd be plodding up the mountain and taking it easy. Or not so easy, if we would be doing the hard load carry the next morning, taking most of our gear up to the Condor's Nest at 16,000 feet, then a couple of days later up to the 18,500 foot Berlin Hut. By now the Americans had joined us, although the initial hares were now moving at a snail's speed and us two old tortoises were out-pacing them. More experienced mountaineers having given me their time and help when I was younger, I felt I couldn't fail to do the same in return for others now.

We left for the summit at 2.00 a.m., when the ice was nice and crisp, intending to have enough time to reach the top and descend again by late afternoon. Aconcagua may not be the most dangerous of mountains, but two Koreans had still died of exposure there the previous week and the Argentinian military were out in force trying to locate the bodies. By mid-morning we had left the youngsters well behind, and compared to the conditions on Vinson this seemed an easy ascent, even if the strain and sweat of the hard climb left me breathless and Neill, who had gone off like a rocket, reached the top fifteen minutes before me. This time we found a simple wooden cross, which seemed far more fitting as we gazed away across the Andes and down towards the planes of Argentina.

An hour into our descent we met one of the lads, finding the going tough yet clearly still strong enough to reach the top, but it wasn't until two hours later and well on our way back to the Berlin Hut that we met the other. He didn't look good to me and by then time was running out for him, so I advised him to turn around and try again another day. He was having none of it however, if only that in his debilitated state he felt this must be his sole attempt, so I reluctantly saw him on his way having lent him my sunglasses, as he'd lost his when he slipped and they tumbled off down the mountainside. I didn't regret my gesture, knowing the young man needed all the help he could get, but was quickly confirmed in my suspicion that a baseball cap pulled down over my eyes would prove inadequate protection from the sun when I rapidly experienced snow blindness. Neill literally had to lead me down the mountain with his ski pole and it was getting dark by the time we returned to the Berlin Hut. Had I been so benevolent on Everest I'd be dead by now, and I should have made more effort to convince the young American to turn back.

I wasn't too scared about my snow blindness, since I know the condition is always temporary, and after a hard day's climbing both Neill and I needed a good night's sleep, but we were worried sick about the boys. It was now pitch black outside, and in the state we knew at least one of them was in we were sure they would struggle to descend and find the hut again. Every ten minutes we'd go outside and flash our head torches up the mountain, and make a noise banging some cooking pans. They'd been climbing for so long that surely their own head torches would have given out by now. We were desperately trying to stay awake and it was only after midnight, by which time my blindness was beginning to ease, when we were starting to give up on the lads that we heard a joyful shout. Shining our lights up the mountain we saw the two of them, waving their arms about a quarter of a mile or so away. They were both in tears when they finally reached the hut, hugging us and thanking us incessantly. Had they come to harm it would certainly have marred our whole trip and in some ways it was more satisfying to have helped them and seen them back safely than to have reached the summit of Aconcagua itself.

We completed the descent the next morning and walked back to Punta de l'Inca in not much more than a day, then at Santiago we said goodbye to the Americans. I've never seen or heard of them again, but it is in the nature of mountaineering that you can help or even save the lives of people you did not know before. The laws of the mountains are unwritten, but it is a code that is normally and should be strictly adhered to. We are all brothers in such an environment. I also don't think I've ever been on a happier trip than that one with Neill, a quick tactical assault where absolutely everything (bar my snow blindness!) went according to plan.

So now I had six summits; McKinley (North America), Kilimanjaro (Africa), Everest (Asia and the world), Elbrus (Europe), Vinson (Antarctica) and Aconcagua (South America). I was now pumped up to finish the job with the 16,024 foot Carstensz Pyramid, a tough rock climb in Papua New Guinea's Irian Jaya and the highest peak in Australasia. Steve Bell at Himalayan Kingdoms again arranged the trip for me. This proved a bureaucratic nightmare, needing various permits from numerous government departments who frequently won't grant them, wanting to keep prying eyes away from a local mine that is an environmental disaster, as well as the police and even local tribal heads. All the same I was off again within six weeks. I was aware I needed to concentrate on planning for my trip to the Antarctic at the end of that year, but Claire was also pregnant and expecting our third child on 20 May. I knew with certainty I must be back before then, with something to spare. Oh what I have put my family through!

It wasn't easy to find a climbing partner. Steve Vincent said no yet again, his days of serious expeditions seemingly over, Neill had used up all his holiday time on Aconcagua and said forget it. Graham Hoyland was working and couldn't get away and Steve Bell was busy elsewhere. I couldn't really think of anyone and in desperation called an electrician friend of mine called Paul Harman. I was a bit concerned that I hadn't done any proper rock climbing for many years, and this would be a long such climb, but although he was a very competent climber the fact that Paul had limited experience at high altitude and had never in his life been to a third world country worried me immensely. All the same, Paul and I arrived in Jakarta on 22 April 1995.

The Carstensz Pyramid is the only one of the seven summits without snow or ice coverage, and there are big differences in the skills and techniques required for ice and rock climbing. With the former you are out on your own, relying just on your crampons and ice axes, and it is potentially more dangerous. In theory at least rock climbing is safer, but you are totally reliant upon your partner. One person puts in protection and anchors the rope while the other leads, climbing up the rock face as they feed out the rope behind them and putting in a running belay for protection as they go. If the lead climber slips and falls they should only be able to do so twice the distance to their last protection, if everything holds of course, the rope ultimately tethered by his second below. At a given point the first lead climber puts in further protection, belays themselves to the rock, and their second removes the nuts and friends, venturing up after them removing the protection along the route, always supported, and so on, usually leapfrogging one another and taking turns to lead. The dangers for the lead climber are always greater, since they can fall further, and the protection they place must be able to catch a falling body, the pull of which upon a rope can so easily pluck that protection from the rock face.

In Jakarta we were met by our guide, Djojo Sumardo, an experienced climber who had reached the top of the Pyramid on three occasions, so at least one of us knew what we were doing. From there we took various flights on increasingly smaller planes, eventually to a beautiful island called Biak near Bali, our destination there to be the Balium Valley – an area only revealed to the rest of the world, apparently, in the 1950s. We landed in a small Cessna 152 aircraft, normally used by missionaries, at a small airstrip in the heart of the valley with mud huts dotted all around it. On landing we were immediately surrounded by the local tribespeople, the women naked except for grass skirts that showed whether they were married or not, and the men entirely naked except for long penis gourds.

I had never been to such a place in my life before and being no sort of anthropologist I didn't really know what to expect, but it was an entirely new experience to find somewhere so completely unspoiled and non-commercialized. Since we were the first outsiders to arrive in their part of the world that year the people were every bit as curious about us as we were about them and we found them incredibly friendly, although of course we could not communicate except through Djojo's translations. Perhaps most refreshing of all it seemed a very egalitarian society, with nothing remotely subservient about the people in any way. They simply lived their lives in the immediate present, with no sense of envy for the things that we might have and they did not. For Paul it was maybe even more of a culture shock than for anyone else, and he had already become increasingly uncomfortable as our trip progressed and he saw the mosquito bites on his arms, and encountered the increasingly tribal food and accommodation.

We then faced a week-long 100-mile trek through jungle inhabited by the most amazing wildlife, from bats and snakes to monkeys and sloths, with the locals acting as our porters. The vegetation was very dense in places, but they made short work of it with their machetes. At 4.00 p.m. each day someone would whistle and they would all suddenly stop, seemingly without any prior arrangement, and spread out into the jungle to return within fifteen minutes, having collected wood and creepers which they used, along with a tarpaulin we had given them, to construct a shelter. This was large enough to shelter the fifteen of them, whilst we remained in our tents to sleep but joined them for dinner, which always consisted of a vegetable called 'uebe' which tasted like a yam. If we were really lucky they would chuck in a bat or rat they might have captured during the day's trek. Paul and I were very conscious of not wanting to upset them, but we did draw the line at this part of the menu so we stuck mostly to our own food that we had brought with us.

There was much laughter around the campfire at night, especially if something funny had happened during the day, and their sense of humour tended towards the slapstick, never more so than when I slipped and landed on my backside. They were also always singing, like boy scouts of an evening, and I'll always remember their wonderful a cappella songs. They were truly lovely people, and if there is one mountain in the world I believe I would return to just for that I think it is there. I was worried however about our lack of urgency and slow progress, as my mind kept going back to a heavily-pregnant Claire waiting for me at home. The ice was really broken when I showed them a photograph of my family, and through Djojo's interpretation they all told us how many children they had. When I explained how soon Claire would be giving birth and that I needed to reach the mountain and return as quickly as possible, this seemed to do the trick. There was a brief discussion between them, camp was immediately struck, and thereafter the tempo of our trek increased and we reached the Carstensz Pyramid within the allotted time.

When we arrived at what would be our 12,000 foot base camp the temperature had dropped from a pleasant 16°C in the jungle to not far above freezing. This didn't seem to bother the semi-naked porters and nor did the conditions underfoot, as they skipped over the slippery rocks carrying their heavy loads in places climbers would normally be roped together. From here

Paul, Djojo and myself would be on our own whilst our porters found a cave where they would make their home until our return. At 2.00 a.m. on the morning of 2 May 1995 we found ourselves staring 4,000 feet up a massive and seemingly almost vertical rock face.

We roped ourselves together and started the climb. Paul excelled himself, insisting we could reach the summit and return to base within the day when I was beginning to voice my own doubts, although he continued to swear at me for getting him into this situation. Over the next few hours we spent much of our time abseiling up and down a series of ridges like yo-yos, some of these abseils very exposed with drops up to 2,000 feet. The altitude was beginning to get to me, but Djojo was hopping up and down the mountainside like a kangaroo.

Part way up I was amazed to see a huge smile and white shining teeth looking down at me. Our efforts had been made slightly ridiculous by one of our porters having run around the back of the mountain and up the other side in his flip-flops to meet us part way, although he clearly had not the remotest interest in joining us and carrying on to the top. By the final ridge before the summit I was so exhausted I removed my pack and left it behind. It took every last ounce of strength in my body to haul myself over that last obstacle, and then a further ten minutes to recover before I could pull my pack up after me, allowing Paul roped on behind me to follow up the mountainside.

From there it was not too hard and within half an hour we had reached the summit. Here a small wooden plaque confirmed the Carstensz Pyramid as the continent's highest mountain, and we stared down through the alpine conditions around us and to the jungle below. Here was the end of this particular part of my journey. I was the third British climber to complete the Seven Summits, and in doing so I had reached parts of the world and met peoples I had never dreamed in my wildest imagination

I might do, when growing up as a boy in rural Wiltshire. The mountains were my first love, and I had time to return home to my second two weeks before Claire ended up giving birth to our daughter Amelia.

ICE

I keep walking, but in my heart of hearts I am despondent and know I'm not going to make it. Things have got a little easier over the last few days, the pressure ridges more infrequent and the mounds of rubble slightly less immense. I've even had the odd day when I managed to cover 10 miles of ground, and you'd think I'd be elated compared to the first few of my journey when I was managing barely even a single mile. But when I planned the trip I knew I had to make those 10 miles or more each and every day over the forty or so I hoped it would take to reach the Pole in record time. Now I've been out here on the ice for thirty-two days, am less than a quarter of the way there, and have used up well over half my food. Worse than that, far more of my strength and will-power have been eroded. In the constant cold my mind has been broken every bit as much as my body.

In this twenty-four hour sunlight you lose all sense of time, but I guess it must be mid-afternoon or so. I'd always thought that I'd look forward to the end of a day, crawling inside my tent and getting some food inside me, but I really think I've stopped looking forward to anything now. I can't chalk off being one day closer to the Pole, because I don't honestly believe I'm going to get there. I just don't see how I possibly can, the numbers don't add up. It all seems utterly pointless now, and I suppose I keep catching myself thinking not so much whether but when I should give up. I've made a mess of things. I'd like to think I still have my pride, but I'm not sure I can even say that now.

Here's another sodding ridge. This one must be about 15 feet high, a wall of breeze block-sized chunks of ice. When I saw my first one, nearly five weeks ago, I thought it was rather beautiful, like some gigantic modern art installation. Now it's just part of an endless obstacle course constantly in my way. I start to zig-zag my way up it, trying to find some purchase and balance on my skis, and pause for breath. My sledge isn't that heavy now, since I've eaten so much of my food, and I thought that would make everything so much easier, but then I'm a lot weaker too which seems to outweigh that. The top at last and I can see clear ground ahead, so at least I have some of that to cross, but this ridge is damn steep down the other side and I'm going to have to be careful negotiating my way down or … Christ, it's moving, collapsing, blocks tumbling down and I'm going with it.

I'm at the bottom and this hurts like hell. My layers of clothing must provide some padding, but I can almost feel the shape of the block of ice where I landed on my side imprinted on my body. Try and take deep breaths, I'm winded, and I know I must also be in shock. I'm doubled up in agony and my ribs are screaming at me. Just give yourself some time, hope the pain eases, then try and get my tent up, but how am I going to manage that in this pain! This really is the end, but just of this journey or everything? I don't know. I have to try and get inside my tent then give myself time to think, once my mind starts working again. I guess I'm lucky one of those falling blocks didn't dash my brains out. Yet if I manage to radio base, will they be able to come and pick me up? I'm scared, but do I also feel something else? Am I relieved, that this finally gives me a way out, an excuse to go home?

* * *

You can never, ever, prepare yourself in advance for the reality of the North Pole. There is nowhere else on earth like it, and however much you try to plan and learn in advance, whoever you talk to who has been there, it is only the actual experience of facing it that can give you a real sense of what it is truly like as a challenge. It isn't in fact a place, in a sense, it is an ocean, but unlike the featurelessness of other oceans the Arctic is constantly changing. There are no maps, there can't be, because the terrain alters from day to day, hour to hour, as the ice moves and huge floating plates crash into each other throwing up piles of debris, and the pressure ridges act as sails pushing the whole ice sheet southwards. At least the South Pole is a continent, and although the ice and snow can be remade there too a map can tell you where you are, it is stable and still. Heading to the North Pole the ocean currents can carry you backwards almost as fast as you can walk, leaving you going nowhere, or sweep you miles away overnight whilst you sleep in your tent.

And it is cold. Of course, that goes without saying, but nothing can prepare you for the temperatures, day in day out, week after week, often –75°C with the wind-chill where every mile an hour of wind makes the temperature seem a bitter degree colder. The South Pole can be colder still, in the depth of winter and at its centre, but no one would try to go there then, they simply would not survive. Because the ground beneath your feet is solid you can attempt to reach the pole at the height of what passes for the Antarctic summer, in December and January, but you can't do the same when setting out for the North Pole. This you must do in early March, to arrive by late April, before the ocean currents leave you with impassable open water.

I'd always felt that when my hero Reinhold Messner reached the top of Everest by the very difficult north-west route solo and without oxygen, as he absolutely proved he had done in 1980, that was for me the ultimate climb. You just couldn't better that in any way. I didn't think about doing it myself, but after Steve Vincent and I returned from climbing Kilimanjaro in August 1981 I was beginning to ponder different challenges, although perhaps also avoiding the other pressing issue of starting to consider a proper career. Although I had not yet climbed Everest, or even really thought I might, I wasn't sure there was much more for me to do in mountaineering, but no one had done lightweight trips to the poles.

Up to then most expeditions had used snowmobiles or dog teams to get to the North Pole, the limiting factor with both being the huge cost of dropping fuel or dog food. Wally Herbert, who sadly rather had his thunder stolen by reaching the Pole the same day Neil Armstrong landed on the moon, used dogs and had supplies dropped by Hercules aircraft. Ranulph Fiennes had his own Twin Otter. I felt if you could keep it small and simple, that would be beautiful. And there seemed to be no real correlation between the size of an expedition and support involved and its actual success. If I could become the first person to walk solo to the North Pole, that might replicate Messner's achievement.

I told Steve about my idea, and he agreed at once to come out and be my main back-up at base camp. My thoughts were still in very embryonic form, and we'd gone out to New York together to set up a company selling outdoor clothing. We both loved the place, and I had ample time to carry out extensive research on the Arctic and the North Pole at the New York Public Library. After six months however, whilst we were walking down Fifth Avenue one day, Steve broke the news that he had decided to return home and marry his girlfriend Cathy, adding that he hoped I would be his best man and he still intended to come with me to the Arctic. I was also missing Claire desperately by this time, so we wound up the business and headed back to England. On the plane home I contemplated my future. With little money and no job I had no clear idea what my path in life would be, yet even then as now I knew I didn't want to be some kind of professional adventurer, but I realized that going to the North Pole was a new obsession for me.

Back home I moved into a flat in Bristol where Claire was studying law. She was only eighteen at the time, and looking back her parents were amazingly trusting in allowing her to move in with some bloke whose only plans in life were to do with such a foolhardy trek. I obviously had to seek help, so I managed to meet Ranulph who had been to both poles, although neither solo nor unsupported, and he was incredibly generous in his advice on things like food, radios and other equipment. I also contacted Wally Herbert, who in my view knew more about the Arctic than anyone else in Britain. Less propitiously, I sought official recognition for my trip from the Royal Geographical Society, but the gentlemen of their committee I met seemed incapable of asking me more than whether I would be wearing a string vest or could change a valve on a radio, which no one in such a position had needed to attempt in more than twenty years. Their support was not forthcoming, and it was privately made clear to me that my lack of a military or public school background was considered a stumbling block. Things have since changed, I'm glad to say, and the institution has completely opened its doors to me.

I obviously had to get sponsorship in terms of cash and equipment, so a vast amount of my time was spent bashing out nearly 3,000 letters on an old manual typewriter. Most received no response at all, maybe a curt or polite no, but just enough did offer help and very soon things like sleeping bags or radios from Plessey started to arrive at our tiny flat, and once that was bursting at the seams at the offices of my father's company in Swindon, where they were stored in a warehouse. My total budget was £40,000, which in polar terms is nothing, but about half of that came from the photocopier company Gestetner and most of the rest from local businesses that had supported me on my previous mountaineering trips.

My starting point would be Cape Columbia at the northern tip of Ellesmere Island, the fastest point from land to the Pole being the line along which there is least drift of the ice south, and my aim was to beat the existing record for the distance of forty-two days. All my research had told me to expect three distinct phases to my 476-mile journey. The first 200 miles, the toughest, would be a constantly changing terrain of ice rubble and pressure ridges, which can be up to 25 feet high. The moving ocean beneath the ice can force up massive fountains of freezing water, or produce icequakes. My belief was that just walking and pulling my sledge I would simply be able to go in a straight line over the top of any obstacles. Setting out at the beginning of March at the start of the Arctic spring, time would be of the essence over this first stage. I would have to reach the 85th Parallel before the month was out, as by the end of April the area between there and the 88th Parallel becomes impassable, since by then the Baltic and Siberian giral currents have broken up the ice leaving open water between the floes. This would be the most dangerous section, since if I fell through the ice I would either drown at once or freeze to death with no hope of rescue. The final section from the 88th Parallel should, in theory, be the easiest, a ski dash over firm ice to the Pole before radioing in and being picked-up by a plane. Oh, and there would be polar bears, who can scent a human lunch 5 miles away.

I'd initially intended to make my trip as pure as possible by navigating just using a sextant and the sun (no stars being visible during permanent daylight later in the trip), but the Canadian authorities made clear this was not an option and I would need to carry with me an Argos, what passed for the time as a lightweight satellite navigation system and would track my position. I collected this in Montreal having been flown there by one of my sponsors, the now-defunct Canadian Pacific Airlines, in first class seats at the end of January 1983. A stretch limousine then took us to one of the best hotels in the city and we hung around there for five days, picking up some last bits of clothing and food, as well as the rifle I would have to carry with me, and nicking their nice soft toilet rolls. Even then I knew it would be a while before I saw any comfort like that again.

From there we flew to Frobisher Bay on Baffin Island. This was only a brief stopover, but getting out of the plane the bitingly cold wind gave me the first indication of what I would be facing. Maybe it wasn't actually colder than the deep freezes I had spent time sitting inside back in England, a vain attempt to acclimatize myself, but it certainly felt so. From there it was on to Resolute, well inside the Arctic Circle and the last place approaching a town before the Pole. Back then it had about a thousand inhabitants, mostly civil servants, and we stayed in a small shack for two weeks further acclimatising to the freezing cold and checking my equipment. An attempt to celebrate our getting this far at least was stymied when we discovered that the bottles of champagne we'd brought with us had all frozen and shattered, a mistake I have never repeated. Apart from being much heavier than brandy I've actually come to consider carrying the drink rather unlucky and to tempt fate. We finally took a small plane to Eureka on Ellesmere Island, where just ten people inhabit a weather station by a long landing strip.

We set up home in a small hut 2 miles away. It was −40°C outside, below freezing within. Steve and I were more used to these conditions, but our radio man Giorgio, or 'Mac' as we called him, took every opportunity to escape to the weather station for a bit of warmth. We were joined by a BBC crew who had been sent to film my departure, and the days that followed were full of mordant humour and practical jokes, an indication of their sophistication being the one where we removed the fur cover from a lavatory seat causing Mac to freeze solid to it the moment he sat down. Against this, all the time I kept thinking that I was about to head off alone into what for me was entirely the unknown.

I very nearly never left Eureka. I woke up in our hut one morning and shouted out to Steve that it was his turn to get the tea ready. There was no answer from the next room so I attempted to climb out of my top bunk, but found I had no strength and slithered to the floor. I felt drugged. I crawled into Steve's room and found him lying on the ground, his face blue and seemingly lifeless. I could smell gas. Barely able to move I managed to radio the weather station then shuffle outside on my knees carrying Steve like a baby, flinging us both down on the snow where we gasped for air. The medic at the weather station deduced we had been poisoned by carbon monoxide from the stove, and although I recovered quickly Steve had to be pumped full of oxygen and took two days to be on his feet again. I felt very guilty at almost leaving his young wife a widow, but Steve just didn't want to be the one person delaying my trip.

Finally, in the first week of March, we took a Twin Otter light aircraft to Cape Columbia for my departure. This was probably the bumpiest landing of my life, and I was convinced the engines would stall as the pilot circled to find a suitably large area of flat ice to get down on. I dawdled on the ice for half an hour with the BBC crew filming me, but I expect everyone knew I was very scared. Eventually after bear hugs all round they got back on the plane and I watched it disappear into the distance back to Eureka. The snowy sunset scene as I looked around me was beautiful, but it was desperately cold and I had never been anywhere so remote in my life. I felt as if nothing here might have changed for thousands of years, that the rest of the world could end and I would know nothing about it. Normally I crave peace and solitude, but here it frightened me. I was the most lonely man on the planet. I suddenly felt as if I had bitten off more than I could chew. It was too late to go anywhere that day, so I erected my tent and prepared myself for my first night alone in the High Arctic.

Working in the extreme cold it took me three hours the next morning to have breakfast and load up. My sledge was only a little over 100lbs, but dragging it as I climbed up and over ridges and rubble almost killed me. There was no respite from it, and by the time I put up my tent that evening I had found only a few yards of flat ice. I'd hoped to average 11 miles a day, but that night I discovered I had travelled a single mile. I realised almost at once how naïve I had been and how totally unprepared I was for the conditions. After three days I had barely covered even 5 miles. Each day brought a new salutary lesson, such as when I cooked my boil-in-a-bag supper using first year ice from which the salt had not yet filtered through. I spat out the first mouthful, the meal ruined as mixed with pure salt water.

After a week I was doing no better. That night I was woken by a sudden shaking as if in an earthquake, with a terrifying noise of first groaning now squealing, and I could hear running water getting louder so clearly closer to me. I got dressed and packed most of my things into my rucksack and onto my sledge in case I had to move quickly, then huddled in a corner of my tent in the dark swaddled in my sleeping bag. I was convinced I was going to die, swallowed up by the frozen ocean. It seemed like a very long night but eventually I must have slept, and when I woke in the morning I scrabbled outside to see what had happened. I had been camped on a flat pan of ice maybe half a mile in circumference, but during the night a pressure ridge had been formed by two plates of ice crashing together. This was no more than 50 yards away, and had it been under me I couldn't have survived. I am not quite sure which was worse, the hours of sheer terror in the dark when I knew something terrible was happening but didn't know exactly what, or actually seeing for certain how close I had come to death. Perhaps it is a cross somewhere between Russian roulette and a lottery, the way you know the incredible forces in the ice can at any time just smash you to pieces. You can't have it in the forefront of your mind all the time, but the knowledge is always there somewhere in the background.

After ten days I had crept up to managing 5 miles on average and was due for my first resupply. This brought not only essentials such as fuel and food but also much needed luxuries like chocolate chip cookies and even a newspaper, but I was very worried as this should have taken place much further north. We only had enough money for three drops, and I was seriously doubting my chance of reaching the Pole, having already surrendered any hope of beating the record in doing so. Everything was proving far harder than I had expected, not least going to sleep aching all over and knowing I had it all to do again the next day. Tomorrow and tomorrow and tomorrow.

Then on day seventeen my Plessey radio died in the extreme cold. This was serious, since I had no way of contacting Eureka save for my Argos, which only had one emergency button to be used should I need to abort. To make matters worse, it had been agreed that if Eureka heard nothing from me for 48 hours they would come and pick me up. Sure enough, the next night a Twin Otter appeared and landed nearby, diverted from supplying Operation Caesar, a Canadian military exercise. The pilot had no spare radio, so decided to take me to the forward missile warning base at Alert on the Lincoln Sea, to which Steve and Mac flew out bringing a replacement. This place was so top secret then, back in the days of the Cold War, that I was even escorted to the lavatory by an armed guard. Since we could not diagnose the radio problem immediately – it turned out to be moisture that had entered the mouthpiece, and was counteracted by using a plastic bag – it seemed sensible that I should return to Eureka and try to do so there, before being delivered back to the exact place from where I had stopped. I was criticized for this at the time by one person, which hurt like hell and did upset me, but today I certainly think it was a valid criticism. You have to take such things on the chin, particularly from people who genuinely know what they are talking about, and I think I've generally been very lucky in how what I've done has been viewed by my peers.

Once I was back walking on the ice again things did become slightly easier, with fewer ridges and slightly less rubble, and wider pans of flatter ice between them. On the odd day I actually managed to walk the 10 miles I'd needed to achieve from the start, but after three weeks I just did not see how I was ever going to get there. I was certainly beginning to behave strangely, talking to myself, which with no one else for many hundreds of miles perhaps anyone would start to do from the loneliness, but I now think I was experiencing something more extreme. Maybe what happened after thirty-two days walking was for the best, as it may have saved me from possible insanity.

I was crossing the 85th Parallel, still many miles from the Pole, and struggling up a pressure ridge piled with blocks of rubble, straining to drag my sledge after me. I reached the top, some 15 feet above the flat ice around, when it just seemed to collapse. First one block started to move, then another, I lost my footing and fell. I hit the ground hard, on my side, and immediately doubled up in pain, completely winded. I crouched there for a few minutes, hoping it was no more than that, but I was in excruciating pain. It got no better, if anything worse, and I knew I wasn't going anywhere soon, so fighting against the agony put up my tent, a task that took me two hours compared to my normal practised ten minutes. Bizarrely, perhaps remembering how once I'd been told that the most revealing pictures can be those you least want to take, I set up my camera and snapped myself sitting hunched forward on my sledge. I looked and felt utterly dejected, in fact wondering if this would be the last picture anyone ever saw of me alive.

After three hours I knew I was finished and radioed Eureka to say I needed to be evacuated, was seriously injured. I was lying in a foetal position, painkillers taking no effect, as Steve relayed questions from a doctor down in Resolute. Was I coughing up blood, perhaps I had punctured a lung? Anything seemed both possible and likely. The nearest plane at Resolute was grounded by a storm for the next two days, and I would just have to hang on in there, but then the storm moved up to Eureka where they would need to refuel, delaying things still further, and carried on up to me. I was running out of food and fuel, terrified that my batteries would die and finding me would be like searching for a needle in a haystack. For four days the wind howled around me, and I was torn between desperately wishing they would set out and risk being unable to land, but also anxious about the £10,000 bill this might land me with, if I was ever in a position to receive it. After another storm hit Eureka it was eventually ten days before Steve managed to convince Operation Caesar to lend their plane, which was then only 60 miles away on their floating ice station. I was a wreck, still in immense pain and having lost a lot of weight, but it was a deeply emotional moment when I finally crawled out of my tent to see the Twin Otter land nearby. I was going to live.

I really didn't understand why the pilot was congratulating me and shaking my hand. I might be alive, but I felt a total failure. 'You've spent forty-two days out here on your own and lived,' he said. 'That's success to me.' Maybe, I thought, and for the first time my mood lifted slightly. 'I'll be back,' I remember muttering as we took off. I was flown up to Operation Caesar, then back down to Resolute, where a doctor diagnosed two cracked ribs, then I had to start taking calls from the press who wanted to know what it felt like to have failed so badly. 'At least I'm a living failure,' I repeated, as I had told myself before. It was good just to be warm again at last.

We flew back to London, a stark indication of our changed status being that we were sent to the end of the queue for stand-by economy tickets on the half-empty plane. I mulled many things over on the flight, but had learned some harsh home truths. I had been utterly foolhardy and simply hadn't had the right equipment or the polar experience to look after myself on the ice. With climbing I had built up knowledge and my skills slowly from the age of thirteen, to the point where I was proficient, but by going straight out to the North Pole I proved how completely incompetent I was there. It was a lesson in my pure naïvety. It was a warm May evening when we landed back at Stansted and it was wonderful to see Claire again, whose support I vitally needed over the next few days I vowed then that despite the living hell I'd experienced I would return to the Arctic, and one day make it to the North Pole.

I was both physically and mentally drained when I got home. I knew I'd made mistakes, but the more I thought about it I came to the conclusion that many of them could never have been avoided, were simply due to the lack of experience anyone in my position must inevitably have. I'd already worked out many ways I could improve my equipment, but in the end I'd finally been beaten by the sort of injury that can happen at any time. I knew I'd have to get back on that horse sooner rather than later, but equally I wouldn't be able to face failing in a second attempt on the Geographical Pole too soon.

An alternative journey would be to the Magnetic North Pole, where all points on the compass converge. This moves over time, due to things like solar flares and fluctuations deep in the earth's core, and in theory should be easier to achieve as it would be a shorter walk. To balance that, if I were to do it solo and entirely unsupported, it would be a genuine first. I'd be pulling a much heavier sledge, so physically it would be very tough, and the psychological pressures would also be great as I'd have nothing I could look forward to other than reaching my final goal. I went and discussed it over a few pints with my old PE teacher Mansel James, and he was very canny to suggest that what I was contemplating might actually prove tougher than another crack at the Geographical Pole. That made my mind up for me. I was going for the Magnetic North Pole.

Since Steve Vincent had now settled down with Cathy and had a good job in the City, I asked John Burgess, a bluff Yorkshireman, to come out as my base camp operator. He taught at Taunton Technical College, but also made rucksacks on the side, which was how I met him when he supplied me with one for my journey to the Pole. He leapt at the chance of an Arctic trip, and we set off in February 1984, a year more or less after I had left for the Pole the year before. Claire was still studying for her degree and was relatively happy to let me go, secure in the knowledge that I'd convinced her this was a far safer trip. This time I'd kept quiet in advance about what I was planning to do, and we flew out of Stansted economy class with less than 250lbs of equipment compared to eight times that the year before. Two days later, we were in Resolute.

Unlike the two months it had taken previously this time I was ready to leave in five days, having ensured every piece of my equipment from my rifle to my Argos satellite was double-checked, the latter being vital to prove I'd reached the Magnetic Pole. I was seen off from Resolute Bay by a Mountie, inappropriately dressed at –40°C in the traditional costume of the Royal Canadian Mounted Police, and then I was walking off across the iced-over beach and onto the frozen ocean. I felt confident, in that I was as well-prepared as I could possibly be, and knew I would not be facing the pressure ridges and tons of ice rubble of the year before, but I was also anxious about whether my navigation skills would be up to scratch, as this would be far more complicated than simply heading in a straight line. If so, I'd be the first man ever to do this solo and unsupported, as even if Inuits had hunted in the area they would undoubtedly have been in groups.

My mileage over the first few days was not too bad, and although at nearly 200lbs my sledge was roughly double the weight of the year before I seemed to be coping well with this hard work. I knew I had about 280 miles to cover entirely by myself, and as well as skirting the coast of some islands and traversing others I would also have to cross stretches of frozen ocean, where there were bound to be polynyas. These are areas of open water surrounded by thick ice, and since they attract seals coming up to breathe they are also the natural haunt of polar bears who come there to feed. On my sixth night I'd been rounding a headland at the tip of Cornwallis Island, preparing to head across a bay, when fast-moving clouds confirmed an expected approaching storm and I pitched camp and battened down the hatches hoping to sleep through it.

I woke about 2.00 a.m to the sound of howling wind outside, but I knew it wasn't that which had disturbed me. I could distinctly hear the noise of pawing and scratching, and when I sat bolt upright I could clearly see the shape of a nose pressing through the tent's flysheet. I grabbed my rifle and started to scream as loudly as I could, then fired off a shot into the ground. I hoped to God this would scare the bear off, but none of it was entirely voluntary as I was genuinely terrified. The noise of scratching immediately ceased, and it seemed as if the bear might have run off. I swallowed hard and plucked up the courage to crawl out of my tent, even though I knew I might see nothing as the white-out conditions of the storm were smothering the twenty-four hour sunlight.

Far from having run away though the bear was still there, standing some 25 yards away and staring straight at me. I fired another warning shot into the ice and the bear seemed undecided as to what it should do, beginning to turn away and starting to move out of my vision, before swivelling round and plodding methodically towards me, looming into my clear vision, its pace then turning into a canter. I knew it was attacking me and I had to defend myself in the only way I could. I'd been warned what I must do in such an eventuality, in order to get the best possible shot: breathe slowly, exhale when squeezing the trigger, and aim for the body rather than head as a bullet could easily ricochet off a bear's dense skull. At this point all the advice I'd been given went straight out of the window. I started screaming 'you bastard', and let fly a spray of bullets. I was hardly aiming, but I hit the bear about 20 yards away. He stopped for a moment then kept coming, swaying slightly before crashing to the ground, and I pumped two more bullets into him.

Adrenalin was coursing through me and I wasn't finished yet. I threw on my parka and marched out of my tent, a little closer to the animal, reloaded and emptied another five rounds into his inert body. My heart was beating like an alarm clock and I was hyperventilating, but I suddenly realized how cold it was and that I had to get back inside my tent to avoid frostbite. I needed to contact base, and I was also worried that there might be other bears around. Although they tend to be solitary creatures, there are certainly areas where they are more likely to congregate. I had no choice but to try and get on the radio, as if you kill a bear in the High Arctic it is something you are obliged to report and, providing a pretty damn good reason for what you have done, arrange for the carcass to be collected. The storm was preventing me getting through on my radio, so I had no alternative but to press the emergency button on my Argos transmitter.

Over the next hour I regained my composure. I knew I couldn't have avoided shooting the bear, it was him or me, but equally I was aware that if I hadn't been there in the first place, in his territory, it wouldn't have happened. I realized I wasn't to blame but I still felt guilty. As my equilibrium returned, I downgraded the message on my Argos to 'Pick-up requested ASAP'. Within an hour a Twin Otter arrived and set down on the ice nearby. When he saw the proximity of the bear to my tent the pilot laughed and agreed I'd had a pretty close shave. I took him and his co-pilot around and pointed out the claw marks, they snapped some photographs and then filled out a statement for the Canadian wildlife authorities. After that we had to strain and lift 500lbs of deceased bear into the high loading bay of the plane, the animal attempting to exact a last posthumous revenge by carrying out a final post-mortem bowel movement.

I wasn't to know it at the time, but my encounter with the polar bear almost instantly became world news. I'd very deliberately kept quiet about where I was going, as I didn't want any advance publicity to put added pressure on me in fearing another failure, but I couldn't prevent the news getting back home. I wasn't proud of what I'd done, but the bear would just become part of the quota that the Inuit are allowed to kill, with the carcass delivered to a village near Resolute. I made my way to the Polaris Mine and camped down in the bay, then the next morning headed off towards Bathurst Island. I knew that my route across that would lead me through what is commonly known as 'Polar Bear Pass', so named because it is an area that supposedly boasts more polar bears than anywhere else in the world. A couple of days later I saw another one about half a mile away, which was plenty close enough for me. Since I knew that bears tended to attack from out of the wind so as to avoid their prey scenting them, I deliberately pitched my tent entrance away from the wind, and left food on top of my sledge parked 20 yards downwind from the tent door. If a bear came sniffing around, hopefully it would at least be drawn to that first.

A week later I felt happy with my progress, and I was coping with the weather and the solitude. I had a routine I was comfortable with and, most importantly, I'd regained my confidence after my brush with death. I was making my way alongside the coast of Bathurst Island and found I was encountering increasing amounts of sticky brown ice, which I suspected might mean I would soon come to open water, so I made a detour towards the actual shore. I was about three hundred yards from it when suddenly my right leg and ski plunged through the ice and into the freezing ocean beneath, sending me lurching over and ice-cold water shooting up my leg. Shouting out in panic I managed to get some purchase to upright myself and pull my leg free, and then scramble to some firmer ice nearby, but all I could think of was getting to solid ground. I sprinted over the ice as fast as any man could dragging a sledge, hurled myself flat-out on the icy shore and promptly threw up.

I'd completely lost it now. If things had been only very slightly different, the surrounding ice less firm, I'd never have managed to pull my leg free, and if my sledge had slipped through the ice it would have dragged me down following it. Physically I was ok, but mentally I felt finished. I knew I'd come close to dying and I think even an experienced Inuit hunter could have made the same mistake, despite their uncanny ability to judge the state of ice. A thin covering of snow had helped deceive me. Apparently far more Inuit hunters are dying today due to global warming resulting in changes in the ice they are not used to. I erected my tent in a state of shock and radioed to base. I didn't care if it was another failed expedition, I just wanted to get the hell out of there. Steve, my radio man, was calm on the other end, and told me to get some hot sweet tea down me and he would call back in half an hour, but when he did I felt no differently. I wanted a plane, and Steve agreed he would call back soon when he had some idea how long that might take. I was getting angry by the time I heard from him again, and wasn't prepared to take no for an answer, but then John came on the line.

He obviously knew the only way he could boost my resolve was to make me even more angry, so he set about me with a typical Yorkshire tirade: 'If you think I've come all this way just to go home because some sissy doesn't like water, you can forget that. You just get walking again in the morning.' I really don't think I'd expected this, the sudden change from sympathy and concern, but it did the trick. I told him to get lost and that I was keeping going, but it was probably a good job I turned off the radio as if I'd heard them laughing on the other end the whole effect would have been lost entirely. It got me back on track however, determined to show them that I could do it. Am I really so easy to read?

As the trip went on my sledge became lighter as I made my way through its supplies, but I was also getting weaker from the constant physical effort and the cold. To make matters worse I developed bleeding piles that made the effort of walking painful, and I resorted to stuffing a sanitary towel between my buttocks. I suppose having had the forethought to bring some with me says a lot about the sort of planning that goes into such a journey. I knew I didn't have too far to go, and when I reached pack ice that I must be near the edge of the Magnetic North Pole, its exact position having been given to me by the British Geological Survey. Now I could only navigate using a sun compass, as the normal magnetic one was rendered entirely useless since it just pointed down at my feet, but on a day in my fourth week I was in white-out conditions again and could see no trace of the sun at all. I couldn't afford a day without making any distance however, so had to work out some other method of finding my way.

I was very pleased with myself at having come up with the idea of using the light meter on my camera to find the brightest spot in the sky, which must presumably be the sun. This was what adventuring was all about, using your ingenuity to solve a seemingly intractable problem, and I set off in what I felt had to be the right direction. After four hours' going I came across some ski tracks, and I stared at them wondering how they could be there. No one had told me anyone else was in the area and I was totally mystified, but as the day was coming to an end I set up my tent and radioed base. I couldn't believe it when they said my position had barely changed from that of the night before, it just wasn't possible as I must have covered a good 10 miles. When my position was reconfirmed, and I was assured I was the only person out here, the truth slowly started to dawn on me. My navigation had totally let me down, the tracks were my own, and I'd come a full circle making no progress whatsoever. Although I was only 20 miles from the Pole I felt utterly dejected at the waste of time, but agreed I obviously had to stay in my tent until the weather cleared and I could see the sun to guide me again.

The next morning there it was, peeping out from behind the clouds, and I set off as fast as possible, hoping to make up for the day before's wasted time and knowing that I was only two days from my goal. I was no longer in great shape, but my sledge only weighed some 40lbs now which compensated a little. The day after I knew should be my last, and part of me was tempted just to ditch everything and make the last 12 miles an easy stroll, but I remembered how the previous year a storm had held-up my evacuation by ten days and something similar wasn't out of the question now. It simply wasn't worth the risk.

After four hours I radioed base to find out how much further

I had to go, and a couple of hours later I did so again, to be told I'd only travelled a couple of miles and then barely one more. This made absolutely no sense, as I knew I was moving at about 3 miles an hour over pretty flat ground. I was beginning to get tired, but each time I called back I was urged on that I just had a few more miles to go. I was apparently still a couple of miles short when they said they were about to leave in the Twin Otter to meet me, so I had better get moving, and from then on I kept my Argos switched on so that they would find me. I was excited about going home, but now utterly exhausted and past caring exactly where I was, so I placed the beacon and flares on top of my sledge and pitched my tent. Within minutes it seemed the plane was there, tipping its wings to indicate it had seen me, and landing on a flat bed of ice nearby. The first question I faced was why I'd walked 10 miles further than I needed to, at which point the truth dawned on me that they'd had me walk straight through the epicentre of the Magnetic North Pole and out the other side, just to make absolutely sure I'd been there. I was angry for about a couple of seconds, and then it was hugs and laughter.

I was going home after thirty-two days on my own, tired and hungry. After an hour drinking the champagne they'd brought we were off, and on reaching Resolute I phoned Claire at once to tell her I'd made it and was on my way back. This time we were upgraded to first class on the way home, a reminder of how differently the rest of the world treats the maybe only tiny distinction that divides success from failure. I also received much positive coverage in the UK press, possibly just a result of a British success seeming such a rare event at the time. I felt I'd earned it however and I'd learned a lot more from my second trip, to the Magnetic North Pole, than I had on that first one aiming at the Geographical Pole. I'd changed lots of things: my skis, the tent, sleeping bags. I'd encountered very different ice conditions, but it was still very hard both physically and mentally. I now felt I had the right to begin calling myself a Polar explorer.

Eleven years have passed, and my life has changed in so many ways. For a start Claire and I are married, and I also have three daughters to support, Alicia the oldest, Camilla, and Amelia the youngest, who was born on 1 June 1995, just a couple of weeks after I completed the Seven Summits. Since I am not a professional adventurer, earning a living has obviously always been a necessary part of life for me, and perhaps provides one reason why I initially concentrated on climbing which meant shorter periods away from home, apart from a major expedition such as to Everest. I suppose having these responsibilities does make you feel grown-up in a different sort of way, more aware of how others depend upon you, but I certainly hadn't lost my thirst for adventure. With our father having died a couple of years previously my brother and I had just sold the family firm, for which we had all worked, to a large American corporation, and I had set up another company called Global Resins. Both these things had forced me to concentrate on work, but I now had definite plans about what I wanted to do next.

I was going to have a crack at the South Pole, and if I succeeded as I intended I would become the first Briton to walk there solo and unsupported. My thoughts had been heading south for a couple of years, spurred on by what I considered a great expedition by Ranulph Fiennes and Mike Stroud to become the first people to cross Antarctica. I'd originally intended to attempt this myself with Roger Mear as a partner, whom I knew from Everest. He had a lot of polar experience having worked for the British Antarctic Survey, although my only previous visit to the continent had been when we climbed Mount Vinson the year before. We did have our differences however, about planning generally and how to do things, and clearly I wasn't the only one who was having doubts about whether we would be the best people to work together on a long trip. I don't really think either of us quite felt we could rely totally upon the other, so although our plans were fairly well-developed it didn't come as a total surprise when in January 1995 Roger told me he'd changed his mind and now planned to make the Antarctic crossing solo. My mind was made up then and there over what I was going to do: I intended to get to the Pole myself.

Having been once bitten I decided to keep my planning pretty secret however. I had to take Annie Kershaw of Adventure Network into my confidence, as she flies people in and out of Antarctica from Punta Arenas, the last major town in Chile, and without her help I would never be starting out or get back afterwards. Because they have often seemed to be so much more successful than us Brits I also decided I'd turn to a number of Norwegians for advice, one of whom was Borge Ousland who has since become one of my closest friends. He is certainly among the world's most accomplished polar explorers and was just about to attempt an Antarctic crossing himself in direct competition with Roger. He still found time to provide me with a huge amount of help in terms of weights and equipment suppliers, but perhaps his most useful suggestion was that I train for dragging a sledge by pulling tyres along a beach, something I have done ever since.

Thanks to the Norwegians I had all the equipment I needed ready by June 1995, when I was still flushed by my Seven Summits success and the birth of a new child. But I also sought advice from Sir Vivian Fuchs who had crossed the continent in the 1950s using a tractor train on the Commonwealth Expedition, and a climatologist called Dr Charles Swithinbank. With the latter I pored over maps and he told me what he personally considered to be the best routes, although he was adamant that any choices must be purely my own as he was still smarting following the criticism he had received from Reinhold Messner after he got into trouble. In my view, any choice ultimately has to be your own, and things can always go wrong, so you never have anyone to blame but yourself. It was a very hectic time for me, as I was also discussing plans for a couple of other future group expeditions, and had the £150,000 budget for the trip to raise. I managed to achieve this mostly through networking, with nearly fifty sponsors in total, although a couple of large chunks made it easier. It may sound a lot of money, but a major part of the sum simply covers the cost of flying in and out of Antarctica.

I was due to leave on 20 October and spent the last couple of weeks training with my tyres and generally getting into shape in France and Germany. Then I had to say goodbye to my family. In some ways I felt most guilty about knowing I would be away over Christmas, and even if Amelia was too young to care about that Alicia and Camilla were already getting excited, with the latter really contemplating the first Christmas she would know much about. Claire and I were both pretty tearful when we said goodbye. I would be back in January, I swore. Apart from leaving my family behind, my major concern was not just my physical but my mental condition after all the work I'd put in over the last few months, both planning for my trips and in terms of the everyday work of business, including the stress of concluding the biggest deal of my life in selling the family business, Robnorganic Systems. Various friends warned me to pull out, but I just didn't feel I could do that.

Roger should have left Punta Arenas a couple of weeks before I arrived there, but had been delayed by horrendous weather. If he was surprised to see me he managed to hide it, but although we'd long since buried the hatchet I still felt motivated to beat him and was furious that Annie was flying him out a week before she would take me. She was fully booked however with a bunch of adventurers already there, including the immensely experienced Russian Fyodor Konyukhor, looking a bit like Jesus Christ with long hair and a beard, who had already made it to the North Pole solo but unsupported. He would now be making the same trip on a similar route to me. I was also thrilled to find Borge Ousland, after all the help he'd given me. We spent time bonding before our respective departures, but I almost didn't manage to leave at all.

I'd picked up my Argos tracking system from Swindon on the way to Heathrow for my flight to Santiago in Chile, due to delays in the Scottish company I'd been talking to sourcing it for me. When I opened the box it turned out to be one designed for a fishing boat, much heavier than the one I needed. I feared I was screwed until I managed to get one delivered to me in Punta Arenas at the last moment by a rival American supplier, due to much help from my cousin Nick Hempleman who ended up being my gopher there, running multiple checks on my equipment. The Argos was so essential because Annie Kershaw had called me into her office to warn me that, without a signal from me within twenty-four hours of setting out, they would come and pick me up, no ifs or buts. Despite my arguments that it could be due to something trivial like a flat battery or sun spots she was adamant that at £65,000 a time they would only be making one rescue journey.

Finally on 6 November Fyodor and myself were flown out, along with Geoff Somers who would be my radio man at base camp and sole point of contact during the trip, an experienced polar explorer himself and someone I trusted. By going together Fyodor and I halved our costs, and we'd agreed that I would set out half a day ahead of him so no one could accuse us of not going solo. We landed at Patriot Hills, the only blue ice runway on the continent strong and flat enough to take a Hercules aircraft. From there we set off the next day on snowmobiles to Hercules inlet, which would be our point of departure and where we would spend our last night together before we set off alone. I was pretty freaked when I compared my equipment with Fyodor's, mine up-to-date and his seemingly army surplus, which felt twice the weight when I tried to lift it. I suddenly felt very weak compared to this ox of a man.

I didn't sleep much that night, worried about the sixty days ahead of me. There would be strong headwinds and endless sastrugi, the Russian word for snow dunes that the wind can blow into mounds up to 20 feet high, a surface like a massively furrowed field that I would find all the way to the Pole. Although I would not have to face the open water and rubble of the North Pole in its spring, here in the Antarctic summer there would be opening crevasses down which a man could easily disappear. In the twenty-four hour sunlight I was up at 5.00 a.m., and after breakfast I said goodbye to Geoff and Fyodor, wrapped the harness of my sledge around my shoulders and set off on what I knew would be the most arduous trip of my life. I was on my own now, and I had to admit that I was frightened. I was standing on pack ice, 50 yards off shore, and ahead of me lay nearly 700 miles of the most barren terrain on earth.

I took up the slack of my 285lb sledge and felt it move behind me. As always I knew that getting through the first ten days would be the most important thing, not pushing myself too hard too fast and knowing that as my sledge got lighter the going would become easier. If I walked for eight hours a day and covered an average of 12 miles, that would take me to the Pole. It was difficult going however, steadily upwards and sometimes with a slope of up to 25 degrees over some sastrugi, and all the time I could see the steam rising from the tents back at Hercules Inlet seemingly no further away. I also remembered that it was not only my brother Mark's birthday but also Alicia's, who was now six. The former I did not really care too much about, he'd cope and perhaps raise a pint for me, but the latter made me feel very miserable and question what business I had at all being here so far away from home. On camping that evening I was further cast down when my GPS revealed that I'd travelled only 6 miles.

The first few days were depressing as my mileage barely edged up, even if I was starting to get into a better routine than on my first morning when I overslept and did not complete breakfast and all my preparations until midday. There were strong winds and visibility was poor so I couldn't even appreciate the natural beauty of my surroundings, or concentrate on something in the distance to help the time pass as I walked towards it. In clear weather you might see 4 miles ahead, but often now it was barely 10 yards to the next clump of sastrugi on which I could focus, and I constantly had to check my compass. I'd also come to my first crevasses, fields of which I knew I could expect to encounter all the way to the Pole. These can be up to 300 feet deep and there are stories of explorers and whole dog teams disappearing forever, swallowed up by these hungry mouths never to be seen again, no hint of where they had gone except perhaps the faint barking of a dying husky.

The first crevasse I came to was about 200 feet long and 8 feet wide. You can normally spot them in advance by the ridge of snow formed by the wind and hanging over the edge, and in this case the yawning fissure was plugged with snow. I tested it with my ski stick and it seemed firm enough to cross, but I chickened out and took the long way round. It was when I realized this had cost me an hour, totally disrupting the rhythm I knew I must establish, that with my heart in my mouth I started to jump across successive crevasses, although I still unharnessed my sledge and just carried a rope to pull it over after me. I grew more confident, even if that was slightly dented when I nearly lost my prodding ski pole as it penetrated the snow surface and I found myself staring into a black hole.

Although I did not allow the crevasses to hold me up too much I was still very worried about my progress, and started to think about what weight I could lose to help me move faster. Perhaps stupidly, I discarded an ice axe and rope designed to help me escape should a crevasse claim me, figuring that out there alone I would have no chance of doing so and would die anyway. This attempt to reduce weight became an obsession of mine, and every day I tried to bury something I convinced myself I would not need.

I had a routine, which you refine and follow vigorously since everything seems to take so much more time in the extreme cold. First the alarm would wake me from a deep sleep, and then it mostly seemed to be about melting snow for boiling water, first for my breakfast tea and muesli with sugar and milk, next to make the soup for my thermos during the day, and then in the evening once again for my dehydrated boil-in-a-bag meal of pasta or chilli con carne. I was depressed about my progress, but consoled myself that in the first four days I had climbed 1,000 feet, a tenth of the way towards the 10,000 foot altitude of the Pole itself. I think that alone in a place like that you do very quickly start to think and behave eccentrically, and I certainly would have looked very odd if anyone had been there to see me. Although I did have modern equipment I have always tended to like sticking with what has been proven, so over a thin wool inner sock on my feet I used a Sainsbury's carrier bag as a vapour barrier (to prevent the sweat moving out and freezing) which poked out at the top like gaiters, then a thick woollen sock and on top of that an old-fashioned canvas boot of exactly the same kind as Amundsen wore when he was the first man to the South Pole in 1912.

During the night after my fourth day walking I heard the wind getting up into a real storm, and when I poked my head out in the morning it was soon apparent it would be suicide trying to move on then. The whole day was lost whilst I sat morosely in my tent obsessing about how far behind schedule I had already fallen. After five days I should have covered 60 miles, been crossing over from 80 to 81 degrees south, but instead I had managed no more than 25. It was only Geoff's confidence in me on the radio that evening which made me feel I could keep going, truly meaningful as he had real experience of similar conditions, knew not only what it was like physically but also what I must be going through mentally.

The next morning the blizzard was still blowing, but I judged that the wind had subsided enough to be manageable, if still potentially dangerous, and I would make an attempt at carrying on. It was slow going, with the wind constantly raising up new undulations in the snow, and my day ended after six hours' struggle. My sledge caught the lip of a sastrugi, stuck fast, and my momentum meant that I was suddenly jerked backwards off my feet by the harness and landed hard on my arse. I cried out in agony, the whole area around my coccyx jarred and shooting pains coursing up my back. I knew I was in trouble. I painfully erected my tent and started to dose myself with painkillers, ignoring the stern warnings on the bottle about the number I should take. Was this trip about to be ended by injury just as my aborted walk to the North Pole had been? I was very close to giving up, miserable and desperately homesick as I felt I'd barely seen my family in the last year due to horrendous overseas business commitments. I was still close to Patriot Hills, and I knew if I pressed the emergency button now Adventure Network wouldn't charge much to pick me up. It would have been so easy to quit then.

I called Geoff back at Patriot base, and he knew exactly what to say. Although I thought I was doing badly I was still well ahead of both Roger and Fyodor. I'd actually completely forgotten my personal race with the former, and evidently I was still winning. He referred to the others as 'poor bastards' compared to me, and although I knew it was guff it cheered me up. I also remembered how my oldest daughter Alicia and her classmates were plotting my progress on a map hung up in their schoolroom, and how pathetic it would seem if the line came to an end so soon. Nor could I forget the warnings of all those who had said I shouldn't come, the friends as well as the doubters, and thought about the prospect of becoming yet another British failure when Norwegians and Russians seemed to find it far easier to overcome these barriers. I reached the decision there and then that as I'd started I was damn well going to finish, or at least wouldn't give up before my food had run out. With that determination the pain seemed to ease and I started to plan. Just get over that first degree I told myself, and after that I would walk an extra half-hour each day, and an additional half-hour after I crossed each successive degree.

I'm not sure how I believed that in my current condition I could ultimately increase my walking day from eight to twelve hours, but it just shows how motivation can blind you to difficulties. I needed it when the morning showed me a total white-out of ice crystals, but I decided to press on even though I would hardly be able to see the crevasses I knew were out there in the swirling cotton wool that lay ahead of me. I suppose I was feeling fatalistic, when I thought of what I had achieved with no more than a few cracked ribs to show for my pains. Far more accomplished climbers than me have perished on Everest, yet I had come through unscathed. I only managed 7 miles that day, but in a sense I had taken some pressure off myself, knowing I would keep going so long as my rations lasted, whether I got to the Pole or not. It also helped having to find practical solutions to problems, and knowing that painkillers would not be enough I fashioned a corset for myself from duct tape and a ripped-up sleeping mattress. Wearing that I waddled across the continent like one of the many thousands of penguins that live around its shores.

The morning of day nine was another blizzard. I was still thinking about how I could reduce the weight of my sledge, as I knew from my Magnetic North Pole trip that if I could halve its weight I might manage 18 miles in a day. Out went my crampons, a big decision for any climber to make, along with my Sony Walkman and tapes, even a spare pair of shoelaces. Having finally got going for a few hours I had one of my longest radio chats with Geoff, and it was the mundane messages that helped me in the middle of the most lonely place on earth. Claire sent her love, and asked if she should pay for some wine that had not yet been delivered? I was also developing a rapport with a girl called Sue, the cook back at Patriot Hills. Since food was becoming such a fantasy I had begged her to make me a blackberry and apple pie for when I came back, and she asked me what she'd get in return. The mildly flirtatious conversation was relayed back and forth, with the whole of British Antarctica listening in.

On my twelfth day I was able to have my first minor celebration, when not only did I finally cross over into the 81st degree but also achieved my best distance so far of 8 miles. It was a purely imaginary line, and there were nine more to go, but after taking off my gloves in the tent and putting them on top of the cooking pan to melt off the snow, I retrieved my brandy bottle from the bottom of my sledge. This I'd made sure I had not discarded, and it had lines marked on it to denote each passing degree. I drank down to the first line whilst scoffing a packet of pork scratchings from my 'special treat' bag. I certainly knew how to throw a party. It was only 1 degree I had crossed, and I had eaten deeply into my emergency supplies for the trip, but if I could achieve 12 miles a day from then on I would still make it. This might not have seemed like a logical hope, considering I'd just achieved my best day so far of much less than that, but somehow this consideration did not strike me at the time. I was up to an altitude of a bit less than 3,000 feet on my way to the 10,000 feet at the Pole, and had many fields of crevasses and plummeting temperatures ahead of me, but huddled up in my tent that night I knew for the first time I was going to get there.

The next day I woke thinking of a fresh start, the pain in my back bearable, even if my superstitious side (my 'Z' stone still around my neck) didn't like the thought of it being day thirteen. It was another white-out, at which times the Antarctic is like a desert, the powdered snow so fine it scatters everywhere, but I still achieved another record of 8½ miles. Yet the day after was beautifully clear, and I could see the Pirrit Hills some 40 miles ahead of me. It is always easier to walk with some objective in sight and an additional mile added to my record was the result. I'd also devised a game to keep me going, based on the fact that the distance from Hercules Inlet to the South Pole is about the same as that from John O'Groats to Land's End, or roughly 680 miles. Pretending I was marching down the motorway, I was now past Aviemore and heading for Glasgow, and each day I mentally marked off the small Scottish town I'd just passed through, this familiarity making my trek easier. And my sledge was getting lighter, both through continued minor disposals and the fact that I was eating it down by 3lbs per day. I was noticeably losing weight, but for now I felt strong even if I knew the hunger would later become unbearable.

It may have taken me twelve days to reach my first degree, but I crossed over into eighty-two on day eighteen, breaking three daily distance records in the process. I wasn't there yet, but I calculated that by half way I would be achieving 12 miles, perhaps more, through the combination of my lighter sledge and additional half-hours of walking. I was also becoming more disciplined, blaming myself for previously being too slack, so reduced the length of my tea breaks and cut out unscheduled ones, along with the inevitable sitting down on my sledge and taking in the contrasting colours of the beautiful scenery. In the mornings when my alarm went off at 6.30 a.m. I wouldn't doze and think about the day ahead, but jump straight up into a kneeling position and get into my routine. In twenty minutes my breakfast and hot drink would be ready, by 7.30 I would be packing my sledge. If I was ready a few minutes early, those would be when I lay down on my thermarest to contemplate the day ahead, whether it would be good or bad, my only quiet pause apart from a couple of tea breaks before I set up camp in the evening.

It was also before setting out that I would always remove my inner tent, dig a hole with my spade, and have a crap before refilling the hole with snow. You don't pee much during the day, and when doing so you make damn sure your back is well to the wind before fishing around in your long johns for something a lot smaller than you remembered, which is the last place you want a touch of frostbite. I've always found it is essential to be regular with your bowel movements however, since there really is no way you could stop for one during the day without setting up your tent. It's cold enough as it is, inside the outer sheet of the tent, and you learn to be pretty quick about it. You also have to be very careful dressing since if something doesn't sit right, your balaclava is a fraction out of place and rubbing your neck for instance, you have to put up with it for the whole day rather than take it off and start again, which simply isn't possible. Everything has to be stowed properly for ease of access – map, compass, munchy bag and flasks of hot drink at the front of the sledge – and weight balanced in terms of both length and width.

Despite all my care I was experiencing my first signs of frostbite by the start of 82 degrees. You can never tell if it is coming, it just suddenly materializes, and you have to keep checking your individual fingers and toes. I would stamp my feet on the ice to create extra circulation, then wrap each finger individually around my ski pole to check I had feeling, devoting an hour during the day to working on each finger, rewarding myself with some salami when I got through them ok. A bigger problem was the inside of my thighs, as it became clear that only wearing one pair of thermals and windpants my legs were getting too cold and there were a series of red patches tinged with blue. I was probably only a day or two away from full-blown frostbite, but although wearing an additional pair of thermals solved the problem it took nearly another three weeks to clear up completely. Worst of all for my vanity it did catch my nose. It's been suggested occasionally that mine is a little larger than some people's, but certainly now it became horribly swollen and bulbous.

By day twenty I had a new distance record of 10½ miles, and even better a huge field of crevasses I'd expected to encounter had not appeared, having obviously either closed up or been filled with snow. I did think slightly mournfully about my decision not to bring a parawing, as for the first time the winds were of the right direction and strength to have made using one a possibility, but I had determined against one due to the extra weight and the fact that there was too much risk of injury when you're out there alone. Fiennes and Messner both had accidents using one, but neither of them was going solo. I am sure it was the right decision, and some people consider the use of a parawing to be cheating slightly anyway, but set against that is the thought that with the right wind and ground you might make 30, 50, even 80 miles skiing in a day. I could have had a double brandy and pork scratching celebration perhaps that night.

Day twenty-four should have been a day of celebration as I crossed into 83 degrees, but it was also 1 December which hit me hard. Apart from my first day feelings of guilt about leaving my family behind I had thus far mostly managed to shut out such emotions, but I knew now my girls would be opening the first windows on their advent calendars, the official start to Christmas for us. I worried whether Claire would be able to fetch the tree, which I normally went and chopped down after we had all traipsed out to a local farm and selected it. I was also disconcerted the next day when a large icy hill some 5 miles across, and clearly marked on my map, simply wasn't there, another indication of the constantly changing terrain which had seemingly just eroded away in that wind over only a few years. But I had a new record of 11 miles, had gone through 4,000 feet in altitude, and was able to change to a larger scale map, which although I was not yet half way there seemed a very significant moment to me. I also caught my first sight of the Thiel Mountains, which I would pass 30 miles to the east, which meant my navigation was spot on. In the distance they looked a little like the Swiss Alps and I knew they reached to 10,000 feet. Most have never been climbed and some not even seen by mankind before, so they acted like an incredible magnet to a mountaineer like me.

On my ground plan of Britain I was now crossing the Scottish border and entering Cumbria, starting to eat up the distance and hitting 11½ miles on day twenty-seven, but the next day I had a real problem. On the high frequency radio that evening Geoff told me that they had not received my Argos position, so if I did not contact base each evening that would trigger an immediate rescue operation, everything could be screwed-up. On 7 December I crossed into 84 degrees and finally achieved 12 miles, but my worry over the Argos was becoming all-consuming. Fortunately I had a spare battery, and that made it start working again, but I had to change the whole pattern of communication. Previously I'd left the Argos on for up to six hours, but I could no longer do that and risk depleting my remaining battery so I had to agree the optimum time to turn it on for no more than half an hour whilst they could pick up my position.

My back was not too bad now, and I was only taking three painkillers a day, but my nose was getting worse. Some polar explorers consider frostbite a badge of honour, like a rugby prop's cauliflower ear, but I certainly did not feel that way. I tried putting tape on it, but that only made matters worse as it became damp and started to freeze. White blisters appeared on the end and it throbbed constantly. It's never really recovered, still goes very red in the cold, and along with the scars and numbness the inside has been damaged. I need an operation to fix it since then, but I can't say it's as good as new now. Roger was still often making only 3 miles a day, and even when he once notched 25 with his parawing he was still well behind me. And on day thirty I crossed into 85 degrees, halfway there and my biggest landmark so far.

Over the course of the next degrees I was gaining altitude, so it was getting very much colder. I'd obviously grown a beard, and it might sound strange how I was bothered that parts of this were as white as the snow around me. Perhaps this concern about growing old was mostly due to anxiety about my strength, and despite my sledge now being 120lbs lighter than when I set out I could tell this was diminishing as I lost weight, at a rate of over half a pound a day I later discovered. Even though the food was disgusting it became increasingly important to me, as did any treats, but I had forced myself to be very disciplined now. When I mistakenly thought I had crossed over into 86 degrees, and had already got out my brandy and pork scratchings only to discover I was still half a mile short, I didn't cheat but put them away until the next night when I would really truly have earned them.

Being alone out there does mean you start talking to yourself, or in my case to my sledge to be exact, which I had begun calling 'Boy' and was interacting with as I might a dog, telling it to get a move on and sometimes offering it bits of Mars Bar. I'd also christened my skis Gandalf and Merlin. On day thirty-nine, when the lip of a sastrugi had caused Boy to tip over for about the tenth time that day, I even administered a severe beating to my sledge with my ski stick, in a way that one never would an animal. This shows just how close to the edge I was mentally, and this sort of frenzy had only ever consumed me once before when I was trying to walk to the North Pole. Once I'd calmed down I was really just concerned how daft I was since I could easily have broken my ski stick, which really would have left me in trouble. The outpouring of emotion must have exorcised some demons however, as the next day I completed 13 miles, my best yet, and I reckoned I was metaphorically now past Manchester with Birmingham not that far off.

On day forty-three I was encountering some of the highest sastrugi of the trip, up to 15 feet, which made the going very difficult. The reference books say this shouldn't be the case as you get further south and less wind is blowing off the Pole, but so much for them. There were also crevasses every 50 feet or so, big ones, which I was now just ploughing straight across, even if my ski stick did often disappear through the ice – although by the time that registered I was safely across. I was still relieved by the end of the day to have come 12 miles and survived unscathed, with the knowledge that the next morning I should cross into 87 degrees. I was beginning to imagine what it would be like reaching the Pole. It had been one of the most dangerous days of the expedition, but I didn't realize yet that worse was to come.

About 9.00 that evening before I went to sleep I had a final pee in a plastic bottle, before tipping the contents out on a specially designated area of ice outside the tent, from where I wouldn't collect snow for cooking. If the ice is solid the urine usually spreads around a bit before freezing, or with powdered snow you hear it fizz before it disappears. This time I heard nothing, but it was only once tucked up in my sleeping bag that this started to nag at me, and although knackered I irritably hauled myself out to check what my sudden suspicion might reveal. There, where I had poured away the urine, was a deep dark hole. I was camped on top of the thin ice crust over a massive crevasse. I thought about it almost dispassionately. The fact that I hadn't already fallen through suggested the ice surface was holding, and moving around was the mostly likely thing that could cause it to give way, which might happen as easily when packing up in the morning as now. I decided to stay put, partly from a fatalistic sense of what will be will be, but also because I felt strangely at peace with myself. I almost sensed that my hero Ernest Shackleton was watching over me, daft as it sounds, or at least I genuinely believe I thought so at the time.

I was a bit less calm in the morning when I awoke and remembered where I was, crawling gingerly around on all fours before getting out and snapping on my skis, then dragging my sledge across the rest of the ridge and away from the crevasse. It was another white-out that I had to trudge through, which was now happening every five days or so. With my eighty-seventh degree celebration that evening I worked out I was down to Worcester, 180 miles or so to go, but since I know the route a lot better I decided now I would pretend to be making my way from Cardiff down to London on the M4, along which I could mark off not just passing towns but service stations. I was up to 8,000 feet and my thermometer read −37°C, but with windchill effect that became about −75°C and any exposure of bare flesh for a moment would mean frostbite.

The next day I heard that Roger Mear had pulled out of his attempt to cross the continent, some 180 miles behind me and at just over 84 degrees. This left me with the real prospect of becoming the first Briton to walk solo and unsupported to the South Pole, but although we hadn't always seen eye to eye I felt genuinely sorry for him. He would have to go home and face the music, which would be so much the worse after all the pre-publicity he'd generated. What people never understand is that, at the time, more people had walked on the surface of the moon than to the South Pole from the edge of Antarctica. I was inexperienced really in comparison to Roger, and although it now meant I had my own genuine chance I was desperately sorry that he'd lost his dream, as I knew exactly how that felt.

The next couple of days were pretty miserable, being Christmas Eve and Christmas Day. I kept thinking about all our family rituals of preparation now going on thousands of miles away, setting out the sherry, mince pie and carrot for Santa and Rudolph, then the kids opening their presents and Claire smiling bravely through it all. I knew she would be worried, and could it really be acceptable to leave her alone for so long, and at such a time? We were going to celebrate Christmas again on my return, but it was the first time in fifteen years that Claire didn't have a present from me. Since I was now averaging 13 miles a day with the additional half-hours of walking, I was getting pretty confident of reaching the Pole in sixty days, so initially I planned to give myself Christmas Day off, but perhaps it was to punish myself for deserting my family that I changed my mind. I'd been thinking for days how I would actually celebrate Christmas, and at least I could hardly complain that I didn't have a white one as I trudged along singing 'Jingle Bells' to myself, but I did decide to make it an additional brandy day and broke open a dehydrated packet of fruit cocktail that I'd saved. It was hardly turkey and plum pudding, but it had to do and was all I felt I deserved.

A couple of days later I was told I could expect a team of five Russian women, who were just doing the last section of the journey after being dropped off at 88 degrees, and asked if I would provide a local weather report to green light their arrival. Frankly I didn't want anything to do with them, worried that any contact would tarnish my solo journey, but Geoff told me not to be so paranoid and reluctantly I agreed. I was still feeling grumpy when they emerged from their plane, but even if after so long alone I wasn't very excited about the presence of female company I doubt my white beard, bulbous nose and the fact I hadn't washed in seven weeks would have made me any more prepossessing. I marched up to the pilot and demanded he sign my diary to confirm I hadn't been given any fuel or food, or anything else that would constitute support, but when one of the ladies offered me a banana I was briefly torn. I couldn't take it of course, for the additional reason that after more than seven weeks of dehydrated food it would have passed through me like a dose of salts. They pitched camp a quarter of a mile away from me, and I never saw them again after I set off the next morning. Soon I'd be crossing the outer rim of the Pole, where the longitude lines end and the final push would begin.

On my fifty-fourth day two things happened that set me back badly however. First of all Geoff told me that after reaching the Pole my friend Borge Ousland had pulled out of his attempt to cross the continent just two days further on. That he had pushed the emergency button was a bad blow to my morale, since he was my hero and I often asked myself what he would do when things seemed to be going wrong. Then in crossing a crevasse my ski pole punctured the surface again and for a split second I thought I was going to topple over, plunge down into the black hole that had opened up next to me. I jerked myself upright and managed to regain my balance, but in doing so I injured my back again and also pulled a couple of muscles in my leg. I immediately had to increase my dose of painkillers once more, but knowing I was less than a week away from the Pole I felt I could get through this now when I wouldn't have been able to earlier in the trip. Sixty miles still seemed like a long way however, and

May 1995. On top of the Carstensz Pyramid, last of my seven summits.

Hot as a furnace. Western Cwm on the south side of Everest, 1993.

Everest 2011. The team in Kathmandu.

Everest 2011. Our truck, having crashed into the ravine. Ironically, out of all of them, it was only Malcolm Walker's barrel that we didn't manage to recover.

Everest 2011. The view from our mess tent at Base Camp.

Everest 2011. Advance Base Camp with North Col and summit above on a good weather day. Actual summit mostly hidden behind ridge, wth cloud blowing off.

Everest 2011. Climbing ridge towards Camp Two.

Everest 2011. Ngatemba on his holidays at the notorious second step.

Everest 2011. Me on summit, another day at the office.

Everest 2011.The four climbers who made the summit: Duffy, Justin, DH-A and Rod.

Everest 2011. Dachhiri Sherpa nearing summit, Tibetan foothills in background.

March 1983. It's all over! Cracked ribs end my North Pole dreams.

November 1995. Before setting off individually for the South Pole, D H-A, Borge, Fyodor, Bernard and Thierry.

January 1996. I've made it! At the South Pole and happy, despite the obvious frostbite on my nose.

April 1998. We encounter more water as we approach the Pole and the thaw accelerates.

April 1998. The last week and the rubble has not abated. Still no sign of the wide open pans of flat ice we had been led to expect.

Mount Vinson 1994. Setting up Base Camp at the start of the season. Very, very cold.

1997. Rune being heavy handed with his equipment. The sledge didn't float very well.

1998. Close to the North Pole. Floating on a small ice floe over an open lead of water.

2003. Geomagnetic Pole.

At the Geomagnetic North Pole in April 2003, the finish, bollocksed but happy. (© Paul Grover)

September 2002. Over Pittsburgh, first failed Rozier crossing of the Atlantic.

September 2003. Mid-Atlantic on Rozier crossing.

October 2004. Rozier altitude record, at the top and not coming down. Mummy, help me!

January 2007. On hot air balloon altitude record, I'm almost too big for the basket.

July 2007. Launch site from St John's, Newfoundland for gas balloon Atlantic crossing.

2007 Atlantic crossing, landing in France.

First drink in a week after my 2007 Atlantic crossing.

2008 Gordon Bennett in Albuquerque. Balloons inflating at launch site.

2011 Americas Challenge. Jon and me at altitude on oxygen, floating across the Prairies.

2011 Americas Challenge in Albuquerque. The winners!

2011 Americas Challenge Albquerque. Me dog tired.

I know how people have failed to reach the summit of Everest by 100 feet. I've seen their dead bodies. Robert Scott and his men died just 11 miles short of their food depot on his return journey. I decided to cut my food rations by half just in case my injuries slowed me down. And it was New Year's Eve when all the family always gets together in a hotel to sing 'Auld Lang Syne'. It was exactly midnight back home in England, and I made a resolution I was going to spend more time with my children.

On New Year's Day, my fifty-fifth, I passed over 89 degrees and now my GPS could barely register the lines of longitude as they merged together and it kept desperately searching for them. A combination of excitement and concern about my injuries meant I pushed myself to walk 14 miles, and I could almost feel the Pole in my grasp. The next day was bitterly cold, but as I cooked my dinner that evening I worked out I had only a further 22 miles to go. I suddenly thought I heard an aircraft noise that sounded familiar, and realized it must be a Hercules landing at the American base at the Pole. The next day was beautifully clear, and with barely any wind it was a real pleasure to be walking in the Antarctic. In mid-afternoon I had stopped for a tea break, when I saw for the first time two distant dots on the horizon. I was 15 miles away, but these I realized were the tips of two antennae. All I now had to do was walk towards them, no need for any map or compass. My thoughts turned to Scott again, since in 1912 he had no idea what he would find at the Pole, and then he must have been crushed to discover Roald Amundsen's tent there confirming that the Norwegian had won their race. Had that not happened I am sure he would have made it back, and I reflected on how much easier it was for me knowing exactly what I would find and with the prospect of being flown home, not to mention all my other knowledge and equipment. What brave men they were.

The next day was crystal clear and at first the antennae

seemed to get no nearer, as it is always very difficult to estimate distance in such a landscape. Then with about 10 miles to go I caught sight of the silver dome at the research base, and the odd colour started to appear, the red of buildings and steam pouring from a roof. It was when I saw the flags, particularly the Union Jack fluttering in the breeze, that about half a mile away I finally broke down, knelt on the ice and wept. The tears first caused my goggles to steam up then to freeze over, and during that last half mile I continued to cry and had to keep wiping my goggles. It was fifty-nine days since I had begun walking on 8 November, and it was now 5 January since by reaching the Pole I had crossed the international date line. I had entered New Zealand time and it was 7.00 a.m. in the morning, so I had effectively lost a whole night's sleep, but I cared little about that. I'd made it. I could hardly believe it, when I thought back to how I'd felt when I first set out.

I frankly didn't really know what sort of reception I might receive from the scientists at the base, and it's often said they view people like me as tourists who get in the way of their research. Certainly no one seemed to be paying me any attention, all had their backs turned and were talking amongst themselves, so I thought stuff them and made my way over to the pole and orb that mark the ceremonial location of the South Pole, a hundred yards or so away from the more simply denoted exact Geographical Pole. I was still crying, but fortunately I had the sense not to kiss it as my lips would have stuck fast, but instead hugged it tightly as feelings of relief and ecstasy fought their way through my tears. Then, one by one, the scientists approached and shook my hand, clapping and cheering. A British scientist fetched me a hot cup of tea, and the head of the research station congratulated me and welcomed me to the South Pole. These guys weren't so bad after all, but had actually been anxious to allow me a few moments alone with my feelings and not to intrude on a moment they knew must be very special for me.

I was invited in to breakfast, but said if possible I wanted to wait for my friend Fyodor to arrive, who I knew had been closing the gap on me after initially falling well behind having started out the half day later. I didn't have to wait long, as he arrived only three hours later, and after I had given him his own space we hugged, both cried, and took plenty of pictures, before needing little persuasion to go in to breakfast. I'd forgotten what it was like to be warm, as it was in the portakabins under the dome, but my first priority was food even though I felt my body falling apart. My nose and back hurt like hell, and I later found I'd lost 36lbs from my starting weight of about 15 stone, but I shovelled a huge fry-up into myself even as I kept apologizing for how bad I knew I must smell. We were assured we shouldn't worry but also encouraged to have a shower after we had finished eating, and even, can you believe it, a sauna. It was wonderful to feel the shampoo and soap send the dirt piling off, our bodies tingling in the hot water, and we were like two excited kids in the shower, with the prospect of the clean clothes we had been given to look forward to. The effects of the unaccustomed food were soon felt, and meant I spent most of the remaining morning sitting on the lavatory, but I also had time to see the doctor who pronounced my nose 'not nice', although she assured me it would heal naturally in time, and gave me more painkillers for my back.

That afternoon I was given a guided tour of the research station, and got caught up in a ridiculous race the scientists sometimes stage on a half-mile course around the actual Pole. Fyodor and I clipped our skis back on and harnessed up our sledges, trudged round the course swearing the whole way, and were then awarded with t-shirts saying we had just completed a round the world race. This was all fun, but I was desperate to let people at home know I had made it, and that evening I settled down to what I was told would be my one allowed call over the satellite phone, which would have to be collect. First of all I had to fetch the base commander to confirm for the operator on the New Zealand side of the continent that I really had permission to make the call, and then I heard the phone ringing. I was so excited at being about to hear Claire's voice, but then there was a click and I heard myself saying 'This is David Hempleman-Adams. We're not here at the moment, but please leave a message.'

Bollocks, where was she?! I begged for one more call, and racked my brains to remember the number of any family member who could pass on a message, but the only one that came to me was Aunt Audrey's. When we tried that it just rang without answer, and I could tell the operator was losing patience with me. I pleaded for one last chance and tried to remember my grandmother's number, writing down the possible permutations on a piece of paper. I thought I had it right and passed it to the operator, who dialled the number. A woman answered and the operator said he had a call from David Hempleman-Adams at the South Pole, and would she accept the charges? There was a pause and then the woman, who I now realized sounded unfamiliar, said in a stern tone, 'You want me to pay for a phone call from a strange man at the South Pole? NO!' That was that then, so eventually seeing the funny side I went off to have a few beers with Fyodor and my new friends.

The next morning we packed up all our equipment to await the arrival of the Cessna from Patriot Hills that would be arriving to take us away from the South Pole. When it arrived Geoff was first out of the plane, and typically reserved Englishman that he is avoided my hug and shook my hand, asking me what all this nonsense concerning a bad back was about. A few minutes later two Twin Otters landed, and disgorged a party of elderly American tourists, snapping away with their cameras. Both Fyodor and I knew what the other was thinking, that this somehow seemed to dilute our achievement in walking all the way to the Pole when anyone could just fly in like this. It wasn't really what we needed, and once they had gone we made our private farewells to the base and the Pole itself, then over to the plane for the six hour flight. We were all big men squeezed into a small aircraft, like sardines, and finally there was a moment of farce as the base commander held us up for ten minutes whilst he confirmed with the doctor that I'd left the trousers he'd lent me with her.

As we took off and circled the Pole I heard the BBC World Service come on the radio and the presenter announced what I had just done. I hadn't come looking for glory, but I did feel a warm glow as I dozed off. There was a party atmosphere amongst the ten or so people back at Patriot Hills when we arrived, and I did get my blackberry and apple pie from Sue the cook, with custard naturally, the thought of which had kept me going during the toughest part of my journey. I suppose the group of elderly tourists couldn't help coming through there, but when the next morning I went into the mess tent and found the place heaving with them I just couldn't stand it and had to walk out. Having grown so used to solitude I simply couldn't cope with a crowd, and although it was good to be getting back to civilization I knew it would take me time to adjust to other people. And them to me. The same tourists were with me on the Hercules back to Punta Arenas later that afternoon, and although I was dressed in clean clothes I still had to wear my same filthy old outer garments. The crew invited me to move down to the back of the plane, away from everyone else, and when we landed the girl from Adventure Network who collected me confirmed what must have been everyone else's view saying, 'Cor, you are a bit smelly!'

My first call back at the hotel from where I had left two months earlier was to Claire of course, and although it was 3.00 a.m. in England this time she answered. Once awake she said she'd missed me, and we arranged to meet in Calais for a family holiday with the girls. Then it was a blissful shower and shave, and time to start paying attention to the twenty-two calls I had waiting from media around the world. Before I left Punta Arenas for Santiago Annie Kershaw also asked me to give a talk to the same elderly American tourists who had dogged my footsteps. I didn't feel I could refuse, and once I saw how interested they were I felt rather guilty about my previous feelings towards these sixty and seventy-year-olds. In their own way they'd done something rather special travelling to the South Pole. Everyone has to set their own challenges. Some people claim they are walking to one of the Poles but only do the last degree, and I would never want to put down those who achieve anything, but the bottom line is that you have to live with yourself and what you are setting out to do. With adventure there will always be purists, but it all comes down to you. You are doing it for yourself and must be your own policeman.

More press calls followed in Santiago. One reason there seemed to be so much interest was that I was only the second person to climb Everest and get to the South Pole, and the first to do so with all seven summits. And only three people, two Norwegians and a Pole, had ever made it to the South Pole before solo and unsupported. Then it was a flight to Paris where my brother Mark picked me up and drove me to Calais to wait for the family. It seems like more than three months since I left, but all thoughts of being away are soon banished as I am crushed under the weight of three squealing small girls hugging me, even if Claire is less than impressed by the frost-bite on my nose.

* * *

There was one thing I was always going to try and do again: complete a fifteen-year odyssey that started back in 1983, manage the one thing that I knew I'd always feel was a gaping hole in my or any other adventurer's list of achievements – finally make it to the North Pole, by hook or by crook. Precious few people have walked there from solid land in the north of Canada, but as I prepared to leave home in late February 1998 I also knew that I was on the verge of something even greater. I stood to become the first person in history to attain the highest summits on all seven continents, as well as all four of the North and South Geographic and Magnetic Poles. Done correctly, in my view, heading north from the edge of solid land in the Arctic, and south in the Antarctic from the shore at the edge of the continent (the Magnetic South Pole is in fact situated over the ocean, so involved a terrifying trip by yacht from Hobart in Tasmania) I am still the only man or woman who can say I have been to all these places doing so properly, rather than simply being dropped-off and walking the last degree or so.

After my first attempt in 1983 to become the first Briton to walk solo to the North Pole had ended in crushing failure, I'd regained a lot of my self-confidence, as well as vital experience, becoming the first person to walk solo and unsupported to the Magnetic North Pole the following year. Since then my business and family commitments had kept me away from these longer expeditions, until I'd returned to them with a vengeance in 1992 leading the first team in a desperate trek to the Geomagnetic North Pole, and in 1996 taking a further group of Arctic novices to the Magnetic North Pole. In between, earlier in 1996, I'd of course become the first Briton to walk solo and unsupported to the South Pole, and I'd made my first summit of Everest in 1993. Now I heard again the siren call of the North Pole. I felt my experience gave me a decent chance of a crack at it. However, I'd made up my mind that it wasn't something I would set out again to do alone.

There are intense rivalries in the British adventuring community, and although I would perhaps claim to be more easygoing than most I couldn't for the life of me think of anyone who would put up with me for two months or, perhaps more importantly, avoid driving me round the bend. So I started to think of other possibilities. The British and Norwegian rivalry in polar exploration goes back to Scott and Amundsen, even beyond that, and frankly they have generally had more success than we have. Although other British adventurers have always seemed reluctant to seek advice from them, I've consistently trusted and respected their experience, equipment and seemingly greater fitness, most of which perhaps stem from their living in a country the majority of which is already covered with ice and snow for much of the year. Why not bury the hatchet and find a Norwegian for a joint national expedition?

My first thought was my friend Borge Ousland, but he wasn't free at the time as he was returning to Antarctica for another attempt to cross the continent, an expedition that he'd failed on at the same time as I made it to the South Pole. Who could he suggest, I asked? Borge offered me a couple of names, and when the first was unable to consider the proposition as he was returning to the Norwegian Navy, I phoned the other, a young man of twenty-six called Rune Gjeldnes. I'd been told he was a member of the Norwegian Marinejegerkommandoen, their equivalent of our Special Boat Service, and this initially made me a little reluctant to make the call – I'm often concerned that the perhaps misplaced courage of military men can be a liability somewhere as unforgiving as the Arctic. Borge had reassured me about Rune however, but when I first spoke to him he didn't really seem very interested either. Although he offered me no real prospect of convincing him, he agreed that if I flew out to Norway we could meet for a drink to discuss it.

We met in a bar in Bergen, one beer turned into two and two into many, and I immediately warmed to Rune and began to think he might be my perfect companion. He obviously had immense experience of polar conditions, having recently skied the entire 1,830-mile length of Greenland in eighty days, but although his reluctance appeared to be waning he was currently involved in a lecture and book tour. What seemed to worry him most was that he would be unable to devote sufficient time to planning the trip, and probably couldn't promise to do more than turn up in Canada at the appointed time. I assured him this wasn't a problem and I was happy to handle that side of things, with a little input from him concerning equipment. I was going to need an answer fairly soon, but agreed to give him ten days to think it over. 'If I come,' he said, 'I have to do all the cooking. I don't trust your English food.' I was hardly going to argue, if he wanted to take on the chore I hated most. When I called as arranged Rune picked up the phone, said hello, then 'Why not?' We were on.

But this was all eighteen months before Rune and I were driving to Heathrow for our departure on 28 February 1998, as we'd already had a first abortive attempt at the North Pole the year before. Although we felt we were pretty well-prepared and had the best possible equipment there were perhaps harbingers of doom from the very start of our trip in March 1997. Rune accidentally left the blue bag containing many of his most important personal possessions on the plane that dropped us off on the ice at Ward Hunt Island. As well as photos, cassettes and a Bible – somewhat incongruous for a trained killer, I felt – this also carried something even more important: ten weeks' supply of tobacco, which for a heavy smoker such as Rune was a disaster of almost unimaginable proportions. He was deeply embarrassed

and determined we must set out anyway, but I knew how important this was to him and insisted we should wait for a couple of
days until the plane returned with a Dutch expedition that was
setting out just after us. When dreadful blizzards set in however,
those two days became eight before we finally left, even if Rune
was now happily puffing away.

I could hardly complain however, as the returning plane also
carried the consignment of travellers' cheques that I'd forgotten
to sign, without which our base man Dave Spurden could pay
for nothing, including any emergency medical evacuation in the
worst case scenario. So by the time of our departure we were
truly quits, but things were no easier once we actually got going.
The ice rubble was far worse than we had expected, and very
quickly we began to have problems with Rune's sledge, which
he insisted should be more heavily loaded as he knew he was
stronger than I am. We had ordered sledges made of Kevlar,
which is also used to make bulletproof jackets and about as
tough as anything gets, but we soon found ours were clearly
constructed from the much weaker fiberglass and they soon
started to show signs of wear and tear. We had no alternative
but to start relaying half loads, leaving what we had carried at
a suitable clearing in the tangled maze of ice blocks, then going
back to collect the rest. For every mile we were moving forward
we therefore had to walk three, across the 100 miles we managed in our first forty short seven-hour Arctic days.

We had no idea how long our sledges could last, despite the
cracks in them being patched-up each night with wire, but we'd
also been held back barely a week after we left by an unexpected
visitor, when a terror-stricken and frostbitten young man called
Alan Bywaters, a twenty-one-year-old student from London,
tumbled into our tent and collapsed. We'd met him back at
Resolute and knew he was planning to set out after us, which
we and everyone else considered foolhardy in the extreme due

to his lack of proper equipment and almost total inexperience. We'd suspected he was following in our tracks for a while, which makes sense if you see a pre-established route, but he told us that he'd fallen into a lead of open water, seen his sledge with his radio and all his equipment vanish, and knew that if he couldn't find us he was as good as dead. We got hot soup inside him and tried to thaw him out slowly, sandwiched between our two bodies in an attempt to prevent hypothermia overcoming him. A plane managed to reach us and evacuate Alan after four days, landing at the third attempt and barely managing to lift off successfully from the short landing strip. We'd expended time and a lot more food and fuel in helping Alan, but we were in no doubt that it was the only thing we could have done.

We were just over the 85th parallel when Rune's sledge finally gave up the ghost. I see a trail of his equipment in the snow as he strides on ahead of me oblivious to what has happened, until I call him back. There's no way we can fix it, what's left is more hole than sledge, and we know that it's the end of this expedition. It's pretty obvious to us both that we can only radio that we need to be picked-up. We're both devastated, but I know I will have to try again next year and my biggest concern is whether Rune will come back with me. We've made a perfect if slightly incongruous team, myself the slightly bumbling businessman and father of three, him seemingly laid-back but a trained killer underneath, but we've just gelled. I needn't worry however, as Rune very quickly forms a pact with me to return, and we immediately start planning how we will do things differently. He also cheers up immensely at remembering that although he'd run out of tobacco the day before, he'd packed a huge Churchill cigar to smoke in celebration at the Pole, and now there is no reason to delay doing so.

It takes a couple of days for us to be collected, by which time our plans are well advanced, and now it's happened we're glad to be out of there. On arriving back at Eureka we're desperate for a proper meal, but having no ready money we seem destined to do without as there's no way we can pay the exorbitant $60 each, until I promise to send the chef a bottle of whisky from England, which does the trick in a place where alcohol is so strictly rationed. A couple of days later we arrive back at Heathrow the day after the general election, a grinning Tony Blair entering Downing Street, and the world seems to have changed in a great many ways.

I took a couple of months off from organizing the following year's expedition to spend the time I'd promised I would with my family, including a visit to Rune's farm in Norway, and I also took Claire to the opera festival in Verona and to Venice. There were many pledges to other friends I had to fulfil, a lot of wonderful but rather expensive meals that needed to be bought, but every one a debt that had to be repaid. The Royal Humane Society announced they were giving us bravery awards for our rescue of Alan Bywaters and, prouder still for me, in October I travelled up to Glasgow to be awarded the Royal Scottish Geographical Society's Livingston Medal. The roll-call of former recipients reads like a list of all my polar heroes: Scott, Shackleton, Amundsen, but also explorers such as Sir Edmund Hillary, Sir Francis Chichester and Neil Armstrong.

In early August preparations started in earnest. We'd sketched out a critical path in terms of planning and this year Rune was able to be much more involved, mostly gathering equipment whilst I chased sponsors, the great majority of whom decided to stick with us. Money would be even more important this year, as we were planning to have two resupplies with a third potential one as an emergency reserve. The first would be after fifteen days at 84.1 degrees, meaning our new and definitely Kevlar sledges would be much lighter over the hardest ice rubble of the first 65 miles. The next twenty days should be easier going, so we would be able to carry more weight faster over a greater distance before our second resupply at 86.3 degrees, the point beyond which the cost of a flight doubles. We hoped to be fit and strong by the final section, which we planned should take twenty-five days but carrying food for thirty.

This year we had more preparation time, but we also had a very clear idea of what we needed. Apart from different sledges we got a smaller and lighter tent and shorter skies, both of which we knew would be an improvement. We pretty much saw eye to eye concerning food, which Rune would handle once again, and clothing where we both generally approved of that based on Norwegian models. I made sure all our sponsorship badges were sewn on our clothing and equipment, which the previous year we'd done late at night in Resolute at the last minute, depriving ourselves of sleep. I was also determined to be fitter this year before departure. I've never been a great fan of training in advance, preferring to acclimatize myself gradually on the ice itself, starting out slowly when it is very cold and the days are short but building up my strength and fitness for when it is a bit warmer and the hours of sunlight longer. That has always been my excuse anyway, although I have to admit I just don't like the effort of training very much, but it had been a bit frustrating for Rune who was incredibly fit when we set off. So it was back to dragging tyres mile after mile again, the only parts I really enjoyed being when my daughters were sitting on them. I also had to deal with the necessity of putting on an additional two stones in weight. I could tell Claire I was off training when I was actually just going down the pub to drink as much beer as I could, which always does the trick.

By the end of January 1998 everything was in place. There'd been less daydreaming this time about what lay ahead of us, because I think we were both entirely focused on what we had to do and confident we would do it. Very often it seems that almost the moment you return home from an expedition you forget about how unpleasant and often downright painful so much of it has been. Perhaps that's an inevitable and essential part of being able to do so again, just as women often say they forget the pain of childbirth. This time we felt we'd thought every point through, knew exactly what it would be like throughout. We were ready for anything the Arctic could throw at us. In mid-February we held a press conference, which I never really like doing in advance of an expedition but is a necessity for raising sponsorship, and then it was the always agonizing process of saying goodbye to my family, made even worse by the fact that my youngest daughter Amelia was due to go into hospital for a minor exploratory operation.

Claire is normally pretty stoic when I go, but this time she was in tears. I felt an utter bastard leaving her to cope alone yet again and even asked if I should call the whole thing off, but she'd have none of it. Even so, I was feeling pretty guilty as we drove out of our gates and headed for the motorway and Heathrow. This had to be the last time I left home for such a critical expedition. Not only was I getting older, at forty-one I could hardly put my body through this much longer, but also as my daughters grew older they were bound to worry more. I just wasn't sure how I could continue to justify this and simply had to make it. I had a lot going through my mind, as I fingered my 'Z' stone on its piece of dental floss that held it around my neck.

At Heathrow we met the third member of our team, John Perrins, a retired policeman who was to be our base-camp manager, as well as TV news crews from the BBC and ITN and a newspaper photographer, all of whom would be accompanying us north. After ridiculous confusion about how we should check our shotgun in with the other baggage I finally just make it to my seat on the plane for the long flight to Calgary. Having been upgraded to business class this time I eat and drink too much, since I know it will be a long time before I see champagne and lobster again. In those days you could still get permission to visit the aircraft flight-deck, so I do that and the Captain kindly prints me out a weather report for Resolute. It makes grim reading, the 40 knot wind meaning a wind-chill factor of –72°C.

From Calgary it is a short hop to Edmonton, where we repeat my regular ritual of spending the night at the Nisku Inn, a hotel surreally built with a fake tropical garden at its heart, as well as sinking some pints in the appropriately named Last Chance Saloon. This will be our last alcohol for several months, apart from our celebratory shots of brandy. We enjoy a large breakfast the next morning, and I've managed to increase my weight to 15½ stone by now, which extra bulk will hopefully give me additional stores of energy. It's about 2½ stone more than my normal weight, but when I returned from the South Pole I'd dropped to only 11. We then board the plane for the long flight to Resolute, having been warned we may not even be able to land there due to thick fog enveloping the airport.

The plane lands at Yellowknife, a former gold and diamond prospecting town, where we see the last trees that we'll encounter before our return, and then again at Cambridge Bay, inside the Arctic Circle and where the ground is covered in permafrost. A short period of daylight has recently returned here, but ahead of us on the ice-cap it will still be permanently dark and even colder. We finally reach Resolute in late afternoon, lucky to land, and the brutal –30°C cold slaps me in the face in the brief time it takes us to reach the tiny terminal building. I feel my eyelashes and the hairs inside my nose freeze, and the tip of my nose throbs. Each renewed encounter with such temperatures takes my breath away, and is always something that at first you wonder if you will ever become used to. People joke about Resolute, 'it is not quite the edge of the world, but you can see it from here,' and as the vast majority of all supplies have to come by air the arrival of a plane is a major social event. Everyone turns up to see those foolhardy enough to venture north towards the Pole, one of the few reasons that this hugely expensively sustained hamlet of a few hundred Inuit hunters survives since the US and Canadian military air bases departed with the end of the Cold War.

We head for the Qausuittuq Inn North, where most expeditions make final preparations and check their equipment. Here you eat the plentiful set meals of traditional home cooking at a long table in the kitchen, cramming in as many calories as you can while chatting with the other adventurers also about to set off, which this time include a couple of Royal Marines about to make a second unsupported attempt, also having failed very quickly the year before. They have been delayed in their departure to the starting off point of Ward Hunt Island by bad weather, and the satellite pictures suggest a further massive snowfall is on the way. I am always cautious about relying too much on such predictions, since the one thing I have come to learn here is to expect the unexpected, the ice constantly changing, new ridges forming, fresh leads of open water appearing or others closing over. When after dinner we pull our crate of equipment into the garage to start the long process of unpacking and checking, everything has frozen solid except for our stash of brandy.

We have a huge amount to do before our departure in four days' time on Thursday 5 March, not least removing all superfluous wrapping and dividing our food up into five-day packs of rations, muesli for breakfast, powdered drinks and soup for lunch, and a dehydrated meal for the evening, plus our munchy bags of nuts, Mars Bars and milk chocolate cut up into chunks to nibble during the day. What concerns me most however right now is that I am feeling dreadful, and if this turns out to be flu rather than simply a severe cold we will have to delay our departure, assuming of course the weather allows us to leave when planned anyway. On the Monday I see the nurse at the health centre who tells me that I have high blood pressure, which probably shouldn't surprise me in view of all the extra weight I am carrying. She prescribes Fisherman's Friends and a course of antibiotics, but I am loathe to take the latter so pack them away in our medical kit in case of emergency. We also test our sledges and shotgun that fires a heavy solid ball, or rather Rune does, since his military training means that polar bear defence has been delegated to him.

We are having trouble with our Argos satellite beacon, and everyone is talking about reported suggestions that the El Niño weather system is causing the polar ice-cap to melt earlier than normal. Could this simply be the wrong year to be making an attempt on the North Pole? I shudder at the thought of this. On a more optimistic note, when we weigh our sledges they come in at 106lbs and 150lbs, since Rune says dragging a heavier one will keep him warm and even up our relative skiing speeds. This is the huge advantage of a supported expedition, since the previous year our sledges were 300 to 325lbs. We'll move faster, but also be less likely to be dragged underwater should we fall through the ice, always my greatest fear. By the Wednesday my cold seems to have lifted, the result of massive doses of paracetamol and vitamin C, not to mention mothering by Joy the cook at the guest house. Borge Ousland phones to wish us well, and we also finally crack the problem with the Argos, where it transpired that we'd been reading the minutes and seconds on each degree as normal one sixtieths rather than simply digitally. It was actually bang on, but this also confirmed to me that you almost need a physics degree to make it to the Pole these days.

By Wednesday evening we have everything ready, and have decided to risk flying up to Ward Hunt Island the next morning. The weather looks touch and go for landing, but it is pointless trying to hang around for perfect conditions and we know that the full moon on 12 March will create massive tides that are bound to break up the ice. As usual I am finding the waiting difficult to cope with, have lost my appetite and feel my nerves are getting the better of me. Even though it goes against the received Inuit wisdom I decide to risk a shower so I will at least set out feeling clean.

We rise at 4.30 a.m. the next morning and eat a breakfast of ham and eggs in subdued silence, it feeling like a condemned man's last meal. After a final visit to a proper lavatory for two months we drive to the airport in the pitch-black. Although we are warned again that low cloud may make a landing at Ward Hunt Island's unmanned, iced-over airstrip impossible we still go ahead and board the Twin Otter, and as we taxi Rune leans round and says to me, 'I've got the feeling we've been here before.' As we lift off he has his Walkman on, and is singing his own idiosyncratic version of the Rolling Stones' 'Satisfaction'. I'll have plenty of time to become familiar with this. We fly north across a white desert lit by a shimmering half-moon as the Arctic sun slowly struggles into the sky, unclimbed mountain peaks beneath us. We land for forty-five minutes to refuel at Eureka and Rune and I feel compelled to admit our nervousness as we walk on the ice together. We just have to get through the first ten days, establish a routine. Airborne again John points out that the position of the sun and moon means a classic neap tide, so relatively gentle currents to disturb the ice of the Arctic Ocean, but in a week's time that will be very different.

When we reach Ward Hunt Island and fly out over the ice-cap however we are shocked to find how broken up the ice appears from the air, although fortunately we see no wider stretches of open water so we should be able to navigate around them. The pilot agrees to attempt a landing on the beach, and at 11.22 a.m. we make a particularly violent touchdown on this tiny cone of land that pokes out into the Arctic Ocean, the most accessible point to the North Pole from its Canadian side. Between us and our destination the only other living things are seals, polar bears, a few arctic foxes and a couple of other teams of explorers. It truly is the most desolate place on earth. The wind-chill is −60°C and my permanently damaged nose is already throbbing again. After saying our farewells we strap on our skis and harness up our sledges, and within not much more than an hour the plane has gone, circling briefly overhead as we take our first few steps out on the ice.

We know what is ahead of us, but in some ways I feel better than last year. Then Rune was a friend, but now he is more like a brother to me. We know how well we work together, and we will need all that. The Pole is 415 nautical miles away, but we will be travelling much further than that around open leads of water and as the ice drifts, east, west and south, more like 600 nautical miles probably. We start walking and within an hour come across a French–Italian–Canadian three-man expedition that we'd got to know back in Resolute. We'd felt then that there was dissension between them, and now it looks as if they might even be giving up on their first day. We head on past them, and set up camp feeling very pleased to have managed 3 miles in an hour and a half. I'm annoyed to detect some slight frostbite on my fingers, a result of filming with the BBC *Video Diaries* camera, as apart from my nose I have pretty much managed to avoid it in the past. Despite that we decide to celebrate our first night on the ice with a swig of whisky from two hip flasks of single malt that we've been given. Supper is Irish stew. Hell, here we are again!

I wake up feeling cold, remembering almost at once that there will be nowhere to warm-up for the next sixty days. It was relatively mild inside the tent last night, only −30°C, but it should really have been some 20 degrees less than that. We've deliberately left slightly earlier this year, when there is less daylight and hence lower temperatures, as that should mean open water rapidly freezes over. I little thought I'd find myself wishing for colder weather, but to a large extent our chances of success depend on that. We both feel the pressure of the sixty days we have set ourselves to reach the Pole, but Rune already seems to have relaxed and settled into a routine of just getting on with the job. I hate getting out of my sleeping bag in the morning, and from that moment onwards I look forward to the moment when I can get back inside it again. We can't ease ourselves into this gently, as the worst rubble and pressure ridges will be over the first 100 miles, but as we are out of practice it still takes us four hours to get going in the dark. Within an hour of setting off we are fed-up, as it becomes clear that our ski bindings have been mounted too far forwards, but for all our swearing we know we will just have to cope until our first resupply. We manage another 3 miles during the day, and in a ridiculous radio conversation relayed between us and John by a radio operator in Resolute we discover that we and the marines are now the only two teams out on the ice, although one member of the other aborted expedition will attempt to struggle on solo, God help him.

The next few days are very difficult. Rune is much fitter than me, the fourteen years between us making all the difference, and I feel exhausted. Our biggest problem is the cold, since we are not heating the tent as we want to conserve fuel. Our thermometer measures down to −55°C, but on the morning of day four it is off the bottom of the scale. Even if Rune is doing better than me we are both tired and miserable, our metabolisms not yet adapted to the cold and we are struggling to digest our 6,000-calorie daily rations. To make matters worse my thermarest, a vital layer of protection as I sleep, has disintegrated in the cold and no longer works just at the time I need it most. Rune gives short shrift to my suggestion that he should lend me his, or that we should share it on alternate nights. At my statement that any good friend would do so he simply smokes a roll-up and says, 'I am not that good a friend.' It takes us an hour to help each other struggle into our frozen boots in the morning. We are making better mileage than last year however, up to 5 miles a day already.

On day five we discover a serious equipment problem, as all three fuel pumps for our stove have stopped working properly. Something is wrong with the rubber washer in each case and they are leaking. If this goes on we will either be unable to cook and hence starve or be asphyxiated by the fumes. We simply can't work out what is wrong. The first two started to leak when it was relatively mild, so the extreme cold does not seem to be the sole cause. We'd checked everything thoroughly before departure, and can't believe in the possibility of deliberate sabotage when we left the pumps out prior to packing, yet nor does accidental damage seem a reasonable explanation for all three. To conserve fuel we agree not to heat our tent however cold it gets, and to accept the cruel sacrifice of foregoing our hot drink before bed. Although this is very depressing we also have a moment of experiencing the sheer beauty that the Arctic can throw up. Rune taps me on the shoulder and points back towards the vapour trails our warm bodies leave behind us as we walk, a ghostly spoor that takes five minutes to dissipate in the still air.

The cold is a mixed-blessing still. I have some frostbite on two toes now, the result of new boot liners I am wearing being just fractionally too small, and Rune has to dress my wounds which may be becoming septic. The temperature does mean we have been lucky in not coming across real open water, until we find our first major lead on day six. There is a science of sorts to determining the strength of ice from its appearance, but Rune adopts a far simpler method of just stabbing it with his ski pole. If it remains unbroken after three pokes then it is safe, if the third goes through you consider risking it – but then he is far less afraid than I am of falling into the icy water below. Salt water freezes at a lower temperature than fresh, about $-4°C$, but although it might be less cold than the surrounding air you lose heat far more rapidly once you get wet. I was terrified to hear about one part of his commando training, cutting two holes in the ice of a frozen lake and diving through one to emerge from the other. Nothing on earth would make me attempt such a thing.

Rune's method of determining the ice's strength seems very rough science to me, but I know from last year that he is right. Having made our way less than a quarter of a mile west we reach a point he has spotted where he thinks we can cross. This time the ice survives until the third poke, and my heart in my mouth I unharness my sledge and ski across without mishap then pull my sledge across after me. This is just the first of hundreds or even thousands that we will encounter, and although it is stressful for me I know it is equally so for Rune in other ways as he feels responsible for me. 'I know how I am going to react, David,' he says, 'but I don't know how you will react.' Apart from this we trust each other completely as a team and we are building a good routine again, starting from the moment my alarm goes off under my ear at 6.00 a.m. and I lean over to wake Rune with a prolonged shout of 'Rooner!' As the cook he must get up first, and he claims to enjoy this time by himself listening to music on his Walkman and smoking the first of his never-ending stream of cigarettes. This only makes the inside of our tent all the more resemble a steam room, our condensed breath filling the air and forming into hoarfrost that covers everything.

I am the main navigator, which is a very complex business. Although we are heading north the compass actually points almost due south, since we are north of the moving Magnetic Pole, and the compensation for magnetic variation even fluctuates during the day as the Magnetic Pole oscillates due to the sun's activity. We can check our position with a GPS, but the batteries for this need to be warmed before it can be used. Often it is easier to navigate by the sun, but that also requires being certain our watches are set to the correct time zone, which will become more difficult when the lines of longitude converge as we reach further north. Rune is better suited to be the point man, finding the simplest route through the rubble and around or across the pressure ridges or leads of open water, the fastest way not necessarily always being the most direct. As the far faster skier he can scout ahead and check the possibilities for our best path, and although we have constant minor arguments about our overall direction and best route we are both astounded how much easier the terrain has been this year, which we know may all change on the evening of our eighth day, Thursday 12 March, with a full moon and spring tide.

And it is truly terrifying when it comes. The titanic forces of the tide produce what seems like an earthquake at sea, as huge pans of ice clash together or are ripped apart. The noise like rifle shots as the ice cracks and the continual sound of falling rubble are frightening, and even worse is the constant vibration. What petrifies us most as we lie helpless in our sleeping bags is that there's no way of knowing if a pressure ridge will suddenly be thrown up 30 feet under our tent, or if the ice will split apart beneath us so we are hurled into the freezing ocean. Despite the night's huge upheaval the state of the ice when we manage to get moving in the morning is not quite as bad as we had feared, but although I do not take a reading I know that overnight we have been swept back between 1 and 2 miles, so we are just making up ground against the continually moving ocean.

Day ten sees us confined to our tent, with high winds and visibility of no more than 18 inches, but we can afford this as we have made such good headway. The next day sees us set a new record distance of 7¾ miles, so it is brandy and a cigar to celebrate. Even our little arguments serve to bond us more closely together. I'd complained that the warm juice we drink from a thermos during the day wasn't hot enough, and the next day's flask is so hot that when I take a mouthful I have to spit it out. In addition to 'Old Man' and 'Kid' that we call each other, I have now become 'Dr Livingstone' after the medal I had received, and Rune is naturally therefore 'Dr Nansen' after the great Norwegian Polar explorer. By the end of day twelve on 16 March we cross our first degree, the 84th Parallel, and last year it had taken us twenty-nine days to reach this far. We only have a couple of days' fuel remaining however, and decide to order a resupply on day fourteen, even though this will make our sledges much heavier again. The rubble is dreadful now, and we just have to hope that we can find a suitable landing strip.

The Twin Otter is a remarkable plane, with pilots saying they only need a flat(ish) 100 feet to land, but even they need 1,200 to take off again. We daren't order the resupply before we have actually found a good enough place, since then the plane might have to turn back and we'd still end up paying for it. Fortunately the skies are blue and clear when we get going, and after an hour we climb a pressure ridge and I hear Rune whooping when he reaches the top. When I follow him I can see what he is so excited about, a perfect pan of ice spread out in front of us. Ideally we'd have travelled more than the mile or so we've come so far today, but we both know this is the ideal spot and too good to pass up, so we set up our tent and radio John to arrange things. The Royal Marines have abandoned their attempt, we are told, and a rescue mission has been launched, although what has gone wrong he does not know. Then it is time to heat up the tent at long last and for Rune to check the frostbite on my toes. I have a big blister on the front tip beneath the nail which looks bad, and I hope it will hold-up.

When we wake on day fifteen and radio Resolute to confirm

the weather is holding we are told that a plane is already on the way. This means a sudden desperate rush to get ready, arranging all our equipment into three piles, one to go back, one to remain with us, and the third to be exchanged for new supplies, as well as all the fuel and food we will be receiving. We have to get this right, and avoid sending back by mistake something we will need. When we finally hear the drone of the approaching aircraft I let off a parachute flare to alert the pilot of our position, very foolishly nearly hitting the plane itself. Rune screams at me and holds his head in his hands, and I know we both have the same vision of the near-disaster that I almost caused. It takes three attempts for the pilot to put-down, our strip clearly not being as long or flat as we thought, but eventually the aircraft comes to a halt. Immediately bedlam ensues, as we rush around dismantling one tent and simultaneously attempting to erect the new one, piles of food and equipment all over the place.

John tells us the Marines have pulled out due to the same sort of fuel leak we've experienced, but are now walking back to Ward Hunt Island for a pick-up having only travelled a total of 12 miles. I feel like crying when it turns out our replacement skis have the wrong bindings and won't fit on our custom-made boots, so they have to go back to Resolute. Within forty minutes the weather is closing in and the pilot needs to leave, saying we've been very fortunate as he wouldn't have landed in the conditions here now. He taxis to the end of the landing strip, and with a roar takes off. Once more we are alone.

Quite apart from the skis things have not gone perfectly. We immediately find a bag of clothing that was meant to go back to be de-iced and washed before being returned to us on the next resupply, so instead of that we will have to order new replacements from the UK. Also I am disappointed that some Italian salami I had ordered hasn't arrived, but apart from that we have everything we could need, including a newspaper. We gorge ourselves on cake, peanuts, even oranges, and now with plenty of fuel and new pumps we turn the stove on full to heat the tent up. The warmth is wonderful, but as we are not used to it our faces puff up. We don't care though: 'Feel that warmth,' says Rune, 'it's as good as sex.' Right now I have to agree, for the first time in weeks we are in a tent not dripping with hoarfrost, and under the roof of the tent it is like a sauna. We lie there stripped to our woollen underpants, our first chance to dry out all our clothing properly. Because I sweat more than Rune does mine is heavily encrusted in ice.

As I sit there reading the *Edmonton Mail* I certainly feel we need these little luxuries that can come with a resupply. Struggling towards the Poles is difficult enough as it is without enforcing even greater privation than necessary upon yourself. Some people might think it somehow isn't 'pure', but it would seem to me ridiculous not to use the modern equipment that is available or to reject the technology and knowledge we have that our predecessors of necessity had to do without. You have to strike a balance between the weight of what you need to carry and how much more bearable something makes our time here. For me now a bottle of brandy is essential for small celebrations, as are plenty of pork scratchings, the salt in which means we don't experience any cramps. Perhaps you have to be a masochist to be here at all, but I don't want to make it any worse than it needs to be.

We know we will have to keep moving fast on the next leg of our journey, to cover the 150 miles and reach 86.30 degrees north for our second resupply by 15 April. On our first day walking again we encounter the worst rubble we've met with so far, and have to haul our sledges up cliff faces of ice up to 10 feet high. To make matters worse we are now pulling more weight than at any time before, with a lot more fuel and thirty days' food, including two emergency five-day packs. Rune is incredibly strong, which makes him ignore my constant nagging about how much spare clothing and equipment he is dragging in his two blue bags of personal stuff, one of which is as large as a rucksack, but although it is a risk we agree to dump ten days' food. The day after is an almost complete white-out with very strong winds, and I have to rely almost purely on Rune's instincts that we are heading north.

That night we cook inside the inner tent for the first time, the old leaky pumps having previously forced us to do so in the outer tent, from which most of the heat escaped. We know our bodies are burning 12,000 calories a day although we can only physically absorb half that, but we think and talk constantly about food and crave even our oil-soaked dinners, squabbling over the portions. We have to suck on our chunks of Mars Bars during the day, as the cold has shrunk the amalgam in our teeth and chewing on them could easily pull the fillings out. Although I now have new boots, which make a huge difference, when he removes the dressing on my big toe to rub in antibiotic cream Rune is very worried about my frostbite. I say I don't mind if I lose the toe, but he says we will abandon the trip if I get gangrene. Over the radio that evening there is plenty of news from home

On day eighteen the dreadful rubble suddenly ends and we have flat pans of ice. To compensate, yesterday's new snow makes the going very heavy and even slows Rune down, so I keep catching him up rather than simply being able to follow on in his tracks. Whenever he slips over on the ice I can't help saying I could do better than that myself, and must keep reminding myself to engage brain before opening my mouth. However much it irritates him, I just can't stop it. On the plus side I seem to be acclimatizing to the temperature and my hands and feet feel better, and I also miraculously discover that I have got used to my skis, the incorrectly fitted bindings now actually making balancing easier, a wonderful serendipitous accident. Rune agrees, and we both decide that we will stick with them this way. When we hear how fast a Norwegian team are moving behind us we also decide we should emulate them and ask for rucksacks on our next resupply, since the ten kilos we could easily carry that way will make a huge difference to the weight of our sledges.

From day twenty-one we decide to walk for seven hours a day, up from our initial five hours although we had already increased that to six as soon as daylight allowed it. It will help counteract the overnight backdrift that is often happening. We've also cut down the time for our breaks and decide to walk on day twenty-two, even though it should be a planned rest, since we are 4 miles behind schedule. During the day I catch myself thinking about celebrations on reaching the Pole, but know I mustn't dwell on this until we hit 89 degrees. It amazes me when I realize that I have spent nearly two years of my life up here in the Arctic, even if that has been spread over fifteen. Despite a decent day's distance the GPS tells us that we have drifted 12 miles west in two days, but the good news is that although my toes still look dreadful I have started being able to feel them again, which is a good sign. Rune's feet, on the other hand, look like a battlefield, the skin falling off both the top and bottom, which he blames on sweat due to the vapour barrier bags inside his boots.

Rune insists on resting in our tent on day twenty-three believing, quite rightly as it happens, that the lead we had camped beside and had seen open from 10 to 150 feet during the day would freeze over during the night. We cross it easily when we set off the next morning, heading north-east to counteract our continued westwards drift. It's our fifth consecutive day of gale-force winds, but it is warmer and Rune says he has slept better since discarding his vapour barrier bag and his sweat will no longer freeze inside his sleeping bag. Then after a couple of hours we are stopped in our tracks. 'It is almost as if we have seen the devil himself,' Rune says. It is the mother of all leads, stretching east and west as far as we can see, a mile or more across, and the sky above us has turned almost black. Has El Niño and the warming weather caused the ice to break up a couple of months earlier than it should do? I will not listen to his suggestion that we strap our sledges together and try paddling across, and it is the first time I have seen waves on the Arctic Ocean, up to a foot high. For five hours we trudge east, and even though we sometimes see the thinnest of ice form the water is moving fast. Eventually we decide we can only camp beside the lead's narrowest point, but for the ice to freeze solid enough for us to cross the wind will need to drop so it stops moving.

In the morning we find we have drifted half a mile north, but nothing like enough to close the lead, and where it was partially frozen there is now open water and overhead we are still shrouded by that ominous black cloud. We set off east in a direction where the sky looks lighter, hoping this might mean the lead has closed there. In a couple of hours we find a place that might just afford a crossing, a jumbled mass of soft ice, debris and pools of water, provided we take the right route through the maze. From a mound of rubble we can see there might possibly be sufficient ice to bear our weight across to the other side, and Rune simply strides across the porridge-ice, his ski poles puncturing the surface with each step, but by moving at speed he does not sink. I don't for a moment think I can follow him.

I have no choice but to try however, and Rune will help me. He unharnesses his sledge and fishes out the video camera, which he sets up on a tripod saying he wants to film this crossing, then he literally runs back across the slush to where I am. Pulling my sledge after me I tread gingerly from patch to patch of ice as he directs me, cajoling me to keep going, not to be frightened and not to stop. I throw him my sledge harness and keep screaming as my feet slip underwater, on a knife-edge between buoyancy and sinking. It is only a dozen feet, and I constantly feel I am teetering on the brink of going right through, but eventually I make it to the other side and slump down in relief. I now feel I need to direct Rune, yet from where I am standing the slush appears 6 inches beneath the surface, but he has crossed twice already and ignores me completely, stepping calmly through the water and crossing in twenty seconds when it seemed like I had taken twenty minutes. We have both made it over and head off again north-east to get back on course.

The rest of the day is beautiful with clear skies and for the first time I can feel the warmth on my back, not caring that I am sweating heavily. We spot a seal, his head poking up through a polynya and the only sign of life since we left. Although the sea fog envelops us and the temperature drops Rune drives us on to continue westing, and despite the fact that I am exhausted by the time we camp we're elated to find from the GPS that we have come 8¼ miles – our best day yet! – and crossed the 85th Parallel. A double brandy day! I am reminded of Peary's words from his first attempt to reach the North Pole in 1906: 'What contrasts this country affords. Yesterday hell, today comparative heaven, yet not such a heaven as most would voluntarily choose.'

On the morning of day twenty-six I wake up feeling dreadful. I know that at 41 I am simply getting too old to be putting my body through the rigours of long polar expeditions, and my weight loss is very visible. To compound my physical debilitation I am also depressed that we have drifted back a further mile overnight. We start walking in another white-out, and it isn't long before I contend with my worst moment in fifteen years' experience of the polar regions. I am crossing what appears to be a solid section of ice across the first lead we come to, and suddenly it gives way beneath me and I am up to my waist in the Arctic Ocean, flailing desperately. I shout for Rune who is only a few yards away, and in a mad panic rip the ice-spikes from around my neck and seek to drive the titanium claws into the nearest piece of white ice I can see. I can't swim with my skis on and feel sure I am going to drown.

Everything seems to happen in slow-motion and our whole expedition seems to pass before my eyes, but before I know it Rune has dragged me from the freezing water and onto an ice floe where I lie gasping for breath. I am desperate for him to set up the tent so I can get my soaking clothes off, but Rune will have none of it. It's happened to him many times, he says, and the only thing to do is keep walking and allow my body-warmth to dry my clothes, otherwise I will never get the ice out of them. He is so insistent I have no choice, but my teeth are chattering for hours during the rest of our day's slog over difficult ice rubble and by the evening I am utterly shattered. My mind now seems dominated by two things, apart from my continual fear of drowning – our continuous drifting backwards and our next resupply, which is threatened by our many days of poor visibility.

Assuming we can walk for just over another week on this leg, managing 9 or 10 miles a day, that will take us up to 86.30 degrees north. If we hang on until then for the resupply that would be great, meaning lighter sledges for the last leg, but it is a balancing act between working out when the weather will allow a plane to come in and if we go beyond that point the cost of a resupply doubling. We will have to rely on John in Resolute to argue our case for us, and keep reminding him over the radio that he must watch the expense. And we are rewarded with some flat pans of ice and easier going, breaking our distance record with our light sledges and achieving 12 miles on day thirty, even finding the drift has suddenly started to work in our favour and carry us north. John tells us that the resupply will probably be delayed until Friday 10 April, due to the weather over the ice-cap and unavailability of planes, but by then we will have run out of food.

We are caught up by the Norwegian Express Team and sit and talk during a munchies stop. By walking for twelve hours a day and sleeping only six they hope to make it to the Pole in a month, the fastest trip ever, and have achieved 20 miles that day. They are clearly incredibly fit, even if two of their party of five have had to drop out. It's disturbing to hear how based on their previous experience they expect the rubble to persist all the way to the Pole, but we can't talk of the conditions all the time and find ourselves discussing the best pubs in London or where to get a decent curry in Oslo. When we get back to our tent John tells us that the air company say the resupply will definitely happen on Friday, another three days' walking first, as low cloud is heading our way tomorrow. I simply don't understand how they can be so certain Friday will be ok, and suspect that although we booked our resupply a fortnight ago they have made other commitments for their planes in the meantime.

The Tuesday and Wednesday are excellent days, we achieve about 11 miles on each, but the latter is one of our hardest as we are running on empty with no chocolate to keep us going through the hours of hard slog, just some hot juice. The most frustrating thing is that we have clear skies, yet the air company believe the weathermen at Resolute who say we should be shrouded in low cloud. How can we feel confident about resupply on Friday when they can't see the real-time weather, and although we will have to pay for the flight we have no real control on when they will come. Rune keeps talking about the goodies we can expect, and the thought of this is driving us both mad. Then at 9.00 p.m. when we radio First Air in Resolute we are told that the aircraft is already on its way and will be with us in two and a half hours. Rune immediately shoots off to prepare the landing strip and I furiously start writing letters to everyone. Then I can't find the

GPS to give our position to the approaching aircraft, and I curse Rune until it turns up in his personal blue bag outside the tent rather than in his sleeping bag where it should be.

We see the plane approach shortly before midnight with the midsummer sun shining brightly. The Twin Otter circles overhead for a few minutes, then puts down first time with an almighty thump. Along with John there are journalists from the *Telegraph* and BBC, and we all hug each other even though I can tell they are holding their breath as I am sure we must smell like sewer rats. The most important piece of news for me is that Amelia has had her operation, and the biopsy has found nothing serious. We also discover that the resupply was brought forward at the last moment as a storm was approaching Resolute, and the plane had taken off in gale-force winds without knowing for certain if they would be able to land here on the ice. We rush around exchanging equipment, a new tent, sleeping bags and a sledge for Rune as his was becoming increasingly damaged, as well as fuel and food for twenty-five days. In less than an hour they are gone, making a very uncertain take-off after aborting one attempt and then barely struggling into the air on the second, just skimming over the top of a pressure ridge by a bare few feet.

It's party time in our clean tent, and we stuff down the cheese sandwiches and cherry pie that we had ordered, with fresh fruit, brandy and, of course, cigars for Rune, who now feels his life has been saved having run out of tobacco for a few days. There are Easter cards from home, and Rune gorges on four chocolate eggs as the party goes on until four in the morning, during which time the unfamiliarly rich food sends him outside four times to go to the toilet. We're exhausted as much by the partying as the late night wait for the plane when we are finally ready to go to sleep, but have decided to take the remainder of that Thursday off, our day thirty-six, as a rest day. We will need our energy for the last leg, and once again we will have heavy sledges to cope with.

Our first day walking again is Good Friday, and Rune is troubled with his vision saying he is almost blind. We are not sure if it is just the temporary yet painful condition of snow blindness, but he has to wear his goggles and fortunately we can at least follow the tracks of the Norwegian Express, which we need as it is another white-out. There is no question that a plane would have been able to land today as originally planned. Rune now carried a rucksack of 15lbs, which leaves our sledges lighter, but we will need time to tell if this makes things easier. We are relatively lucky with the leads, but the full moon of the night before has broken up the ice, the noise of it grinding and crashing together having kept me awake for hours. When Rune's eyes seem to be improving the next day, we come to the conclusion that it was probably the massive excess of sugar in the chocolate he ate that caused the problem. Even though he is better red splodges on the ice make me worry that Rune is bleeding for some reason, but they turn out only to be the tobacco juice he has been spitting out from his constant chewing. We've headed too far east, following the Norwegians, but still crossed over the 87th Parallel.

Day forty, Monday 13 April, starts well, but we soon find ourselves struggling through alternating rubble and then across leads, dozens of them, although later in the afternoon the way opens up and we seem to be crossing old multi-year ice with humps but little debris. Then suddenly I stumble and fall, smashing my wrist down on some thin ice a long step down from an ice floe, worried at first I may have broken it. Rune rushes over, but I get no sympathy. 'Get up David and get a fucking move on,' he shouts. I've never heard him swear directly at me this way before, and ignoring the searing pain I scarper the 10 feet across the lead towards him. A crack in the ice splinters at my feet, and sensing his urgency I ski after him for five minutes, until we are finally clear of the fault in the ice-sheet that my fall had triggered. This is not the end of my bad day though, as when clambering over ice rubble I slip and my sledge that was balanced precariously behind me rams into the small of my back, making me scream out in agony. My back was bad enough already, but now it hurts all the way down its length.

We will also soon be crossing the Lomonosov Ridge, which rises almost 4,000 feet from the 9,000 foot depth of the Canada Abyssal Plane that has stretched all the way here from the coasts of Canada and Alaska, before the seabed then plummets into the trough of the Pole Abyssal Plane almost directly beneath the Pole and the deepest part of the Ocean at 15,000 feet. The Lomonosov Ridge is the strongest influence on the water movements in the Ocean, and the colossal currents may mean we have to fight against drifting back 2 or more miles overnight from the direction in which we need to go. To compensate we increase the length of our walking day and manage a new record of just over 12 miles even with our heavy sledges, but it is hot work and we vent off all the zips on our jackets and trousers even though it is –49°C with the wind-chill. It is the first day my goggles icedown due to the warmth, but because he walks without his face mask Rune catches some frostbite on his left earlobe.

Day forty-three is a huge relief, the wind having dropped so it at least seems warmer and there is no back-drift. We equalize the length of our sessions rather than starting with a longer one, making them an hour and twenty minutes each, which seems more manageable. Also we decide to stop for a more substantial lunch than just chocolate and hot juice, and find that gives us more energy through to the end of the day. We are thrilled to manage our best mileage yet again of 13 miles, but concerned still to be seeing the tracks of the Norwegian Express as they should be at the Pole already. On the radio that evening John tells us they have set the emergency code on their Argos beacon. Since they have no radio no one knows exactly why, but there is concern that reports in the Norwegian newspapers, from a pilot that recently flew over the Pole, say they have been stopped by a lead 10 miles wide and 2 miles across. If this is true, our chances of reaching the Pole may have gone, as such a stretch of open water will probably never freeze over now the sun is up twenty-four hours a day.

My back is hurting me desperately, not to mention my thighs and toes, and the huge amount of ibuprofen I am taking not only upsets my stomach and prevents me eating properly but is also making me physically sick, so I leave frequent pools of freezing vomit in my trail. We have to start notching up regular large distances now though, so I know I must do whatever it takes to get through this. The weather is good however, but the warmth makes me sweat and it is a constant balancing act between having my goggles soon ice over from my perspiration, or going without them and risking frostbite and snow blindness. I find my mind wandering, not just to the perhaps natural thought of whether I will get an upgrade to business class for my flight home, but to the more prosaic question of how my football team Swindon Town are faring. Rune frequently upbraids me for the general coarseness of my language, which genuinely seems to upset him. He is far more religious than me, although I admit I am praying for good weather and terrain, and he feels my constant swearing is disrespectful towards the awesome power of the natural world around us. Even if he can't deny he has adopted many of my English expletives he says that doesn't mean he considers me a good influence, and I vow to try a little harder.

Towards the end of the day we spot a tent about a mile away which we are certain must be that of the Norwegian Express. Since we know they are safe due to their Argos message, perhaps superstitiously we avoid them and press on as fast as we can. Rune is ruminating on how many days it might take us to reach the Pole from here, saying he will remove the skins from his skis to reduce friction and that now is not the time to try and conserve our health or energy, but I have always felt any Polar expedition is a marathon and not a sprint. We should set our sights on crossing the 88th Parallel tomorrow, and then concentrate on the final 120 miles, which Rune still feels we might achieve in ten days. The next night, despite terrible rubble most of the way, the increase in the length of our walking day to nine and a half hours sees us shoot past the Parallel and notch up 12 miles, and time is now of the essence as I am desperately worried about whether we can beat the open water that will inevitably come with the thaw. We hear on the radio that the members of the Norwegian Express have ultimately been defeated by all their skis disintegrating under the demands of travelling up to eighteen hours a day.

On Sunday 19 April, day forty-six, we take a break and stay in bed until 10.00 a.m., then spend the rest of the day drying out our clothes, repairing equipment and chatting. It seems warmer in the tent, but the thermometer says otherwise, still −34°C outside, so perhaps we are just getting fully acclimatized. Inevitably our conversation turns to what the other would do if one of us was injured and could not continue. From the start Rune had minimized the news he was receiving from home so any bad reports wouldn't make him turn back, but I had always said that I would go back if Amelia's condition had proved dangerous. In that event Rune would probably have come with me, but we feel near enough now to say that if either of us was injured the other would drag him to the Pole on his sledge. I tell Rune that if I needed a medical evacuation I wouldn't let him on the plane, would break his fingers in the door if necessary. If nothing else could be done I believe that we are so far in that the other should continue alone, but Rune is typically modest, saying that this is my Grand Slam and it would be pointless him going on without me. That night we speak on the radio to a pilot who says the ice conditions to the Pole look good, but we both know what might appear fine from the air can be a jumbled mess at ground level. We'll believe it when we see it.

We find that we've drifted back a mile and a half during our rest day, but we needed it, the last one we will have before this final dash to the Pole. The terrain is dreadful all throughout the day with rubble and partially frozen leads, and we are also floating eastwards unusually quickly, all of which I am sure are due to the effects of the Lomonosov Ridge. For me it is a day of injuries: firstly I experience a heavy nosebleed for the first time in years, which makes me worry about the high blood pressure I was warned about before we set out, then my sledge once again rams into the small of my back making my damaged coccyx even worse. Finally and worst of all I slip on some blue ice and strain my thumb. It bends back to touch the side of my hand and for a while I worry it is broken, although I manage to keep skiing despite the intense pain. When Rune tends to it that evening with alternating warmth and ice the treatment works and the swelling subsides, but I am still worried I may have fractured it. We've achieved 13¾ miles however, despite the conditions, and at this rate we are only a week from the Pole.

My thumb keeps me awake during the night, which I could do without. We are both very fatigued, desperately needing all the rest we can get, and Rune tells me that he has been throwing-up all morning due to the food last night disagreeing with him. Our injuries and weakness as our weight has dropped mean we fall over far more easily in this dreadful terrain, and we constantly wonder if we will ever find the big pans of flat ice that we've been led to believe we should be encountering by now. In mid-afternoon when clambering over a pressure ridge I slip and fall partially into the water, my arm and shoulder submerged but my legs still on the ridge and snagged in rubble. When Rune eventually sees what has happened he unhesitatingly dives into the lead and treads water with his skis as he helps me out, before I finally do the same for him. It's seeing something like this that makes me realize how truly incredible this young man is, unquestioningly doing something that most people would think might kill them. We have to walk hard all the rest of the day to drive the moisture from our sodden clothes, but when the sun comes out if feels beautifully warm and we have completed a distance similar to yesterday.

Our radio seems not to be working the next day, and despite taking it apart that evening I can find nothing wrong with it. We can only hope our Argos position will show we are still making progress, that John won't panic and try to airlift us out. With another record distance of nearly 15 miles we can't help starting to think seriously about the possibility of making it to the Pole. Now and the next day we have finally come to some small pans of flat ice, the wind has dropped and it gets warmer as the day wears on, leading us to strip off several layers. We crave the warmth, yet fear the inevitable thaw that it must bring. Towards the end of the day we see two seals, which worries us as it can mean only one thing – open water – and in a few minutes we come to the largest lead we have seen in days, a huge stretch of broken ice. We don't feel injury can thwart us now, but clear water certainly can, yet we manage to cross it and by evening also the 89th Parallel.

The next day, 51 of our trip, is a Friday, and we are faced with a dilemma. We both want to push on, could increase the length of our walking day, but Claire and Alicia are due to arrive in Resolute on Tuesday, intending to come and meet us at the Pole. If we get there early we will just be sitting around, or still having to walk every day to maintain our position there as the drift constantly takes us away from the Pole. Although part of each of us feels more confident of eventual success, I keep warning Rune not to be complacent as things can go wrong now as easily as at any other time on our journey. We are both madly fantasizing about the food we will have when we get home – beef sandwiches for me, a massive omelette for Rune – and our luck seems to hold up today, since although there is plenty of open water we always find good crossing points, but Rune's navigation seems to be going astray. It is increasingly difficult as you near the Pole, and I'd found on my trip to the South Pole that my ski sticks could affect the magnetic variation on my compass which is nearly 180 degrees now. When I tactfully suggest this to Rune he first glowers at me then, after taking a solar reading, veers off at a right-angle to his previous direction.

We're close enough now to start fretting about whether there will be a flat enough pan of ice near the Pole to land a plane, or whether a really large area of open water could be sitting there making the Pole impossible to reach at all. We're maintaining the same sort of distances, and I am crossing leads now on the sort of spongy ice that I would absolutely have refused to risk just a few weeks ago. On Saturday afternoon the sun is suddenly hidden by thick cloud and we are soon in almost complete darkness, with the temperature plummeting back down to –36°C and the wind then picking up. We keep going but after managing 13 miles decide enough is enough and we should camp. We have a little more than 25 miles to go in a straight line – not that such a thing ever actually exists here.

I am very worried about what the weather will be on Sunday morning, and we start walking in bitter cold and a total white-out. To make matters worse the break-up of the ice is the most extreme we have seen so far, which just shouldn't be happening as we are well past the Lomonosov Ridge. Then in the early afternoon the cloud starts to break and we can see the sun low in the sky, which lifts our spirits and makes navigation much easier. With the weather improving our luck also seems to change, and the leads we come across are either frozen or have simple crossings, and eventually our wishes come true as the landscape opens up to leave a clear vista westwards towards the northern horizon. It is almost as if the Pole is illuminated by a spotlight, tantalizingly close, leading us to add an extra forty minutes to our normal workload.

Late in the day we see the tracks of an Arctic fox, and even if that means polar bears could also be nearby it provides some comfort not to feel entirely alone here. I am frankly bored of this hellish landscape and my fifteen-year battle with this awful but strangely beautiful place. We both want to get back to civilization. A gale on the Monday leaves us thankful for our mileage the day before, and we make dreadful progress with our navigation confused and even the GPS proving misleading, as the lines of longitude converge the nearer we are to the Pole. I am particularly cold, having ripped a hole in the backside of my windproof trousers when I almost castrated myself with my left ski the evening before, but I can't be bothered to mend it so close to the end. We've eventually had enough and camp that night some 2 miles from the Pole, although Rune is not pleased and feels we should keep going. I am partially motivated by a feeling that, since they have supported us for the last three years, we shouldn't arrive at the Pole whilst the BBC crew that is coming to meet us are still in the air from England. At the same time, another part of me feels it is arrogance and courting disaster to stop when almost within touching distance of our goal.

I wake at 5.00 a.m. on Tuesday 28 April, day fifty-five of our journey and exactly a year to the day since we were lifted off the ice at the miserable end of our last expedition. We're late start-ing, in heavy wind and an almost total white-out, so navigating by the sun will be impossible. Rune has switched on the Argos beacon and puts it in his rucksack so it will record our track right to the Pole, and we both clip on radio microphones to record our feelings. After walking for an hour we take out the GPS to check our position, but although it normally takes about thirty seconds for this to appear on the LCD screen in five minutes there is still nothing. Nor does Rune's spare GPS work either. I'd warmed the batteries that morning for these last few miles, so what can be wrong? Here at the Pole the GPS should pick up more satellites than anywhere else, but it is getting no signal at all. Could the satellites be turned off? The last time that hap-pened was during the first Gulf War, and tensions in the Middle East had been mounting again when we set off. It dawns on me horribly that we have heard nothing from the outside world for almost a week, and anything could have occurred. Nuclear war could have destroyed civilization for all we would know about it.

I frantically try to think what we could be doing wrong or different to before, and then it occurs to me that we are both wearing the radio microphones. Perhaps they are affecting the signals. I switch mine off and walk away from Rune, and sud-denly a series of dots appear on the GPS screen as the satellites are detected. Thank God, we are a mile closer to the Pole, and will be able to find it after all. An hour later we are just over a mile away, and the next time we check barely half a mile. I'm marking our position on a small-scale plotting chart, which is the only way we will be absolutely sure we get there. Now it is only 300 yards, and we have our first disagreement when Rune insists I should go ahead, which I refuse. We walk together, side by side, with the GPS in my hand as we count down the last 100 feet, and at 2.00 p.m. we decide we are as close as we can reasonably get within the accuracy limitations of the system. We've made it, at last, and my fifteen-year odyssey is finally over.

We hug each other furiously, and Rune sees me cry just as he did the year before. He quotes Amundsen's famous words on reaching the Pole ahead of Scott, 'Polen er naad. Alt vel' – 'the Pole is reached. All well.' Then we repeat what we have said every night of the expedition when we pitched camp. 'God save your Queen,' says Rune to me, saluting. 'God save your King,' I reply. We're getting dangerously cold so set up our tent for a late lunch and with the intention of doing absolutely nothing else for the rest of the day, but while he is getting the stove ready I hear a shout from Rune. He has taken one last reading, and it suggests that we have drifted even closer. Our tent is perhaps no more than 10 feet from the Pole as the whole world revolves beneath us. We film the GPS screen and settle down to our brandy and cigars.

It was only the next morning that our radio miraculously started to work again, and we heard a friendly voice that turned out to be that of the person guarding the fuel cache at 86 degrees, awaiting the planes that would be coming to pick us up. Rune felt very firmly that we'd done enough walking, but I desperately wanted to be as near to the Pole as possible when I met Claire and Alicia, as well as the BBC and ITN journalists and Robert Uhlig of the *Daily Telegraph*. We spent a ghastly seventeen hours walking overnight to find a landing strip that the pilots would feel they could put down upon, and our tiredness could almost have done for us both at the very end. I feared for a moment I'd lost Rune when he suddenly disappeared beneath the water before he finally resurfaced spitting ice-cubes, but eventually we managed to rendezvous with the planes and I was hugging my family and friends again, drinking champagne and filming interviews.

When we finally took off for the long flight back to Eureka

I felt I could no longer speak, withdrew into myself and could only stare out of the window. The ice looked so beautiful from above, but we flew over so much open water I knew that we would never have made it if we'd had to cross those last two degrees even a week later. I am so glad to be going home, to civilization and the comforts that we've been without for so long, but it is only when I leave the Arctic behind that I realize how much I will miss it once I have gone.

Returning to the North Pole on that third attempt I was a far more mature animal than previously, and I wasn't sure then if I actually wanted to try any more solo expeditions. On that second trip with Rune, even if we were supported, we felt it was a greater achievement than our unsupported but failed attempt, and it saw Rune become then the seventh Norwegian to reach the North Pole and me only the fourth Briton, or actually the first using just their own skis rather than dog teams or snow mobiles. We needed to get there, and if two resupplies were the only way to do so then that was the lesser evil. Would we have made it the first time without our sledge problem and helping the kid? I think we would, we'd done the first third, the hardest part. But the Holy Grail for me was the Grand Slam. A couple of other people were trying for it, so I thought if I don't get this out of the way now I'm never going to do it. That was the real pressure I felt, in finally reaching the North Pole at my third and what I felt must be my final attempt. Global warming will only make it harder, if not impossible, for others to continue doing so in the future.

There was one challenge in polar exploration I felt I'd left unconquered: a solo and unsupported expedition to the Geomagnetic North Pole. Although in 2003 at the age of forty-six my head told me it was probably time to put polar trekking behind me, my heart said, 'Bugger that, I've got no choice, I've got to do it.'

One of the main reasons I wanted to make this attempt was

the fact that I'd failed previously on a solo expedition to the Geomagnetic North Pole. The geomagnetic poles are antipodal points where the axis of a best-fitting dipole intersects the Earth's surface. This dipole is equivalent to an extremely powerful (and large!) bar magnet at the centre of the Earth, tilted at an angle of about 11° to the axis of rotation that points to the Geographic Pole, and it is this theoretical dipole that comes closer than any other to accounting for the magnetic field observed at the Earth's surface. In contrast, the actual magnetic poles are not antipodal – that is, they do not lie on a line passing through the centre of the Earth. The place in the northern hemisphere where this bar magnet then met the Earth's surface, the Geomagnetic North Pole, was positioned at 79.12° North 71° 12 West, although the fluid motion of the Earth's outer core means that both the Magnetic and Geomagnetic poles are constantly moving.

In 1992 I'd led the first team to walk unsupported to the Geomagnetic North Pole and I'd subsequently wondered whether I could repeat this trip solo and unsupported. I made my first such attempt in 2001 and on that occasion I'd had two choices to decide between: whether to go through the Sawtooth Mountains, a jagged snowcapped mountain range, or to take the longer route. Being a lazy git I'd chosen what I thought would be the shorter, easier way. However, maps don't always show you everything, and my journey was up and down like a yoyo; there were large ice boulders and not enough snow cover. Within four days or so I'd torn the bottom of my sledge, the runners had come off and I'd used up far too much food. That was the end of that trip and I called up a plane to come and pick me up. I'd only been out a few days and felt a terrible failure yet again, having travelled less than a third of the total distance. Once I'd got over the initial disappointment though I wrote down all my mistakes, and the lessons I had learned in the process. Now I wanted to return and do things totally differently, so as to achieve my goal.

I spent over a year organizing and training for this second attempt and Rune helped me sort out all my kit and with my preparation for the expedition. With new plans in place and equipment ready, I set off in March 2003 during the Iraq War. I was leaving a couple of weeks later than on my previous trip so it was slightly warmer. This time I'd also decided to tell hardly a soul about where I was going and to keep it that way until I knew for sure I was definitely certain to reach the Geomagnetic Pole.

I'd decided against attempting to go through the Sawtooth Mountains again, but to take the longer way around. I flew to Resolute Bay and then on to Eureka, the desolate meteorological outpost on Ellesmere Island, and found things had changed a lot since my previous trips. In Resolute there was now just one man at the weather station. In the eighties there were twenty people manning the Eureka base, but now there were only four. They used to let us eat anything for free, whereas now there was a steep price on absolutely everything. To transport my sledge down the two-mile strip onto the fjord they were going to charge me $300. If I wanted to stay the night in Eureka it would have cost me more than a room at The Four Seasons Hotel.

I decided I might just as well sleep in my tent, as I'd have to get used to that soon enough. The following morning, on 17 March, I set off dragging my sledge a couple of hundred feet down from the weather station onto the Slidre Fjord. This time however I skied in completely the opposite direction to the way I'd gone before. It was a beautifully still day then, and it took me just another four days to reach the spot where I'd been picked up at the end of my previous failed attempt. I had vivid memories of my broken sledge and dashed dreams, and was determined to make it this time. I always find that having failed at something once is a huge motivation not to do so again.

I was skiing on nice flat ice in –30°C, slowly getting into a rhythm and routine, and from there on it was all brand-new territory open before me. I had to ski right to the end of the fjord where it met a glacier and from there I needed to get onto the ice-shelf covering Ellesmere Island. My biggest anxiety was this: how was I physically going to climb onto the ice cap, which is 50 feet high in places? I kept trying to work out in my mind any way I could possibly haul up my hefty sledge, without ending up in a crumpled heap below.

One day I was having some snacks from my munchy bag when, from the corner of my eye, I saw something move. I looked around and there was nothing there. Then I looked again and in the distance I spotted a herd of musk ox. Next minute, they were gone; I'm pretty sure I must have scared them off. I was, though, skiing in the heart of polar bear territory in the spring, when they emerge from their dens after hibernation desperately hungry and searching for food, then head out towards the sea ice in search of seals to gorge upon. On the Penny Ice Cap, however, unless a bear has climbing experience, or an ice axe, you shouldn't see one! But I wasn't going to be complacent as I'd already seen plenty of polar bear tracks around the coast and was always on guard. I'll readily admit that after my previous encounter I'm a bit paranoid about polar bears, and each night I slept with my .306 rifle close to my side. This had been thoroughly checked before I left home, the grease removed and teflon powder used, because if you have any moisture at all in the rifle it possibly won't fire, which is the last thing you want to happen with a bear weighing half a ton charging directly at you. I kept the gun in the bell-end of the tent, which I left slightly open, and I still took the additional precaution of always leaving some salami and chocolate on my sledge parked in front of the tent. If a polar bear was sniffing around I hoped I'd be woken by the noise.

On Saturday 22 March, a few days into the expedition, I received a radio message asking me if I would give a statement about the death of my friend Terry Lloyd. Terry was an ITN reporter, one of the handful of people that knew where I was going, who had been planning to come out and interview me if my trip proved successful. I learned that Terry and his team of two cameramen had been caught in crossfire near Basra in Iraq, but only later discovered that the coroner recorded a verdict of 'unlawful killing' by US forces. I was desperately upset by Terry's death, which immediately sent me into a spiral of depressing thoughts about loved ones who had died, including my father, my uncle and various other close friends.

Being alone out on the ice you have no shortage of time to dwell upon such things, although strangely enough perhaps less than when you are part of a team and all the tasks are divided, rather than having to concentrate upon everything yourself. After a while I gradually managed to pull myself together. I needed all my mental strength and energy to focus on dragging the 150lb of provisions and equipment across that wilderness. Technically the route was pretty challenging as I had to scale ice walls, climb rocky outcrops, traverse shifting glaciers and abseil down frozen waterfalls. I certainly couldn't have done it without a background in both mountaineering and considerable polar experience.

As the trek went on I grew increasingly tired as I found myself having to climb up the side of a glacier, which was getting progressively steeper. Eventually this became a 60 degree slope so there was really only one option, to construct a pulley system and hoist up my sledge half its load at a time. I removed my skis, wore crampons, and used ice screws and an ice axe to do the job. I pulled up half a sledge-full first then came back for the other half. It took me the better part of half a day buggering about, but after that it was a fantastic feeling finally to be up on the ice-shelf as I experienced its pure remoteness. No one else, so far as I knew, had ever crossed this land as part of a solo expedition before. On the downside, I did begin to wonder how I could ever be rescued if I got into any trouble, since there were no helicopters for 500 miles. A Twin Otter could only land at the bottom of the fjord and from there it would take four or five days for anyone to reach me. I just had to push these negative thoughts aside and press on.

It took a further three days for me to cross the ice cap on Ellesmere Island, then I came down to the foot of a valley where it met the sea. From here I saw another fjord, the other side of Ellesmere Island, from which I could see across to Greenland. My next big challenge was crossing a treacherous glacier, lowering the sledge down, sometimes 4 or 5 feet at a time, sometimes 20 feet.

At the end of one day I came across a frozen waterfall some 20 feet high, and began lowering the sledge down again, trying to get a good strong hold with my ice axe. To my right was what appeared to be a nice big soft snowy bank, so I let the sledge down first and then jumped down after it. I landed on the bank about 10 feet below, which turned out to be ice-covered rock as hard as steel. There I was expecting to sink up to my knees in powdered snow, but instead I found myself smacking into solid ice. My leg buckled twisting horribly beneath me, and the pain in my right ankle shot up through my body. For a while I thought it was all over – longer than I like to think, but it certainly seemed a long time. I was convinced I'd broken my ankle or leg and that, once again, the Arctic had finally beaten me.

I was tempted to radio for a rescue plane there and then, but was damned if I was going to give up immediately so dragged myself to a flat section of the ice. Whilst lying on my side I clumsily erected my tent and crawled inside, then dosed myself up on painkillers and began inspecting my swollen ankle. Initially I thought about putting some ice directly onto it, but the ice was far too cold for that and I didn't want to end up getting frostbite, which really would mean the end of things. I had to heat up the blocks of ice on my stove until they were warm enough to begin melting, and then apply them to my swollen and bruised ankle. The ice slowly began to reduce the swelling, then I strapped up my leg as tightly as I could bear and tried to get some sleep.

After a miserably restless night I awoke to find I did have more movement in my leg than I'd expected and feared, so I forced my bloated foot back into its boot and slowly got going. I was either likely to be crawling or hobbling, so I got my ski sticks out for additional support. It was very painful going but I convinced myself that if I could actually move my ankle then it was unlikely I'd broken it. I slowly got to the end of the river valley, which opened into a fjord. Once I reached the bottom it was much easier terrain and I knew I was probably just three days away from the Geomagnetic North Pole. Each day I took more painkillers and at night I slept on the coast, near the sea ice where polar bears travelled. I made sure my rifle was always by my side, just in case I had any unwanted visitors.

After reaching Copes Bay, located in the Nares Strait on the east coast of Ellesmere Island, I then skied and scrambled across 50 miles of sea ice. The Geological Society in Scotland gave me the exact position of the Geomagnetic North Pole, and once I decided I was definitely going to make it I called the base station at Resolute Bay, asking for messages to be passed on to reporters at ITN and Robert Uhlig at the *Daily Telegraph*. These messages made my expedition public for the first time. Slowly I made my way up Smith Sound, the Arctic sea passage between Greenland and Ellesmere Island, and finally reached the Pole on the afternoon of 11 April. Here I was, after thirty days traversing about 300 miles of ice. I spent half an hour or so gazing around at the spectacular scenery and vast expanses of sea ice that stretched out before me in every direction. This was an incredibly poignant moment, as I felt certain in my heart it would be the last time I ever embarked on such an arduous solo polar expedition. I was definitely getting too old for this sort of thing.

A Twin Otter plane circled above me for a while, which began to worry me in case the pilot couldn't land, but I later discovered I was being filmed! Once inside the plane I slowly removed my boot, inners and socks, and began to inspect my right foot properly for the first time. I found it had turned a rather alarming shade of black, and Robert Uhlig nearly threw up at the gruesome sight. Then I did some interviews, including one with Radio 4's John Humphrys. I admitted to him that I'd told hardly anyone, including my own family, that I was on an expedition to the Geomagnetic North Pole, I'd simply said I was going off skiing. In truth, I hadn't wanted to frighten them, but I ended up being demonized by a lot of women in the country. It might sound like a terrible way to behave, but my family are used to it and to be honest I am always terrified that some journalist will doorstep one of my daughters and ask if she is worried about me when I am off on an expedition. There is no ideal way to handle this, but it seems to work best for us like this.

When we arrived at Resolute Bay a doctor looked at my spectacular foot, diagnosed a broken ankle and put a splint on it. I'd had a stressful and gruelling few weeks, but at the same time I knew I would miss the wilderness. I'll always remember how pristine the virgin snow appeared; the sun low on the horizon with an orange glow, varying shades of blue all around. I was truly privileged to witness such sheer beauty. I decided to dedicate the record to my friend Terry Lloyd who, like me, had found a rare peace in the Arctic and Antarctic.

Back in England I went straight to Cirencester Hospital, where an X-ray confirmed I had indeed broken my ankle and that it would take several weeks to recover. Emotionally, I knew what had happened: I'd blocked out the pain determined to finish the trek and not be a failure again. I was very lucky to be alive however.

I'm often asked what, of all the things I've set out to do, is the toughest challenge, and it is something I've thought about a lot. Both times I've tried Everest I have succeeded. On each occasion I've set out to reach the South Pole, long-distance, solo or other-wise, I've made it there. The one place that took me three attempts to get to, from the coast, was the North Pole. If you look at the numbers, very few people have ever successfully completed expeditions to the North Pole compared to the other big treks. My great hero Messner, for all his incredible achievements, took a shorter route than me in Antarctica, and with another person, but nevertheless he achieved it. The one thing that he's failed on in three attempts, and has said he'll never go back and try to do again as it's just too hard, is the North Pole.

Because you want to avoid the greatest drift and open water you simply have to go at the coldest possible time of year, and that can mean temperatures of −40°C plus wind-chill for three weeks, on a constant morning, noon and night basis. It doesn't warm up at all. The limiting factor is the light, so you have to go late enough in the spring when there is at least twilight and a plane can drop you off. For the South Pole, because it's a solid landmass, you can go at the warmest time of the year, the summer, and it can be relatively warm. The sun's always up, and the temperatures need not be so brutal. Of course, at the Pole itself you are at 10,000 feet, so it is colder due to the lapse rate where you lose 2°C for every

1,000 feet you go up, but in the summer on the coast at sea level you definitely get temperatures sometimes above freezing. Of all the things I have done, and perhaps no one else can truly say this with the same conviction of personal experience, the North Pole is the greatest challenge of them all.

AIR

I know I've made it. I'm somewhere above 41,000 feet, and no one has ever been higher in the open basket of a Rozier balloon, or any other sort for that matter except in a pressurized capsule. It's about 7.00 a.m. on a bright, clear morning and I can distinctly discern the curvature of the earth. I don't really look over the side, but in the west I can see the Rocky Mountains through the deep blue skies, and there is a slight haze, a shimmer to the light. My god it is cold though, about −80°C, and that really is the ambient temperature because in a balloon there is no wind-chill effect as you are just blown along with it. I've never known it this cold, not at the poles, not on Mount McKinley, and I know at these temperatures it is dangerous to hang around. Everything becomes brittle – metal, plastic, could just snap at any time. If a flying wire goes, that's it, curtains, goodnight Vienna! I'm bundled up in about five layers of protective clothing, fleece, down jacket, three sets of gloves, and in the tiny basket there's no room to move around to keep warm, even if I was prepared to risk doing so. At this altitude I'm almost at the point where I should be wearing some sort of pressure suit, to be honest.

I've counted fifteen seconds so I can be certain the barograph will have recorded where I am, that the record can be ratified. I don't want to make any mistake with that and have to do this again! It takes a reading every four seconds, but I want to be absolutely certain. Now it's time to get myself down as quickly as I can, and I'll be back for breakfast. I pull gingerly on the rope to open the gas valve at the top of the envelope, and hold it for three seconds. Don Cameron, who originally built this balloon for me, had told me the horror story of a flight he'd been on when the rope came away from where it was attached to the valve, the whole thing ending up with him in the basket. Ever since hearing that I've never forgotten it, and I'm frankly petrified should it happen now as there'd be no way to get down. I want a nice slow descent, but nothing happens, no movement downwards, so I pull on it again a little harder and longer this time. Nothing! In fact, looking at my electric barometer, the pressure reading is continuing to drop so I'm actually still going up.

I'm confused. How can I be releasing gas and still rising? Could I just be imagining it, if maybe my oxygen is not working properly and I'm getting hypoxia? I start to panic slightly, but know that will only make matters worse so try to keep calm. I've probably got another hour or so of oxygen on my main supply, and don't fancy having to swap over to my back-up wearing all my gloves in this cold. Once my oxygen is gone so am I. This isn't like Everest, where the effects of oxygen deprivation creep up on you. I'm not acclimatized and I'm far, far higher. This would be more or less instant, in which I find little comfort. I may have a parachute but I can't take my bulky oxygen supply with me, and even if I initially survived getting clear of the balloon and the free-fall after baling out I'd be dead before I reached breathable altitude. What am I going to do? Slow down, think carefully, I've got to try and work this out.

I'd never tell any of the fraternity this to their faces, but perhaps you don't have to be terribly clever to climb or to attempt polar challenges. You need to learn from experience of course, particularly with the latter, but there are times when you really just have to get your head down and keep going. I soon discovered things were a bit different with ballooning and you had to be rather more cerebral about things. In the five years before Bertrand Piccard successfully made the first round the world flight in the Breitling Orbiter 3, there must have been something like twenty-two failed attempts from people like Steve Hilton, Richard Branson and Steve Fossett. Perhaps that very quickly became part of ballooning's appeal for me, and also the fact that it is really unheard of for anyone to have major achievements in three such entirely unrelated fields. It's very unusual for anyone to move seriously from mountaineering to polar, or vice versa, but I can't think of anyone else who has added a third such string to their bow; maybe the odd sailor but never aviation. I very soon fell in love with the sport, which I found attracted a rather different type of person to my other adventuring: lovely and quirky, perhaps more thoughtful, the sort of people who like the challenge of working together as part of a genuine team effort.

Having said that, I really only started ballooning for just the one flight. With most climbing and polar trekking you have to learn your trade as you go along, but I didn't get my balloon pilot's licence just to fly around England or anything like that, although I've done a fair bit of it since, but purely to attempt one trip. After just failing in my second attempt to reach the Geographic North Pole in April 1997, it having been a terrible struggle and fearing I might never make it under my own steam, I'd started wondering if it was possible to do it another way, in a balloon. This had tragically been attempted by one of my great historical heroes, the Swedish pioneer Salomon Andrée, exactly a century earlier, but the huge advances in meteorology in the hundred years since then made me think it might genuinely be possible. Back then the state of knowledge about prevailing seasonal wind patterns at different altitudes, and of course the inability to see them in real time, effectively left adventurers in a state of total ignorance. Today things were very different.

I was originally taught to fly by a Bath-based balloonist called Terry McCoy. Terry took me flying around his local area and I soon got the ballooning bug; I loved the fact that you can feel the wind against your cheeks and also the simple sense of freedom that comes from using the wind currents. Brian Jones, who had been the co-pilot on the Breitling Orbiter, was the instructor who took me on my check-out flight for my pilot's licence (I got my fixed-wing licence later on in 2003) and has since become a good friend. He was the perfect examiner because he continued to use even the test as a teaching experience and was very positive in everything he said. Brian is the person who has taught me pretty much all I know about ballooning.

In the UK, 99 per cent of balloons are of the hot air variety with a modern burner and propane tanks as fuel. When you heat the air in the balloon it rises, if you stop doing so it comes down. You really can't get anything simpler than that. As with all balloons they are classified by their volume, from AX-01 (with a hot-air variety) having a volume of less than 250 square metres, up to AX-15 the massive size of more than 22,000 square metres. The next type up is a gas balloon (AA-01–AA-15), where you have a semi-permeable cell which doesn't allow any gas to escape and is sealed at the top and bottom; there is a little valve on the top and you use a lighter-than-air lifting gas. These days we use helium or hydrogen for that and sand as ballast. If you want to go up you drop sand over the side and, to come down, you pull a rope which lets gas out of the top via a valve.

The third type is a combination balloon known as a Rozier (AM-01–AM-15), where you have both hot air and at the top of the envelope a closed gas cell. This is the most effective type of balloon for longer distances. When you heat the hot air with the

propane burner that in turn heats the helium in the cell, causing the balloon to rise, and the heat of the sun on the balloon
during the day will do the same. I'm afraid you can't really get
away from the fact that ballooning is a pretty expensive sport;
a brand new balloon big enough to fly four people costs about
£30,000, plus around £300 per flight for the gas and insurance.
Partly to get my hours up, I made the first hot-air balloon flight
across the Andes with only three hours P1 (the pilot in overall
charge of the balloon, or solo as I was in that case) experience,
which in retrospect was probably one of the most stupid things
I've ever done. The first time I flew a Rozier was on my flight to
the North Pole.

Salomon Andrée's journey in 1897 ended in failure, his balloon coming down on the way from Spitsbergen to the North
Pole. He and his two companions died in their attempted return
on foot south to civilization. My North Pole flight was audacious
I suppose mainly because no one knew if it could be done, but
in a sense I was never really too worried and felt it was relatively safe. It required a great deal of planning, but I was pretty
sure I would come out of it alive. It could have been very dangerous if the only possible weather pattern would have taken
me away after the Pole towards northern Iceland, leading to my
worst nightmare of having to drop into the ocean, but realis-
tically I would never have allowed that to happen and would
have put the balloon down on the ice way before that. Then it
would just have been a question of erecting my tent and waiting
to be rescued, although I obviously wasn't keen that should need
to happen. As it transpired the wind took me all the way back
almost to my initial departure point on Spitsbergen.

The things I am probably proudest of achieving, both in
terms of planning and execution, are my two Atlantic crossings in a Rozier and then a gas balloon, and my Rozier and
hot-air balloon altitude records. For many people the Atlantic

crossing will always seem the ultimate challenge, as it was in the pioneering days of aviation back in the 1920s, and in both cases the quest claimed many lives. Despite that, during my Atlantic crossings I felt pretty comfortable most of the time because I knew the planning had been right, even if many people seemed to think I was mad. For me the most dangerous thing I have ever done was certainly my Rozier altitude record, because there was absolutely no room for error. With the Breitling Orbiter, which coincidentally held the record previously from the end of their round the world trip, the pilots were inside a pressurized capsule, sitting in shirt sleeves in nice comfy chairs. That was still a great achievement and, maybe in comparison, to take off in a small open basket sitting on a fishing stool might seem on the verge of foolhardy. I would be within a whisker of it all going horribly wrong, if I ran out of oxygen or something on the basket didn't work properly.

The idea for my first world altitude record was hatched whilst hanging around in Canada for seven weeks in the summer of 2003, waiting to get the right weather for the Atlantic crossing on which I was about to embark. I was planning to use the same balloon for both, the very one that I had also flown to the North Pole, so it was a trusty old friend by now. This was a Rozier mixed balloon, so with a gas cell and also using hot air, of the AM-08 class, which means an envelope of between 2,200 and 3,000 square metres. My particular balloon was built by Don Cameron in Bristol with a 90,000 cubic foot capacity.

The existing record for that class was held by the great ballooning icon Per Lindstrand, who in 1996 had taken it to 34,943 feet, which also took him up through six further classes all the way up to AM-14. The absolute record, AM-15, was held at 38,732 feet by Bertrand Piccard and Brian Jones in Breitling Orbiter, from their landmark round the world success in 1999. They hadn't set out to break the altitude record, it was simply a coincidental by-product of being in an absolutely massive balloon and also comparatively very light at the end of their trip.

It has always been the case with distance and duration aviation records of all kinds that you need to exceed the existing mark by 1 per cent to break it. This is probably just an historical throwback to the days before GPS when such things were more difficult to determine exactly, and for the sake of consistency has never been changed. However, with altitude records, the required margin is 3 per cent, since for various scientific reasons altitude has always been, and remains, slightly harder to judge very accurately. To break the Breitling Orbiter's record, taking out all seven classes above me, I would need to reach 39,894 feet. Of course, with that necessary margin needed to break an altitude record, the higher the mark is set the progressively harder it is to break in the future. The challenge I wanted to set myself was to achieve a point that might prove impossible ever to beat, or at least that might stand for a very long time.

The figure we decided to aim at was 41,000 feet. I knew that would be very hard, but if I managed to achieve it no one else would be in the record books anytime soon. This would be something very special I felt. I wouldn't hold the record for anything below a Rozier AM-08, but I knew no smaller balloon could ever have any prospect of getting higher, it simply wouldn't be large enough to generate sufficient lift. By taking away all the other classes above me, however, I would technically be breaking eight world records. To use a boxing analogy, it would be a bit like a flyweight beating a heavyweight, and normally a good big 'un always beats a good little 'un. The thought of this had really got my competitive juices flowing.

It took a hell of a lot of planning, and for six months Tim Cole (in charge of the bottom end), master balloon-builder Bert Padelt (in charge of the top) and I worked our socks off. I'd known them both since Bert first contacted me with an offer of help before my second attempted Atlantic crossing out of Pittsburgh, and he had introduced me to his friend Tim. At the end of the day it all really boiled down to a very simple equation. From our cubic capacity we could calculate how much weight the balloon would carry at any given altitude. If you inflate the envelope at sea level it will generate a defined amount of lift, but if you go to 5,000 feet it will be somewhat less and at 10,000 feet even less still. If you take this up on a graph to the world record level we were aiming at, you can see the exact amount of weight you can afford to carry. The calculation itself isn't that difficult, but packing everything you need into that weight limit certainly is, particularly for a bloke like me. Lighter boxer shorts were a start, but that was soon followed by no beer and definitely no second puddings.

It was obvious from the start that the flight would have to take place in north America, since it is just so much easier doing things there. Being such a huge country, even with crowded skies it means there are wider open spaces between the flight paths, and generally speaking air traffic control (ATC) is that much more accommodating. Of course there are still strict rules you have to follow, permits you must apply for and clearance you need from ATC at any given time and altitude, but if possible they will try and find a way to let you attempt something, whereas in the UK the default position always seems to be that you can't bloody well do that here, a 'not on my watch' rather than a 'can do' mentality.

We'd be taking off from Greeley just outside of Denver, Colorado, for the simple reason that this is where Tim lives, but with the added advantage of the fields there seeming to be the size of Wiltshire. I was fed up of trying to land a Rozier balloon on a postage stamp, smashing my way through any number of things before I could come to a halt. It was from here that Tim and Bert had done five other altitude and test flights for all of Steve Fossett's trial launches, and as a team I am convinced they are simply the best. Bert had flown out by the time I arrived in Denver at midday on Monday 22 March 2004, and after such a long build-up everything happened very quickly. I'd got there with the expectation of flying on Thursday, but now I found that the weather had changed and it would be first thing the next morning.

I would be flying in a very small, two-man wicker basket, the base a rectangle of about 4 by 5 feet, sitting on a fishing stool and with two Worthington propane gas tanks and three oxygen systems crammed in around me. That night we went through everything for the tenth time, planning for any possible contingency, all the things that could go wrong. If this fails, we do that, if that freezes we switch to this. We'd built-in double redundancy throughout, but I was still nervous about how things would function in the extreme cold, and particularly about the oxygen apparatus which was unlike anything I had previously used other than in training.

There are big differences between the physiologies of individual people, subtle variations within the human body, and you train in a barochamber to recognize hypoxia. Since in a balloon you are going up very fast without any form of acclimatization you need oxygen from a much lower level than when climbing a mountain, almost from the start at Greeley where I would be taking off from a ground altitude of about 10,000 feet above sea level. There are two different types of oxygen system, and how high you are planning to go determines which one you need to use.

The rule of thumb is that at 10,000 feet you need 1 litre a minute, at 20,000 feet 2 litres and at 30,000 feet 3 litres. You can certainly safely go up to 20,000 feet on what is termed constant flow oxygen, the type I used on Everest, but if you intend venturing beyond roughly 30,000 feet the air pressure and your physiology reach the point where constant flow oxygen ceases to work and you need what is termed demand oxygen, similar to an aqualung, where oxygen is forced into your body at a rate roughly three times that of constant flow. Pilots using oxygen at altitude will always be on a demand supply. If something goes wrong you don't have long, just as happened to the golfer Payne Stewart and his entourage who all died when the cabin pressure and oxygen in his private plane failed. I would be aiming for a lot higher than that.

So for my altitude record I needed demand oxygen, with a back-up system should the initial one fail, and also a spare constant flow supply in case I additionally needed that on the way down. At the rate I would be climbing I'd be at the height of Everest in about forty minutes, certainly not stopping on the way up, so I would also need to pre-breath for an hour before I took off, to get my body attuned and the red corpuscles in my blood well-saturated with oxygen. Unless you do this properly to force the nitrogen out of remote areas in your body, you could very easily end up getting extremity pains or even the bends. And since you are using up so much more oxygen than would be the case on constant flow you are very aware about the limits of your supply in the time you have to get up and down. Each cylinder lasts about two hours.

The other thing that would be new for me was that I was going to have to take a 'geometric altitude' with a barograph, which could be different to the altitude that might register on my altimeter. The barograph reading needed to be adjusted on a computer programme to take account of the temperature and air pressure. When that dropped to 185 I knew I would be at 41,000 feet. I'll admit I was nervous and didn't have the best of night's sleep, not just because I had to be at the balloon, literally in Tim's backyard, at 4.00 a.m.

When I turned up the next morning everything was ready to go. One last weather check and the helium started to be piped into the balloon. TRACON, the authority that co-ordinates all American ATC, were contacted and told I would be taking off at 6.00 a.m., and I was provided with transponder codes and radio frequencies in return. Bert had given me a clear flight profile, that I'd be rising at about 500 feet per minute until I gradually slowed down and would top out, hopefully at the altitude record. I was weighed off to reach 41,000 feet, and now I had to start an hour of pre-breathing before lift-off. The really scary part was when I had to take a deep breath as the bottle was changed and switched over to a new one in the basket. Just one breath off the bottle, I'd been told, would put all the nitrogen back into my body and make my hour of pre-breathing a complete waste of time. Then suddenly it was time, and Tim said the Balloonist's Prayer.

May the winds welcome you with softness. May the sun bless you with his warm hands. May you fly so high and so well that God joins you in laughter and sets you gently back into the loving arms of Mother Earth.

I was airborne and everything was working perfectly. I gradually got rid of my three bags of sand, passing through two sets of clouds on what seemed like a non-stop elevator ride to the top. But it was soon clear there might be a hitch. I started off talking to air traffic control, and when I got to 20,000 feet the ATC told me to change my transponder code and call up another guy to get further clearance. I was being handed over to another ATC responsible for the air space in a higher altitude band. He seemed disconcerted by my wishing to pass through and wanted to know where my approval was. This made no sense to me, as Tim had been meticulous about getting permission for my flight from the Federal Aviation Authority (FAA) three weeks ago, yet the ATC knew nothing about this. His view was clear, I didn't have approval to pass through his altitude band and had to stop.

He didn't seem very interested in my explanation that I couldn't do so, that there is no hanging around in a balloon and you are just going up. My only alternative was to cancel the whole trip. I was violating the airspace, he said, and should contact this number when I landed. Here, I knew at once, was a massive problem. With any world record regulated by the Fédération Aéronautique Internationale (FAI), if you break a local aviation law then the record is void and will not be ratified. Tim is absolutely pedantic about such things so I was certain he must have cleared everything, but right now that appeared to count for nothing. Unbeknownst to me, right at that moment this ATC was bringing to a halt all traffic going into Denver airport, and starting to direct the planes in on another flight path and onto a different runway.

I was certainly worried about what the ATC had told me, but right then there was absolutely nothing I could do about it. I kept going on up at about 500 feet per minute and it was just like being in an almost completely silent lift. The burners weren't on except for the pilot light, and normally in a balloon that seems quite serene, but this time it felt more and more spooky and scary. As I got higher and higher it became increasingly cold, and I was thinking to myself I just want to get this over and done with. As the temperature dropped and things froze I knew that absolutely anything could break or malfunction, I was flying by the seat of my pants. My rate of ascent was decreasing, and the reading on the electric barometer slowly ticked down, 200, 195, 190, closer and closer, and then through the 185 I knew I needed.

I stopped at 182, and waited the fifteen seconds for my two little black box barographs to do their stuff and record the pressure. Now it's time to get the hell out of there, but when I pull on the rope to let some gas out from the top of the balloon nothing happens. Bert had told me I could expect to begin descending slowly, pick up speed later on then slow down again when coming in to land, but I seem stuck here. Another pull for a further three seconds and still nothing! In fact, when I look at the barometer if anything I am still going up! For the life of me I can't figure this out and I don't want to go up any further. Think damn it, think! Now I've got ATC asking me what my intentions are, and I feel like telling them I wouldn't mind carrying on being alive.

I was definitely starting to panic and on reflection I am amazed at how lucid my thought processes were, but gradually it began to dawn on me what must be happening. Balloons tend to be white, and on some round the world journeys they even have reflective material on the outside. The reason behind this is that you want to minimize the difference in outside warming temperature between day and night, and I recalled how on my North Pole trip even the effect of a blue logo on the side of my balloon had been considered and calculated. It's normal to expect the heat of the sun to make a balloon rise later on in the day. There wasn't a cloud in the sky though, and what none of us had considered was how much greater the influence of the sun would be at such altitude. It was the solar gain heating the helium in the balloon that was making me rise further, or at least counteracting the small releases of gas that would normally be enough to take me back down.

Having finally worked this out I decided I had to pull the rope longer, so this time I kept the valve open for a good ten seconds and then did it again. Very gradually at first the barometer reading began to creep up, then suddenly I started to drop and pick up speed, coming down at 500 feet per minute just as I had gone up. God it was great to be on my way down! I bottomed out a bit at about 20,000 feet, when I pulled the rope again. By this time

I felt very relieved and comfortable, since although I would still need oxygen I would be fine switching to constant flow if my supply failed now.

Unlike the patchwork pattern of fields I was used to seeing below me in England, the ones I was descending towards now were vast. There was a nasty amount of drift and I could see a big radio mast that I seemed to be heading towards, which I didn't fancy at all. By 500 feet above the ground I had stowed everything for landing, but I could see high tension wires about a mile away and I was doing 12 knots or so over the ground. It was time to dump her down and at about 100 feet I pulled the rip on the top.

This part is always slightly scary. Unlike the rope attached to the valve on top of the balloon, which allows gas out slowly, this rope is attached to a piece of fabric that opens a vent and lets it all out. Obviously the last thing you would want to happen (as it would be the last thing you ever did!) is for this to come loose when you were at any altitude, and as a precaution it is tied in place with dental floss. The two ropes are also different colours to prevent them becoming confused, and the rip rope is kept completely out of the basket until you are coming in to land and need it. The absolute importance of the rip panel being secure, however, can also make it difficult to pull out, and on both my North Pole and Atlantic flights I couldn't actually do so. I was hanging onto the line, jumping up and down, but it simply would not break, and I eventually had to stop the balloon just by keeping the valve open and letting the gas out slowly. This time it popped right out and I dropped like a brick. Although I bent my legs as I hit the ground it still took the wind out of me, and I then had to hurl myself to my knees. The burner suspended above my head came loose from its harness and crashed down on top of the basket, narrowly missing bashing my brains out.

Hopping out of the basket I now felt pretty pleased with

myself. I'd been airborne for not much more than two hours, and was somewhere near Akron about 70 miles from where I'd started in Greeley. I knew my ground crew would be on their way and should arrive soon, along with some media that we had organized. It was just a matter of waiting for them, standing there in all my cold weather gear, down jacket and big boots, but it wasn't more than a minute or two before I saw these flashing lights approaching in the distance. A squad car screeched to a halt and out jumped a great big sheriff, whose first words were 'Sonny, I'm going to bust your ass!'

Pretty soon there were four squad cars there in the field with me, plus an ambulance and a fire engine. The sheriff said he'd been contacted by the FAA and he was going to haul me in, arrest me for violating air space. He'd taken out his handcuffs and was about to slap them on me when a shrill voice piped up, 'you take your hands off that boy, don't you dare touch him!' My ground crew had rolled up, and this was the FAI observer Barbara Moreton, a delightful, tiny old lady in her seventies then. The sheriff wasn't really prepared for this sort of stern but diminutive resistance, expressed in a voice that would clearly brook no opposition, and seemed to calm down a bit. What I really needed was a drink, but my water bottle was frozen solid.

We spent two hours milling around in that field, with sheriffs and state troopers, and pretty soon two FAA inspectors also turned up. After what seemed like endless discussion between them the FAA guys said they would handle things from there, and asked to see my passport, insurance, registration, permits, pilot's licence, everything! The British media later said I was going to be put in jail, although I am not sure how likely that might really have been, but from what I was told there did seem to be a genuine prospect of some sort of prosecution. Eventually however, when they had presumably concluded I wasn't going to do a runner, they decided they would let me go for the time being.

We all drove back to Greeley, getting there by late morning, and everyone felt pretty sombre. We couldn't celebrate properly, and although we went out for a steak that night it seemed very muted and hollow. I knew I'd broken the record, but the whole thing might be null and void. Tim said he had absolute proof of all the permits he had applied for, but the fact remained that everything still had to be subject to the approval of air traffic control at any given time and altitude, and they were insisting we had violated their air space. Obviously the whole system is designed for aircraft that can change their height and direction, rather than balloons where there is little fundamental control, but unwittingly we had changed the whole traffic pattern of Denver airport.

We had to write a report, with all times and relevant facts about the whole thing. When we downloaded the trace it showed I had been stuck 'at the top' for more than ten minutes, which surprised and rather frightened me even if it had seemed like an eternity at the time. Tim had all the reference numbers for the permits, and everything went into the system of the FAA investigation. Their adage sometimes seems to be 'we are not happy unless you are unhappy,' but a month later they came back and said we were completely exonerated. Tim had been deeply upset that he might have done something wrong, but they apologized and admitted that it was their system which had been at fault, which I frankly think is something the Commercial Aviation Authority here would never do. We had been meticulous, but it was still a big ask for the FAA to come out and admit they were in the wrong, yet they did it.

It was a huge relief as I am not sure I would have gone back and done it again. Everything had worked perfectly, apart from my sheer terror when I thought I wasn't ever coming down, and it is one of those very rare occasions where I think I can honestly say I wouldn't have changed a thing, except perhaps a flask of hot tea for when I got back to the ground. Sometimes though, you just feel you've been lucky to get away with something. I still hold the record and don't think anyone will achieve that additional 3 per cent needed to beat it for a very long time. The weights just don't allow it, and to have a crack someone would certainly need to be a lot lighter than me.

I also wanted to set an altitude record in a hot-air balloon, and my experience of doing that couldn't really have been more different. The one I had set my eyes on was actually a very old record, going back to 1978, a mark achieved by Carol Rymer Davis, a tiny little lady who sadly later died when I was racing against her. A great deal had changed in balloon design since she set her record, which made me think I would be able to beat her mark. The fabric was now much tougher so it could be thinner and therefore lighter, and oxygen systems had also become more efficient and smaller. The balloon I was going to use was built by Bert Padelt and was an AX-05 class, which meant it had a volume of between 900 and 1,200 square metres.

Most people are a lot heavier than Carol and certainly I'm no lightweight. I thought the only way we could overcome this difference in weight would be to cut whatever else possible down, make everything a lot lighter, and our planning was all about paring things down as far as could be safely done. For instance, we designed a basket with a rigid composite floor but only fabric sides. This was a lot lighter than a traditional wicker basket, in which you certainly feel a lot more comfortable – the fabric would obviously give you no sort of protection if you came down at any sort of speed or smashed into anything.

In the New Year of 2005 we went out to the huge open plains of Calgary in Canada. Snow lay deep over the endless fields stretching as far as the eye could see into the distance, and it was very cold. With all our planning and having done the weight calculations we were confident we'd be able to beat the record easily, and I'd be going up with four tanks of propane. I intended to use a constant flow oxygen system, which is lighter than a demand apparatus. I'd be on the cusp for safety with this, and a lot of people would say I should have had demand oxygen, but with my experience I felt comfortable doing so. Anyway, a day of good weather arrived and we were ready to go. I talked to ATC, up I went, and only made it to about 25,000 feet. We'd missed the record by a good 5,000 feet, which is a big chunk of altitude. When I came back down again we were all utterly confused about how I could have been so far off, and trooped back to the hotel to mull things over. What else could I lose to get my weight down further, other than chop my legs off?

By the next day though we had changed a lot of things, half a dozen or more, some of them very tiny, but one was certainly significant. We'd decided that I could get by with a lot less fuel than I had taken the day before, so instead of four propane tanks we could cut that down to two, pressurized with nitrogen. This would save us a lot of weight and up I went again, but we were still 2,000 feet away from our target. By the next day the weather had closed in with no prospect of another open window appearing, so that was it. We had to pack up and go home.

Back in England we put our thinking hats on, even if this did often involve meetings in the pub. We were determined to have another bash the next year, so we went over everything again and looked at how we could improve things, to achieve more lift as well as cutting down the weight even further. Bert Padelt also provided a lot of input from his home back in the US. The main thing we came up with was the idea of putting a radio thermistor at the top of the envelope, which we could use to keep a check on the temperature there. With a hot-air balloon, if you use the burner too hard and overheat the air you can very easily burn out the top of the envelope, end up with just blue sky above you and drop like a stone. With the thermistor we could push things to the limit but know exactly where to stop. This would help us a lot we thought.

When we got out to Calgary again in January 2006 we were confident that all the changes we had made would be enough. We'd probably tweaked about thirty little things by now, reconsidered everything, taken out anything not absolutely necessary and looked at any way we could do things differently. And everything worked perfectly, so it seemed. I was able to get clearance from ATC to go all the way from the ground, which was much simpler, up I went and there it was, I'd broken the record. Barbara Moreton was our observer again and she sent the barographs off to Don Cameron at his office back in Bristol, who would check them officially on behalf of the FAI. It felt great, we all celebrated and home we went with another record under our belts.

Then a couple of weeks later there was a bolt from the blue. I got a call from Don saying, sorry, but you haven't actually broken the record. The conversion on the barographs hadn't been done correctly to take account of the very low temperature and we'd actually missed the record by a sliver, just 250 feet. I was devastated, but as usually happens with me I just felt all the more determined to go back and get the job done properly at last. It was infuriating and deflating however, having to return again when we all thought we'd already cracked it.

Knowing we had to do it once more hadn't meant we'd stopped thinking however, and by the time we went out again in January of the following year, 2007, we'd made another five or so very minor alterations. The most important of these was that we were feeding oxygen into the burner so that it would burn more efficiently and there was less danger of it going out. It's really horrible when that happens and you have to climb up out of the basket to light it again, with ice all over everything. I obviously don't have a bad head for heights, but I really don't think anyone would feel terribly happy having to do that.

The first day I was ready to go up I went, and it was a very good flight. Perhaps I was just getting used to it now. We passed through the record and the additional 3 per cent I needed, and then managed to put on an extra 500 feet to make absolutely sure. I wasn't going to miss out by a tiny bit again and I wanted to be completely certain. I came down a lot faster than I'd planned however and the basket started to spin. Thankfully I just had enough fuel to control it, but I hit the ground hard. Two engineers who'd been working nearby were sitting in their truck, and told me later that they didn't want to come over and just called the police as they were convinced I must be dead, until I crawled out completely winded. My retrievers were still miles away. You don't feel it at all when you are up there, you could light a candle and it wouldn't blow out, but the wind had been so strong that I'd been travelling at 120 miles an hour over the ground at the top during the hour and a half I was in the air.

Back at the hotel with Barbara there we hooked the barographs up to the computer. What the hell was going on? There was absolutely no trace at all. The only explanation could be that it had been so cold, about −50°C, that the device had simply failed to work and malfunctioned. Things only got worse. It turned out that Barbara had forgotten to put the batteries in the spare one, so we had absolutely no readings to confirm that we had broken the record, even though we were completely certain that we had. It wasn't something we could have checked ourselves – and believe me, we would have done if we could – because as pilot and crew we weren't allowed to go anywhere near the barographs under FAI regulations, to ensure no one could tamper with anything. This is something they are a bit too precious about, in my view. Barbara was in tears, and to be honest I briefly almost felt like killing her myself.

I just had to go and do it yet again. Luckily the next day, 14 January, the weather was just the same, cold but clear. We fitted chemical hot warmers on both barographs, watched Barbara put the batteries in and ensured they were long-lasting lithium ones, then checked they were working properly and that we could see traces on the computer. This was now my fifth flight and it was the easiest of all, if only in part because I knew I could do it. I went straight up and came straight down again, with a gentle landing that just kissed the ground. This time I was sure the record was mine at 32,480 feet. We rushed back to the hotel to check the traces were ok, and there they were, that was it. Now we genuinely could celebrate, and I took the whole team out to a restaurant in Calgary for massive steaks and too much beer.

There is no such thing as an easy world record, but this was an incredibly satisfying one in terms of the way it was achieved, perhaps the most satisfying of all mine. It had been overcome in lots of small increments, and was a real example of group effort, perhaps a bit like how in a more serious situation Apollo 13 was nursed back to earth after disaster struck. It had needed real teamwork, and we'd not only had to work very hard to break it but think a lot about how we would get there.

As I've already said, in my view the ultimate challenge for a pilot since the great pioneering days of aviation in the 1920s has always been flying across the Atlantic. A lot of people died trying to do so in a balloon and there were perhaps twenty attempts before the first successful crossing, many teams simply disappearing without trace. Then finally in 1978 three guys from the American ballooning centre of Albuquerque, Maxie Anderson, Ben Abruzzo and Larry Newman finally achieved it in Double Eagle II, taking off from Maine and landing in a field north of Paris six days later. The first two had tried and failed the year before, being hauled from the sea, badly frostbitten, by a rescue helicopter just off the coast of Iceland. Finally making that crossing was a great achievement, comparable to that of Lindberg first doing so in an aeroplane, and huge crowds welcomed the American trio on their arrival. This was something I desperately wanted to do myself, and even if the actual crossing had been made before I intended to be the first person to do it in an open wicker basket. This might not be an official record of any kind, but it seemed to me that it would in many ways be an even more significant achievement and very much in the spirit of adventuring that I have always tried to follow.

It took me three attempts though. I used pretty much the same team throughout, including Gavin Hailes to launch the balloon and relying on the meteorological advice of the Belgian Luc Trullemans, who I really believe is the very best in the world at what he does. I'd first met Luc through Brian Jones back in 2000 when I was planning my trip to the North Pole, and he's rather famous back home in Belgium as a handsome TV weather presenter who all the girls seem to love. I was also doing things relatively on the cheap, as I was using the same envelope, basket and burners as I had on my flight to the North Pole, but I was a little worried about any damage the balloon might have sustained on my previous trip so decided that I would start from Pittsburgh in the Midwest. If anything went wrong early on I far preferred the idea of still being over land, rather than having to ditch in the open ocean and the balloon (and quite possibly myself) being lost at sea.

So in early September 2002 we pitched up at a little airport, Allegheny County, with its art deco tower. It was a place just used by small jets and private pilots, and a guy called Steve Phillips lent us his hanger where we could get everything ready. We had full tanks of gas and were prepared just to sit around for the right weather, but within four days Luc reported we had the perfect slot ahead of us, and even though I was barely over my jet lag we said let's take it. As always they started to inflate the envelope in early evening and at 10.00 p.m. I took off into the darkness. It was a slightly surreal experience, and very unlike the 24-hour sunshine I'd had on my way to the North Pole, flying in virtual silence apart from the occasional puff of the burner and the constant chatter of air traffic control. Now I could see the lights of Pittsburgh and its surroundings spread out below me as I flew at about 8,000 feet above them.

I had an autopilot system which works on barometric pressure. This obviously can't alter your direction, but is designed to maintain the exact height you want for the weather pattern that will take you in the direction you plan, as wind speeds and even direction can be very different at varying altitudes. This only works on a downward cycle, as there is no way for it to let gas out of the balloon (and nor would you want it to), but it will just gently puff as required to keep you at the right level. It's a very clever system since it learns as it goes along, pushing you up a little too high the first few times and then settling down to exactly the right amount of burn, picking up changes in your height far earlier and more exactly than a pilot could do themselves.

In the morning, when the sun heats the gas in the balloon, it has no control, so you have two choices about times to choose for catnapping. Either you can do so with the autopilot operating, although this can obviously be dangerous since if it failed whilst you were asleep you might come down and crash before you woke up, or you can do so when you know the balloon is slowly rising, but then you have the opposite threat that you don't know when it will stop and without an oxygen mask you could easily die of hypoxia in your sleep. I would usually try to grab a few hours' sleep in the early morning, just when there would be a bit of gentle lift, but there was too much going on up the East Coast for me to do so now with the ATC of Pittsburgh,

Newark, La Guardia and Boston to deal with. It also seemed that all the pilots wanted to speak with me, but although the skies were very busy the Americans are generally pretty good at giving you clear air space, ensuring nothing comes within a mile or so of you.

After my first night tracking up the east coast it was clear that the autopilot wasn't working properly. I already felt very tired, and talking to the guys back in the control room in Bath they said it would be stupid to set off across the ocean. The only sensible decision was to fly through the night and then find somewhere to land at first light, so at once I had to switch from trying to maintain a maximum speed and direction east to moving as slowly as possible and keeping away from the coast. When first light came and the sun rose it was a beautiful morning. At 5.30 a.m. I was tracking north-east over New Hampshire, with the trees below just beginning to turn into their early autumn colours, but I couldn't see anywhere to land, no fields at all.

In the distance I could hear a siren, getting closer and closer. I was flying at roughly 100 feet and moving at about 10 knots, prepared to put the balloon down into any open space I could find. I rolled up the sides of the basket and got the trail rope ready for landing. I also pulled in from below the dipole and transponder antenna, since the last thing you want to happen is have those get tangled in any electric wires as you could very easily be electrocuted. I'd changed over the propane tanks to ensure I was on a new one, which you always do to make sure you don't run out of fuel just at the critical moment you are coming in to land. Now I was flying virtually as if I was just in a hot-air balloon. Everything was stowed away. The sirens now seemed to be approaching from the opposite direction, and looking over the side I could see two cop cars, an ambulance and two fire engines. Back and forth they went. 'What's going on?' I asked Dave Owen back in Bath. 'They're chasing you, you twit,' he replied. Unlike me, they couldn't travel in a straight line and had to follow the small country roads.

Eventually I found a field and thought I would bang it down there. One technique people sometimes use when landing a balloon is to hit the top of a tree to take out the speed, remove the momentum. This was great in theory, but not something I'd ever actually done before. I smacked the top of this big tree, and just stuck in it, suspended and swaying disturbingly, the field I'd been aiming at just the other side of me. Pretty soon the emergency services rolled up, and were rapidly joined by a satellite tv truck. The firemen got out their ladders and one climbed up to ask me if I wanted a lift down. I said no way and climbed down the tree, to be met at the bottom by a reporter. 'Is anything hurt?' he asked. 'Only my pride,' I replied. Pretty soon there was a fairly large crowd of people there, and then this little old lady pushed her way through with a cup of tea for me. This turned out actually to be Steve Phillips' mum, and it transpired I had come down right by where she lived. A couple of hours later Steve himself turned up with the trailer. We got the balloon out of the tree by chopping it down, packed everything up and took it back to Pittsburgh, where we stored everything in the hanger for next year.

We were back at the beginning of June the following year, 2003, because I felt I wanted to be there at a time when the hours of daylight were longer. We'd had all our debriefs and thought we'd solved the problem with the autopilot, but we didn't really change much else. We'd returned to the same little airport, although this time we planned to take the balloon down into a valley to give it a little more protection from the wind for actual lift-off. Although I was no longer concerned about the general condition of the balloon I was obviously very anxious about the autopilot and whether or not it would work properly.

We'd received some sponsorship from Krispy Kreme Donuts

and as part of the deal they sent us a large box of their wares every day. This was great the first morning when we all tucked in and scoffed about five each. On day two this probably dropped to three, then one, and after that we couldn't stand the thought of even looking at any again. We ended up giving them all away. The donuts were doing my waistline no good, and it looked as if we would have a lot of sitting around to do.

This time we seemed to have no sort of luck with the weather at all. Whenever it appeared that I might have a great track heading out east, that always coincided with big thunder storms that would be waiting for me over the ocean just off the coast, which I suppose shouldn't have been a great surprise as these are always going to be more likely in high summer. At one point it looked as if we'd found a great track and had got so far as filing our flight path, when a guy came over from the FAA office over the road accompanied by a sheriff. Apparently my proposed path would have taken me directly over Camp David, and I was informed in no uncertain terms that even if the President was not in residence at the time I would be shot down if I attempted flying overhead. Clearly I wasn't going to risk that, but I still had to sign this piece of paper acknowledging what I'd been told.

Finally towards the end of June it looked as if our luck had finally turned and I was able to set off. I was tracking out north-east and getting up towards Hartford, feeling much more confident this time, when Luc came on the radio. The weather had unexpectedly gone to shit out over the Atlantic and the wind would now take me up across Greenland and Iceland, so there was no alternative other than to land. Once again I had to switch from trying to find the fastest path to getting on the slowest possible one.

Just outside Boston I found a big field and pulled off the best landing I've ever made by a country mile. It was 5.30 a.m. and

I just kissed the ground, stood the balloon up and let the gas out. A farmer came out to say good morning, closely followed by his daughter dressed still in her night clothes. When they invited me in for breakfast I jumped out like a shot, nearly losing my balloon which made an attempt to take off again without me. Having been picked up and brought back to Pittsburgh, I realized this clearly wasn't working and beginning to get ridiculous, as we were waiting in vain for the rare combination of two completely different weather systems, one to track me up north along the coast and then another to take me out east over the Atlantic.

So over a beer on our return to Pittsburgh, we decided that we would set up base a lot further north and east, at Sussex near St John in New Brunswick, Canada, from where, when the right weather pattern arrived, I could go straight out over the ocean. The two previous aborted attempts had at least given me more time in and made me feel more comfortable with the balloon, and I felt confident that everything should work – otherwise I'd be taking a swim, but that rather goes with the territory. If you are setting out to cross the Atlantic in a balloon there is always the prospect that you might have to ditch, but you simply have to be prepared for that eventuality.

We went straight up there in early July of the same year and established home in a small hotel and an office that had been set up for us by Lorne White who was then teaching me to fly fixed-wing aircraft. He's someone I miss a lot, since he died just afterwards on a flight in Africa. We had the helium tanker that had needed to travel all the way from Toronto, and Bert Padelt and Tim Cole came up. Then it soon turned into Groundhog Day. It's not as if there's a great deal to do in the area, and each morning would start with a breakfast of blueberry muffins, cappuccino and orange juice, which we always bought from the same place and bizarrely cost a different amount every day, so they were clearly just making it up. That was then followed by a lot of sitting around. Everything was ready to go but the weather just wouldn't come right, and as it got later into the season and began to get colder I was starting to think we might miss out again.

Then finally, in the last week of September, Luc said 'you're off'. There was no messing around and I took off late at night and headed out straight over the ocean. I was dressed in my immersion suit and wearing a parachute initially, and this time everything seemed very different. Unlike over the US there was very little air traffic control to worry about, and I had what seemed like an excellent track over Newfoundland and then the Atlantic. Early on it seemed as if I would be taking a very northerly path that would eventually see me end up in Lithuania, if I actually got that far, but then the wind direction changed and brought me further south.

I was about three days into the flight, maybe 500 miles out of Ireland and sitting there enjoying a lovely day at about 14,000 feet, when all of a sudden the basket just dropped twenty feet. Christ, I thought, has a flying wire snapped or the flap come away from the top the balloon? My knees were really wobbling, and I got my life jacket and everything else ready in case I genuinely was coming down, before I put through a call to the control room. We simply could not work out what had happened for ages, but eventually from checking the flight schedules the guys concluded that I'd just been hit by the sonic wave from Concorde, breaking the sound barrier as it came out of the UK. I'd heard absolutely nothing, but my god I felt it.

Later that evening, and still several hundred miles short of the Emerald Isle and what would technically complete my Atlantic crossing, I was moving through thick cloud. I could see long icicles forming around the mouth at the bottom of the balloon's envelope, and I knew this was seriously bad news. If you can see ice there, then you could be damn sure there would be a whole lot more inside and at the top, formed by moisture condensed from the water in the air by the propane burner. The autopilot was working very hard, firing the burner almost full-time to maintain my altitude, and it was pitch black. My variometer which stated my height had an alarm fitted, and suddenly it went off with a shrill warning. I was starting to come down fast, perhaps at 500 feet a minute, all due to the extra weight the ice had added to my balloon.

The burner seemed to be doing nothing to compensate for my fall and there was only one thing to do. Luckily I was still well short of land so I was able to cut away six tanks of gas which dropped into the sea below. I couldn't see anything beneath me, and it did cross my mind for a moment that should I be unfortunate enough to pick out a fishing boat with my aerial bombardment I could end up facing a murder charge, but I really had no alternative. Losing the weight of those tanks stopped my descent, but I'd fallen to about 5,000 feet which also changed my direction as I'd found a different wind pattern. Over the next couple of hours I was crouched there with my helmet on, as the melting ice kept coming down in sheets, chunks bouncing off and around me, and I was standing in the basket ankle-deep in slush.

When I finally hit the coast over the Dingle Peninsula the Irish ATC came on the radio and said 'Welcome to Ireland'. It was time to start thinking about where I might finally land and I had various alternatives in mind. Although I'd originally been intending to end up in Europe I knew that having lost so much gas I would never be able to cross the North Sea, so it was a choice between putting down in Ireland or keeping going to northern England, although the country isn't all that wide at that point and with the wind really picking up wouldn't actually present the largest of targets. If I carried on it would still be light when I crossed the Irish Sea, and I really felt I wanted to get properly home and land in England, so that was the decision I made.

It was pretty rough up there now and I was coming in fairly low ready for landfall. I was wearing my immersion suit still, in case I came up short, but despite the poor visibility I could see the coast. It was 5.00 p.m. and awful weather, the rain now falling. In the distance I could see the lights of Blackpool Airport and I wasn't alone in the sky, a police helicopter buzzing around, a couple more following and several fixed wing planes that I assumed were carrying media. I couldn't mistake the landmark of the Blackpool Tower. Dave Owen and Clive Bailey, who was also in the control room, suggested I should try and land on the beach, but my response to that was 'are you crazy?' I was travelling at about 12 knots now, and if I made a mess of attempting to hit, and more to the point actually stopping on, the sand I could very easily take out the whole front of the Blackpool Illuminations. That really would have made me popular.

The police helicopter tried to direct me towards a golf course over on my left, getting a terse response that I had no choice in the matter and was going wherever the wind took me. Fortunately I was now over some fields just the far side of the town, and knowing this had to be it I came down and put out the trail rope, then tried to pull out the top of the balloon. You always know this might be difficult if it is secured too firmly, as the alternative could prove far worse, and on this occasion it just wouldn't come out at all. It was going to be one hell of a struggle coming to a halt in the wind that was now blowing.

I hit one hedge hard, but the big volume of my balloon meant the wind just dragged me straight through and into the next field. I bumped over that and into a barbed wire fence, but again I was plucked right out the other side trailing strands of wire behind me. Not too far away on the other side of the next hedge I could see some big high-tension electric wires, and I was already starting to think that if I couldn't stop before them and went through that hedge too it would be time to shout 'Geronimo!' and jump for it. This was a big hedge with a ditch in front of it, I hit it hard and … Stopped! I could feel the wind tugging at me, plucking at the balloon, and was it going to hold? Luckily there was a farmer nearby who drove over on his tractor, and I asked him to take my trail rope and tie it around the closest tree.

I now managed finally to rip the top off and let out a lot more gas, so I truly was stationary at last and not going anywhere again. There was a lot of activity around me with helicopters overhead, and a crowd of kids from the local houses had started to gather. I don't really blame them now and I'd probably have done the same, but I was pretty pissed off at the time that they started to nick all my stuff, maps, compasses, anything they could carry off. People from the media were there by now who wanted to interview me, and I kept having to nip back and try to shoo these little blighters away.

I'd called Clive after I landed, and he got a guy he knew in the Lake District to drive down and pick everything up on a trailer. By 9.00 p.m. it was just me standing there alone in that field, in the dark with drizzle falling. I was still in my immersion suit of course, with no pockets, and realized that I didn't have any money. I was beginning to feel a bit daft and wondered what on earth I was going to do now? I must have looked a bit of a plonker, but this chap pulled up in his car and I asked him if he'd give me a lift into town where I could find an ATM machine. It looked like I'd be spending the night in a local bed and breakfast. He asked me where I actually lived and I replied that was all the way down near Bath. I was stunned when he said he'd need to ring his missus first, but if she said it was ok maybe he could take me. After making a few phone calls he came back and said fine, let's go!

I guess he must have felt sorry for me, but blimey this was

kind. I remember climbing into his car and putting my seat back, just getting onto the M6, and then I must have dropped straight off and gone deep asleep. The next thing I knew he was shaking me awake, and asking exactly whereabouts near Bath I lived. We'd obviously driven all the way down the M6, onto the M5 and then the M4, and were just now coming up to my local roundabout. All the time I'd clearly been out like a light, and most probably snoring my head off. Now this was embarrassing, that he'd had to drive all the way without conversation if maybe not in silence. I told him where to go and he took me from there right to my front door, which we arrived at about 2.00 a.m.

I invited him in assuming he would be staying the night, but he said no, he'd just have a cup of tea then needed to get back as he had to start work at 8.00 a.m. the next day. I must admit I felt this was absolutely wonderful and one of the things that epitomizes Britain. I wrote to him afterwards and sent him lots of bits and pieces, and he was interviewed and appeared on the front page of his local paper, so I hope he felt that giving me a helping hand was worth it. It certainly was a great way for me to get back home, and a wonderfully unexpected end to my third and finally successful Atlantic crossing.

You can generally judge the sanity of any particular expedition by the response it receives when you explain to people what you are planning to do. Before my flight to the North Pole it was 'Hmm, interesting.' For my previous transatlantic flight the reaction was 'Awesome!' When in 2007 I suggested I was intending to do the same thing in a tiny Gordon Bennett-sized balloon everyone said 'Are you absolutely nuts?' This would be an AA-06, and if I made it the smallest gas balloon in which anyone had ever crossed the ocean.

On my Gordon Bennett Race experience in September 2006,

when I flew from Belgium to the Russian border with my co-pilot Jonathan Mason, we'd been able to carry enough ballast to last us for four days. I therefore suspected, on paper at least, that it might be possible to fly across the Atlantic in the same amount of time. I also knew that two world-class pilots, Benoit Simeons and Bob Berben, had flown just over 2,100 miles from Albuquerque to New Brunswick. With that trip they held the current world distance record for the same AA-06 size balloon, but they had been flying over land. With a perfect weather track could I cross the greater distance over the Atlantic? My crossing in 2003 with a much larger Rozier AM-08 had only taken me three days, but that had been on a much higher flight track; this would be a seat of the pants job.

I again asked Bert Padelt if he could build me such a balloon, as he had done for my hot-air balloon altitude record earlier that year. He said, 'Hempie, I have always wanted to try that flight in that size of balloon.' He thought it was right on the limit of what was possible, but was adamant it should theoretically be achievable. Having worked with Bert since my first unsuccessful attempt to cross the Atlantic from Pittsburgh in 2002 I now considered him by far the most skilful balloon manufacturer in the entire world, and the basket he designed and built for me at his studio in Pennsylvania was an exquisite piece of art in my view. He's a unique individual and a master craftsman, his workmanship and skill second to none. I'd started referring to him as the Balloon God, a name slightly belied by his appearance, since he's on the short side and has a bald head usually concealed beneath a baseball cap. Ballooning seems to attract a lot of Alpha males, but Bert is simply kind and hard working, and I've never once known him to lose his temper.

I also knew I had to work with Luc Trullemans again, the Sky God as I now called him. What I admire most about him is his uncanny knack of predicting minute very local weather patterns, and since 2000 he had become a good friend, almost like an older brother to me in some ways. I asked him the night before we met for lunch in Belgium if he could look at historical tracks from St John's on Newfoundland in the summer; I'd need a flight profile of 5,000 feet after take-off, 7,000 feet during the second day, 10,000 feet on the third day and 13,000 feet the fourth. After two weeks Luc said he'd given up, he just had so many possibilities. I'd waited two months for my last weather window in New Brunswick.

My logistics director was Nigel Mitchell, an old friend who as managing director of Chase de Vere, had sponsored an earlier flight of mine. With his boyish grin I've come to rely on him, he and Bob Wilson becoming my retrieve crew on several balloon expeditions. Nigel flew out to St John's for a recce and everything seemed in place to fly from 1 July, 2007. It is always practically impossible to predict the exact day of any balloon flight, as there are so many different factors to take into consideration. One of the most difficult issues with this flight from Newfoundland was its extremely remote location. The truck containing our helium had to travel all the way from Toronto via a ferry to St John's. This cost tens of thousands of pounds and I knew that the clock was ticking as time passed.

We landed late on a Friday evening just before midnight, then on Saturday morning over breakfast we looked at our first weather data for a possible take-off time. Monday night immediately looked as if it would be perfect, but the minute we were given that as a possible launch target we were thrown into panic stations. There was so much we had to do in very little time: fit out the basket, fill the sandbags, put batteries on charge, get helium onto the field, perform the radio checks, prepare the food, do the Argos tracking system checks. Six hours later Luc called to say, 'Looks good for a flight straight over to Bristol.' My God, this was really going to happen fast! It was a hectic rush for everyone, but I actually prefer not having to spend too long hanging around.

Back in England the control room team, Flight Director Clive Bailey – who I consider to be one of the best control men in the world – and Air Traffic Control Co-Ordinator Kevin Stass, were busy getting ready at Toshiba HQ in Weybridge, Surrey. It's always useful to me that Clive is a balloon pilot himself, and since we've known each other a while he's very familiar with me indeed so he can easily judge my moods and seems able to second-guess my feelings at any time, which can be vitally important when you are severely stressed and things appear to be going badly wrong. As an excellent meteorologist he is also able to quiz Luc on flight paths. Clive is one of the most hyper men I know, like an untrained Labrador on Red Bull with so much energy he makes everyone else feel slow, whereas Kevin is the complete opposite being calm, collected and low-key, and that seems to make them a perfect combination.

On the day of the launch I was getting mixed messages about the weather tracks we could expect. Bert Padelt said he was convinced we had an absolutely perfect one we shouldn't miss. However Tim Cole, whom I of course also trusted hugely, warned 'Whatever you do, don't take off!' I told Bert what Tim was saying and he contacted Luc Trullemans, who insisted, 'Go! These are the best conditions you will ever have.' Then Bert came back to me and asked, 'What do you want to do?'

By this stage they had started to fill the balloon with gas. I spoke to Luc myself and told him, 'Tim doesn't want me to fly. Are these valid concerns?' Since Luc was the meteorologist who had helped me fly safely to the North Pole and back when everyone else said I stood no chance of getting there, he was a man I literally trusted with my life. In the end I followed my gut instinct and Luc's advice. After kissing a cod for good luck (a weird local superstition, but I wasn't taking any chances) I was ready to fly. At 11.30 Zulu (GMT) Monday night, I slipped into my immersion suit and put my lucky bead in my mouth. I also wore a parachute, as the very start of a flight is when your balloon is at its heaviest, and if a seam is ever going to split it most likely would be then, although you take it off after a couple of hours. Bert said the Balloonist's Prayer and I was away – 00.00 Zulu.

It was pitch black, I was surrounded by mist and fog, and I felt like I was going straight up in a lift. For a while I could hear a warning horn in the distance, and then there was complete silence. I thought, 'Christ, am I making the right decision?' Up through the thick cloud I went and then, suddenly at 3,000 feet, it was like turning on a light switch; up above were brilliantly gleaming stars and a full moon. I was on my way.

I had to stay north of a nasty weather system. The first day I was hanging around at 5,000 feet at only 5 knots. Luc had 'parked' me so I wouldn't catch up with some bad weather heading over into Europe. That first day out of Canada was very hard because it was such slow mileage. I was only moving at 2 or 3 miles an hour, still within spitting distance of land, and sometimes I could hear helicopters passing beneath the cloud. So far to go, and the constant fear in my mind was that I would run out of ballast half-way across. I was genuinely worried that I might have to land in the sea. Occasionally I contacted Luc to ask him what was going on, but he just said, 'Don't worry Hempie, this is exactly where I want you.' He kept reassuring me where I would be in a few hours' time and he was always bang on the money.

However with nothing much happening it gave me plenty of time to think. I have often been asked, 'What do you fear most on a balloon trip across the Atlantic?' My biggest anxiety has always been, without any shadow of doubt, that I might have to ditch in the North Atlantic, in pitch blackness with a swell, lose my dingy and get tied up in the flying wires. In the run up to the flight this had become a frequent recurring nightmare for me. The truth is I frankly don't like water very much at all and I'm not actually a terribly strong swimmer. This fear of drowning meant that every hour I was flying the balloon I kept rehearsing my ditching drill like a mantra:

Contact the control room with latitude and longitude.
Switch on the McMurdo (a satellite tracking beacon).
Do up immersion suit, put on life jacket, clip life raft to me.
Get grab bag full of radios ready.
Take seasickness tablets.

Meanwhile, back at the control room in Weybridge Clive and Kevin, plus two pilots, Graham Duff who I'd later take to Everest and Jordan River Scott, all got themselves into a great routine and did their best to keep me calm. The second day out my speed started to pick up and I went through the 15 knot barrier for the first time. I even managed to catnap quite well for the first couple of hours in the morning. All through the flight I slowly climbed, picking up speed as I went. Bert had given me a flight profile all through each day and night, with exactly how much sand I would use until I landed – he was not 20lbs out at the end. I suspect that even this difference was probably because I didn't lose as much body weight as expected during the crossing, as well as the fact that I'd given him a slightly false take-off weight, my pride having got the better of me. Luc had also given me a flight plan which was split up into detailed weather forecasts for each six hour period, giving tracks and speeds. I spoke to him every day, partly for a sociable chat to stop me getting too lonely but also to go over the weather data in depth. When I eventually landed he was just 10 miles out.

If you count the sandbags after day three and the answer is

right on the money, when Clive tells you the first blush of light will hit the horizon at 6.00 a.m. with sunrise at 7.20 and it is, when Luc tells you at 4.00 a.m. you will be tracking on 095 degrees at 45 knots and you are, it all gives you a feeling of complete confidence, but certainly not arrogance or complacency. So many balloons have gone down in the sea within sight of land. I still prayed, I still had my lucky bead in my mouth when trying to find a track. I always shivered uncontrollably from the cold at night. I never stopped fearing the big black hole below waiting to swallow me up.

I became increasingly tired during the flight because I was getting no chance of any decent REM sleep, which is always one of the greatest physical challenges in long-distance ballooning when you are confined within a very cramped basket. This certainly started to influence the way I was thinking, and in many ways is more debilitating than physical tiredness. Coming over the halfway mark, into the 20's of longitude, I saw a plane coming straight for me. I panicked, put on the strobe light and tried repeatedly to contact them on the VHF radio. This was the most frightening moment of the flight and perhaps of any expedition I have ever been on.

I knew that there shouldn't be any planes in the vicinity and I couldn't begin to understand how there could be an aircraft with its landing lights on slowly heading directly my way. I switched the VHF to an emergency channel and prayed the TCAS (Traffic Collision Avoidance System) in the plane would alert them to my presence. Why on earth did the pilot have his landing lights on? As my terror grew I contacted Kevin at HQ and begged him to tell me if they maybe had a plane up filming me for some reason. I was getting frantic, hyperventilating, desperately trying to think of anything I could do to avoid being mown down by this approaching jet. Clive came back on the phone to me and said, 'Hempie, there is absolutely nothing out there!' After five minutes of mind-numbing terror, when the plane didn't seem to be getting nearer as I would have expected and I slowly realized that I couldn't actually hear its approach, it finally dawned on me that in fact it wasn't at all an aircraft but the planet Venus I was seeing, big, bold and bright. I felt an idiot at having made such a mistake, but was almost weeping with relief at the same time.

By the third night I was tracking in at 50 knots, gobbling up the distance. Whilst I was above the clouds, I could still judge the speed by looking down at them. I knew I'd beaten the AA-06 distance record over the sea, but actually by this stage I don't think I was remotely interested in breaking any records. All I desperately wanted now was to be over land. I was utterly exhausted and fed up of being on the edge with the possibility of still landing in the waves below.

My path had taken me well south of England and coming up towards Nantes in France, in the early hours of the morning, I started to run parallel to the coastline. I immediately started to panic that I was about to start heading back out to sea. I was so tired and completely shot, I really didn't know where I was going. Clive said, 'Don't worry, just keep giving us your position.' I knew I had to put my faith in the team, but it seemed an age before I finally made landfall. Ironically, Jordan River Scott was then doing his day job flying into Nantes, and we chatted through air traffic control to keep me company and take my mind off my fears. Kevin had sorted me out a clear motorway corridor through France. I was desperate to land as soon as possible, but the ground speed was zipping along and I'd agreed with Clive that sunset at Dijon would give me the slackest winds for a safe touchdown. Fail on that and I would be rushing headlong into the Alps, my biggest anxiety now.

I got my orders in from Clive: 'Slow down!' Down 3,000 feet, 20 knots still. Over the hills I was gradually descending, but then it became very thermic. The wind speed was getting far too high. I was rapidly approaching the Swiss–French border and I was now very light. A spoonful of sand over the side and up I went! Approaching Nolay and above an uphill sloping field the other side. I was going very fast at 50 knots again now and all I could see were vineyards beneath me, and as I dropped I was tossed violently around. I threw out some sand and shot up immediately. I saw the Nolay church spire approaching and thought, 'I must miss it!' I decided I had no option but to land into the hillside and, true enough, I smacked into the side of a 45-degree slope. It was like being in a car crash without a seat belt on.

I landed at 15 knots, trail rope out. The balloon was so small at 37,000 cubic feet that people must have thought it was nothing more than a small hot-air balloon out on a brief pleasure flight. How many locals these days go and see a hot-air balloon landing around Britain? Zero. When the Americans landed in France in the seventies, after becoming the first ever successfully to cross the Atlantic in a balloon, there were thousands of spectators waiting to greet them. My only visitors on arrival were nine bemused cows.

Within no time at all my loyal ground crew Nigel and Bob turned up with the Union Jack flag and a bottle of champagne. Then the cavalry arrived: German, French and British media. My feet were badly swollen due to the lack of any real movement in the cramped wicker basket, but despite this minor inconvenience I felt pure relief to be back on solid earth. On reflection, I'd been quite naïve about the trip. I had thought that if I needed to ditch in the Atlantic I could simply inflate my life raft and bob around for a few days until someone came to get me, but I didn't see a single yacht or ship during my entire crossing until I reached the coast of France.

Except for the first morning I'd had to rely on half hour-kips – anything longer and I could have woken up to find the balloon falling into the sea. And the sleep deprivation had made me utterly paranoid. I was petrified that in my sleep I would accidentally pull on a release rope and expel all the helium from the balloon, and that would definitely have been that. Clive told me I'd broken five distance and duration records. Normally I'm actually quite unconcerned when someone breaks one of my records, but this time I certainly felt I wanted to keep hold of them all for a while. I've been on some challenging flights but, without a doubt, this one came closest to the wire.

In one way at least ballooning is similar to climbing, in that it has many different facets and there are a great variety of ways in which you can participate. A climber can simply want to tackle the technical challenges of an indoor climbing wall, or short climbs when bouldering, but at the other end of the scale they can set out to become involved in high-altitude mountaineering with the different necessary skills to tackle rock and ice. With ballooning at its most basic level you have private pilots off on a jolly flying in hot-air balloons. That's what I am much of the time, even if I do have a commercial licence, but although I sometimes take passengers I don't fly people for a living in any sense.

Many of the balloons you see in the UK will be doing just this, particularly around Bristol which has a large number due to the location of Cameron Balloons, who build many of those that appear in the skies above England, but in the summer you'll see them all over the place. Then you get the commercial pilots who offer rides, the ticket stating that the flight will be exactly an hour, plus or minus to allow for the weather, as any more than that would use too much gas and eat into their profit margins. The more people they can fly, of course, the more they earn. You'll see a lot of almost surreal sponsored balloons, either amusing or ugly depending on your taste. You can probably imagine the one that is an advert for Wonderbra, but there is also a supermarket shopping trolley that flies about. Then you have the gas pilots who just do long distances, mostly in Europe. These are a bit defunct now, although every decade or so people start to talk about them again as a cheap way of moving freight, and they have had a revival recently with coastguard operations in the US. I suppose you might liken most of these to the commercial mountain guides you get in the Alps. At the very pinnacle are the sports balloonists, the real long-distance flyers, who try to cross the Atlantic, fly around the world, or take part in the great balloon races.

Hot-air ballooning is the oldest form of aviation – going back to the days of the Montgolfier brothers in the late eighteenth century – but it took a great leap forward only about fifty years ago with the developments of a couple of American engineers. As part of NASA they were experimenting with burners and propane, and although it might seem relatively low-tech they came up with the sort of cylinder we use today. Gas ballooning, on the other hand, has been going on in Europe for well over a hundred years, which explains its far more widespread prevalence on the continent, where it has become a great tradition.

Many of the original European clubs used town gas to inflate their balloons, and would have an underground pipe running from a factory to provide hydrogen or coal gas, which might be free but very flammable. You can turn up at many places in Germany, Belgium, Switzerland or France and find a launch field, pristinely cut like a bowling green, with a club house and sandpit, and a balloon meister who will inflate and set up your balloon for you. In these countries today there are hundreds of balloonists who go out every weekend and fly for hundreds of miles. Gas ballooning is a wonderful sport since, unlike in a hot-air balloon where you might fly for an hour or two and the limiting factor is your amount of propane (when that runs out you have to land), with a gas balloon you can be up for several days and get forty-eight hours in the air for exactly the same cost.

The physical art and experience of flying a gas balloon is also very different. With a hot-air balloon you will usually have the burner going virtually continuously, and you can hardly hear yourself talk or think. A gas balloon, though, is totally silent. You hear dogs barking in the distance, trains running miles away, and you almost feel as if you are floating on a magic carpet. It is the most serene form of flight, absolutely fantastic. You still have a retrieve crew, of course, usually of two so that they can take turns driving. They will hang around for a couple of hours after you take off until you have a rough sense of where you are heading, then set off following you like the clappers. With retrieve crews it tends to be a matter of great pride to try and keep up with a balloon, and at night they obviously can't see you. Even if you are only travelling at 20mph, you are moving in a straight line and it can be a devil of a job keeping pace.

I'd only had a very limited number of hot-air balloon hours under my belt before I went to the North Pole, but after I had completed that journey I suddenly had a huge number of Rozier gas balloon hours on my licence from that trip. I thought I could do anything as a result, but I still actually knew very little about the elite end of ballooning even though I was now planning to cross the Atlantic. It was while waiting in Sussex for my third and finally successful attempt at that first of my Atlantic crossings, that Bert Padelt told me a whole lot more. He'd hoped to remain with me until I finally left, but he explained he had a prior commitment and had to leave as he was flying in the America's Challenge Gas Balloon Race, which is held out of Albuquerque each year. This was complete news to me, I'd never heard of it or anything about balloon racing, so Bert explained everything to me before he went.

The Gordon Bennett Cup is the most prestigious event in balloon racing and the oldest aviation competition in the world. It was first held well over a hundred years ago when it flew from Paris in September 1906, although there was a long hiatus from 1939 when the planned event to be hosted in Poland was overtaken by more historically significant events, until it was reinstated in 1979. James Gordon Bennett who first sponsored the competition was a newspaper proprietor, his father of the same name having founded the *New York Herald*. No one really seems to know where the expression 'Gordon Bennett' denoting amazement or surprise actually comes from, but it probably has something to do with how newspapers at the time were always trying to come up with new scoops and angles to publicize themselves, and the son was perhaps most famous for having dispatched the reporter Henry Stanley to find Dr David Livingstone in Africa in 1871.

Gordon Bennett junior sponsored various different sports and there were in fact originally three other Gordon Bennett Cups, much less long-lived, for biplanes, racing cars and sailing schooners. Gordon Bennett senior had been born in Scotland and his son was something of a playboy as well as a sportsman, with a rather dissolute reputation. A famous if possibly apocryphal story relates how he was engaged to a British woman and, during a drunken dinner in England, rather than withdraw in more seemly fashion he had chosen to relieve himself in the grate of the fireplace, causing his prospective father-in-law to cancel plans for the wedding on the spot.

The basic rules of the competition are very simple and have never really changed, although there is a huge amount of associated protocol and messing about involved that has always driven me barmy. All the balloons must have a capacity of no more than 1,050 cubic metres, and a great deal of checking goes on to ensure everyone is following the correct specifications and rival teams frequently challenge each other over breaches. Each national association may enter three teams, who represent their country rather than simply flying as individuals, and both pilot and co-pilot must be citizens of that same country. Pilots need to have a minimum of fifty hours flying time in command of a balloon, be authorized for night flying, and at least one of each team must be able to communicate with Air Traffic Control in English.

The winning team is the one that travels the greatest distance as the crow flies, which of course you don't, from the starting point, and there is no time limit, but there are many different grounds for automatic disqualification. This happens if you land in water, or also if you break one of the air traffic control regulations of any country you happen to fly over. This can be a major problem in Europe because some countries, such as Italy, do not allow night flying for balloons. An even starker issue is that others, like Russia or Belarus, don't allow entry at all into their airspace. A military helicopter from the latter actually shot down a balloon flying in the Gordon Bennett Cup in 1995, killing the two American pilots Alan Fraenckel and John Stuart-Jervis who were competing for the Virgin Islands, so we take that danger pretty seriously and any risk of crossing their borders means you have absolutely no choice other than to land.

The competition has always been hosted by the national association of the country from which a team won the year before, now changed to two years previously, a little like the Eurovision Song Contest. They decide the most suitable place to fly from, in terms of support a particular town might provide and the likely weather conditions that should lead to the best possible race, and it always leaves on the Saturday night closest to the weekend of the full moon in the first couple of weeks in September. In many European countries where there are numerous excellent and very experienced pilots, such as Germany or Switzerland, competition to fly can be desperate and cut-throat, and the former has a very complex system for selecting who takes part based on a premier league of pilots, with points awarded for hours and distance flown in the preceding year. There never used to be enough British teams wanting to take part, so if you wanted to fly you could, but nowadays it has become more competitive here partly, I feel, because I have managed to raise the profile of the sport.

I first flew in the America's Challenge Gas Balloon Race in 2005 with my co-pilot Jon Mason. This always leaves from Albuquerque in October and was first held in 1995, having almost exactly the same rules as the Gordon Bennett. The balloons have the same capacity and the winning team is also the one that flies furthest, the one major difference being that there is no limit on the number of national teams entering and they allow the pilot and co-pilot to be from different nations, which has caused them quite a few problems over the years. Since America also has a lot of pilots desperate to compete in the Gordon Bennett Cup, it acts in the same way as their Olympic trials with the top three placed American pilots being selected for the other event. It wouldn't matter if you had won the Gordon Bennett five years in a row, if you don't get that top three in the America's Challenge you won't get picked the next year. Since the pilot always selects his co-pilot, there have been cases of relative novices picking co-pilots who are far more experienced than them, from Germany say, attempting to use the rules to beat the selection process.

Albuquerque is a place I absolutely love to fly from, which no doubt has something to do with the fact that in the five times I've done so my worst showing has been to come third. At the start of my first competition it almost seemed as if we were jinxed however. Although he was also competing himself Bert had very kindly lent us one of his balloons, and his wife Joan was going to retrieve for us, but just before we were ready to leave she got a call that one of her boys was sick so she had to rush off. We just thought, oh well, we'd hitch-hike back or hire a van. Then, when the balloon was inflating, the gas entry nozzle shot out and broke Jon's finger. What an absolutely great start that was!

We took off into the night and for various reasons a lot of the other balloons in the competition landed very quickly. Heading north we crossed over the Canadian border, and eventually landed in woods nearly 2,000 miles from where we had started. We were pretty amazed that on our first outing, and from about twenty-five entries, we came third. It's actually fairly likely that we could have pushed on and won the whole thing at our first attempt, since the balloon that did so was only about 50 miles ahead of us and we still had some ballast left, but we'd found a suitable landing spot and felt we should use it. If we'd carried on it would probably have meant coming down in much thicker forest, and it seemed like rather poor etiquette to borrow a balloon from someone and then trash it in the trees. We were absolutely delighted with third place anyway. In some ways it hadn't been a terribly eventful flight, but getting back was another matter entirely.

We got a lift in the middle of nowhere from a guy called Mike. He called some friends of his who came out with a pick-up truck and drove us back to the nearest little town where they lived, then found us rooms in a small hotel. The next morning we went to their factory where all our stuff had been held overnight, as we had to set off back to Albuquerque, since with a rostrum finish we needed to be there for the awards ceremony and all the usual backslapping. We hadn't thought it would be difficult, but it soon became apparent that no one was prepared to hire us a truck that we would then be taking over the US border. We seemed stuffed, until Mike said he'd drive us down in his truck to the US border himself. It was about a three-hour drive, but once we'd crossed the border and found a truck hire company Mike changed his plans again. We'd got on really well and because he was just divorced, perhaps a bit lonely and at a loose end, he said he'd come all the way with us back to Albuquerque.

We took it in turns driving the 1,800 or so miles back, stopping only for comfort breaks and to grab some food, in not much more than a day, one of us usually sleeping whilst the others swapped behind the wheel. Only about six hours after we arrived, Mike said goodbye and drove all the way back by himself. We heard later that when he returned the truck just before the border the manager there who checked the mileage was furious, cussing out the idiot he was certain must have recorded it incorrectly before we left. There was no way, he was convinced, we could have driven over 3,500 miles in three days, but we had. Since he so obviously wouldn't have been believed Mike said he didn't bother trying to correct the mistake. We kept in touch after that, and Mike and a friend of his even came over to Europe to retrieve for us with my Shogun in our first Gordon Bennett race.

In 2006 the Gordon Bennett Cup was held in Belgium and Jon and I were rather nervous as we knew we'd be flying north and then crossing the North Sea. I'd flown over the Atlantic of course, but not then in a balloon of this size, and Jon certainly hadn't done anything like it before. To make matters worse there is always a great deal of hanging around, as the regulations state that you have to be there several days before the race starts (one year they actually tried to disqualify me when I arrived a little late). At the opening ceremony there is a huge amount of razzmatazz, and everyone is obliged to stand to attention for the singing of the anthem of the Fédération Aéronautique Internationale. There is something slightly fascistic, or at least rather Ruritanian, about the whole affair. At the opening ceremony they also draw lots by country for the departure sequence, with the teams then going one at a time in that order so they are separated from their compatriots.

On the evening of departure all the balloons are weighed-off and a checklist of each one conducted to ensure that everything is according to the rules. There is often a fair bit of shenanigans and arguing about this, since all the pilots want to keep as much ballast as they can because an extra bag of sand either way can make all the difference between winning or not. The Launch Master is anxious to get rid of you as fast as possible, as each balloon is brought over to the podium about three minutes apart. They play your national anthem, he says 'hands off', and off you go up and away, slowly if you have managed to stay heavy or like a rocket if you've been conned out of too much sand and you are light. You need to be certain you aren't too heavy however, since if there is any problem in your getting away you go straight to the back of the queue.

We left at dusk and headed into the darkness. In the total silence as we ascended the noise of the big crowd rising towards us was deafening, but slowly that faded. For an hour or so we could see the strobe lights of all the other balloons ahead and behind us, but after that the distance between them gradually increased and we seemed to be totally alone. Our path took us over the Channel to England and I vividly remember going over Norfolk, hearing people outside in their gardens having barbecues and then the voices of people as the pubs emptied out. It was just incredible the way sound travels upwards. You could discern every word of the argument a couple were having. Quite a few balloons landed there, obviously chickening out from heading off across the North Sea, but we were determined we weren't going that way. It was misty now, so we couldn't see any other balloons or anything below, but we could hear the intercoms on the oil rigs telling the workers their lunch was ready. It was a very eerie feeling, and because Jon is a psychologist I always have the slight feeling when flying with him that I am being observed.

There seemed to be two tracks that the balloons which had

carried on were splitting between. One headed in across southern Norway and Sweden, and most people decided to take that route and then landed as it was nice and flat there with few hills. We chose a more difficult northern route up past the Shetlands and came in over the mountains north of Bergen. By this time we were really tired, and were buffeted about by heavy turbulence over those mountains. We knew from our ground crew that there were only four teams still flying, all on slightly different tracks now, so we were in with a chance. We then crossed Sweden and into Finland, but we were running out of anywhere to go.

Neither of us felt terribly confident about landing the balloon, as a gas balloon is a much harder thing to put down safely than the hot-air variety. Most German pilots, with so much practice, can bring themselves down on a postage stamp, but we hadn't had many landings and there are a lot of trees in Finland. From the information provided by our retrieve team, who were able to follow what was happening on the official website, it was clear to us that with our track there was now no way we could manage better than third place, but that was still the highest ever for a British team. We absolutely had to land before we hit the Russian border or be disqualified, or worse still shot down, and as there was no point pushing on further into Finland we looked out for a suitable landing spot. The winning team eventually landed just before the Russian border but much further north than us up near the Arctic Circle.

As we were coming in I got the trail rope out and let it down, and then we saw a lake approaching and I had to haul it all the way in again. That really is back-breaking work when you are feeling shattered after three nights without sleep. We'd seen on the map that there was a village nearby called Minnervi Verni, so we might be able to get some help and wouldn't be stranded in complete wilderness. We hit the ground in a marshy area, let the gas out of the top of the balloon and made everything secure.

Once we were down we contacted the Gordon Bennett control centre who are always very professional and know exactly what to do. They said they would ring the local fire brigade and try to get someone to us as soon as possible. The emergency pack they provide for each pilot includes a phrasebook with useful things to say in every European language. I found the phrase in Finnish that said, on behalf of the Gordon Bennett Committee, these two guys are pilots flying in our competition and please will you provide them with whatever assistance they need and that you can. At least, I think that's what it said, but obviously I didn't know a word of Finnish and it could just as easily have been something much less complimentary. I went so far as to phone up my friend Rune and asked him if he could speak any Finnish, but not even he could.

We hung around for a while twiddling our thumbs, and after an hour or so this guy turned up on a four-wheel-drive quad bike. From the full gear he was wearing he was clearly a fireman, so I handed him the phrasebook and pointed at the appropriate sentence, smiling in what I hoped might be an ingratiating fashion. 'Welcome to Finland' he said, in impeccable and what seemed entirely unaccented English. When I complimented him on this he explained the reason for his fluency, saying that he worked for Santa Claus as one of his gnomes. I assumed he was taking the mick, but he then told us how Minnervi Verni is famous worldwide for the Santa's grotto that they have there each Christmas. Apparently, every winter you get up to 10,000 English-speaking people who come for the experience, reindeer and everything. He might be a fireman by day, but in the evenings he was also one of Santa's little helpers.

After about five trips with the bike he finally got all our stuff to the nearest road, at which point Mike and his buddy, our two

Canadian retrievers, arrived to meet us. They'd known we would be heading towards Scandinavia, and even with that head start had done an incredible job of getting to where we were within hours of us. With a top three finish Jon and I had to fly back via England to Brussels for the closing ceremony, which is always held on the Saturday a week after the racers set off. We'd never have made it by road, as that would have been a four or five day drive. I almost wish we hadn't bothered.

When we reached Brussels we immediately found ourselves involved in an incredible amount of hassle. It transpired that one of the four teams that had gone through Norway had done so without contacting ATC, and the Norwegians had been obliged to close down their air space. Now they were threatening to prosecute the whole Gordon Bennett organizing committee unless they found out which particular team had transgressed. I knew we had talked to ATC, and it should have been perfectly easy to prove it from the unique code on our transponder, but we were virtually frogmarched into a room and made to fill out all our logs and give the exact details of our track.

Jon had just got married and was terrified that he might suddenly be facing a legal bill of up to a million quid, and I wasn't too chuffed with the idea either. Surprisingly it turned out that the culprit was one of the German teams, but I still think the Belgian authorities and their Gordon Bennett Committee treated us appallingly. I've never forgotten or forgiven this, and it was pretty clear from the start that they were pointing the finger at us as the guilty party without any evidence whatsoever. We were certainly much less experienced than the other three teams, and I can only assume that our getting third place on our first attempt had put a lot of people's noses out of joint. We were absolutely thrilled by what we had managed to do, but this behaviour definitely made it feel as if a bit of the shine had been taken off our achievement.

* * *

The race from Waasmunster in Belgium in 2006 in which we'd come third had been won by a Belgian team, so the 2007 event was scheduled to leave from Brussels, but the whole thing had to be cancelled due to bad weather. Without a winning country for their national association to host the 2008 event the rules stated that they had to look back to the last non-Belgian winners, who were Richard Abruzzo and Carol Rymer Davies in 2004. They had hosted the event from Albuquerque in 2005 (which had obviously been won by Belgians), when due to the local weather the race was unusually held in October, at the time the America's Challenge is usually flown, and which this year the Gordon Bennett Cup replaced. It all sounds very complicated, but rules are rules, particularly in the case of the Gordon Bennett committee. With a couple of placings in races to our names now, and the event due to fly from Albuquerque again in October 2008, we naturally wanted to take part since we'd done so well there in the past.

Although we were the only people wanting to enter, we still had to apply to the British Balloon and Airship Club to be nominated. I'd written to the chairman to tell him that we planned to be there, and he ticked me off in no uncertain terms saying that we still had to go through the formal application process again, even though there was no one else up against us and there could have been three teams anyway. Aaargh! What is it about balloons that makes people behave this way? Anyway, we were selected, as the only team flying for Britain, and off we went to Albuquerque. We borrowed a balloon and basket again from Bert, as that was cheaper than me buying my own or hiring one, and we had Tim Cole there to inflate for us. We arrived a couple of days early, and my two now old friends Nigel Mitchell and Bob Wilson came out with me to retrieve. Nigel has become a bit of a lucky charm for me, as I've always been placed when I have had him with me there.

We took off in the evening somewhere in the middle of the line, amidst all the fanfare of national anthems. I'd had the weather forecast from Luc, who'd said keep it low. The first couple of days will be very slow, and then you will begin to pick up speed. That night was certainly low and slow, but we started to head down towards Mexico and the White Planes missile testing ground. That is most definitely a no go area, and entering that would have disqualified us at once. I called up their ATC on our satellite phone and asked if we could come over? He said no. We'd have our transponder on and wouldn't land? The answer was still no. Even if we just skirt the edge? Look, he said, you're not getting this are you. No means no. You'll just have to land now. In the end we missed it by about a mile.

We then started to head back up north, and a full day after we had left, when other balloons were way out over the prairies, we found ourselves back over the launch site in Albuquerque again. In a whole day we'd effectively gone nowhere, zero miles! Nigel and Bob had washed their hands of us, assuming they'd have a pretty easy retrieve, as we were in last place by a country mile. But because we'd kept things low we'd hardly used any ballast and continued to stay down at only a couple of hundred feet. We threaded our way north through a pass between the Rocky Mountains and the mountains of Albuquerque, very beautiful country, heading up towards Santa Fe and back into the prairies.

It was now the middle of our second night, about 10.00 p.m., and I was flying the balloon with Jon asleep in the bottom of the basket. We were creeping along at about 5 knots, and I was chatting to our control room back home. Suddenly Clive Bailey came on the line. He's fairly excitable at the best of times, but now it was obvious he was just back from the pub and had a few drinks inside him. 'Luc says climb', he shouted, 'and you have to do it now! Lose 20lbs.' Action stations! I didn't want to use any sand ballast if I could avoid it, so I looked around to see if there was anything else we could dump. We had two big tractor batteries to run our radio, and one of those would have to go. Jon was still too groggy to consult, so I heaved one up to the edge of the basket and looked down. It was a clear night and I could see open fields below, so over it went. I actually heard it fall all the way down, and then there was a muffled thump. Immediately I felt the fabric of the balloon start to move and we began to climb at a hell of a rate. We shot up a couple of thousand feet, which put us on a completely new track at a much higher speed. Luc was dead right.

Heading out over the plains the next day we knew a lot of other balloons had already landed, having used all their ballast flying high over the mountains, and we were starting to creep up the field, picking them off one by one. It was very hot, and we had to put up sheets around the basket to protect us from the sun, but we had a peaceful day as we took turns kipping and drinking cups of tea. At various places we had to talk with military ATC and ask their permission if we could come through, and they were always eager to have a chat. One guy said they had a sortie flying through in ten minutes, and we heard him speaking with his pilots and asking them if they were ok with our location. We didn't hear them coming, but suddenly two fighter jets shot beneath our basket, screaming past with an incredible noise which scared the living daylights out of us.

On our fourth day, we were at about 10,000 feet, when suddenly we hit a snowy squall, the temperature dropped and we just fell from the sky. That meant throwing out a lot of ballast, but we knew we were doing well and were determined to keep going if we could. A big German rival of ours had just landed, and we were now briefly in the lead, but still had a very good Austrian team behind us. By the time it had got dark we were over Madison just north of Chicago, coming up to the Great Lakes. We only had one bag of sand remaining, and had to ask ourselves if we really wanted to cross a body of water as large as Lake Michigan, which is huge, at night?

We were down to 8,000 feet, and when you cross colder water there is always a drop in temperature which means you lose a great deal of lift. Apart from the battery earlier in our flight I'd already cut off and jettisoned half our trail rope. You aren't supposed to throw out anything apart from sand, and knowing the Gordon Bennett Committee it wouldn't totally surprise me if someone reads this and tries to disqualify us retrospectively, but everyone does it. Anyway, we didn't think we could make it all the way across the Great Lakes, so the only sensible thing to do was try and land as near as possible to the shore. Second place is better than a kick in the arse.

But it was solid woods below as we came in, Jon spooning out the ballast. We were very light now, well into our last bag of sand and just a little water left. Although it was pitch dark and the balloon totally silent, the incredible thing is that all the animals below could clearly sense our presence, and we heard the deer racing to and fro beneath us, the birds flying up. They know you are there, just skimming the treetops. I put the spotlight on, very glad to see a cornfield to put down in, and with what was left of our trail rope dragging behind we managed to hit the ground and come to a halt, half a bag of sand remaining. We really couldn't have got any further.

It was midnight. I contacted Clive, spoke to the Gordon Bennett control room in Albuquerque and gave them our co-ordinates from the GPS. Second place was great, but the Austrians were still flying. Seeing the lights of a farm in the distance we took our passports with us and headed in that direction, but began to worry that turning up in the middle of the night at a lonely house in mid-America was a recipe for getting our brains blown out. We shouted to alert anyone inside that we were there, but no one answered so we trudged off to find the main road. Whenever we passed another farmhouse we'd shout again, and now lights flicked on and dogs came out to bark at us, but no one emerged to ask who we were or what we wanted. We'd begun to think we might as well head back to the balloon when in the distance we heard a siren approaching. Obviously someone had decided to call the police, and we knew they were coming to get us.

We stood in the middle of the road with our hands up, and the police car screeched to a halt 30 feet from us and trained its searchlight into our eyes. Once we'd very politely confirmed his question that we weren't carrying any weapons, that we were just pilots who had landed nearby, he came and checked our passports and after that he was as nice as pie. Putting us in the back of his car he drove to the nearest hick town, and found us a motel where we checked-in at 1.00 a.m. Before we went to sleep we called Nigel and Bob, to say they should meet us there as soon as possible. It was actually my birthday, but we were so shattered we just crashed and went to sleep.

The next morning I emerged from the shower with a towel around me, and saw a note had been pushed under the door. I assumed it must be from the motel people, but it was actually from Nigel and Bob and I've kept it to this day. It only had two words on it, and just said 'you've won'. I thought they were taking the mick and phoned them up, but it was true. The Austrians had landed an hour after us, but just short of our distance, and we had indeed won the Gordon Bennett. I woke Jon up and gave him a big hug, somewhat to his surprise at first I imagine. Not only had we won, but we were the first British team ever to do so. After that we went out for a big breakfast, then to retrieve our balloon and thank the deep-sleeping farmer for the use of his field. It was a fun drive back to Albuquerque, and I remember a song by Elbow – who had just won the Mercury Prize – blaring out on the CD, which was our anthem that year. We were driving a big van and took three-hour turns at the wheel, whilst the others could kip and lounge in the back. We felt like kids on a road trip.

In Bert's balloon Lady Luck we'd flown for seventy-four hours and covered 1,100 miles. Of course, our winning the Gordon Bennett Cup presented a headache for the British Balloon and Airship Club, as they'd now have to host the competition themselves. This would actually be in September 2010, since the rules had just been changed to give national associations two years for planning, which we'd certainly need since it would be for the first time in England and everything would have to be done from scratch. Everyone was very excited about it of course, and Don Cameron set up and chaired a committee on which I also sat. Lots of cities wanted to act as host, and the Duke of Edinburgh even offered us the use of Smith's Lawn, a polo field just outside of Heathrow, although this didn't really feel like a terribly sensible location to fly from in view of other airborne traffic. Eventually everyone agreed on Bristol as giving the best package.

There isn't any prize for winning the Gordon Bennett, other than the cup itself that you have to hand back the next year. If you are borrowing a balloon, as we had done previously, you can probably do the whole thing fairly cheaply without spending a great deal. When hosting in Bristol though we certainly splashed out a lot, since we wanted to make a show and have our own marquee and toilets, something you definitely value if taken short just before lift-off. Having competed quite a few times now I can definitely say the sole British-held event thus far was the best organized competition I've taken part in, with a lavish champagne reception at the Wills Building, and the Civil Aviation Authority also came up trumps by agreeing to close an area of airspace for us between 11.00 p.m. and 6.00 a.m. We also had the largest field since the war with thirty-two entrants. We had a deliberate attitude of wanting as many people flying as possible, unlike say the Germans who often seem to use any excuse to try and disqualify you. To that end we did a lot of pre-checking well in advance, things like licences, insurance and medical certificates, to try and resolve any problems before people actually turned up.

This time I was flying with a new co-pilot, a neighbour of mine and a proper commercial airline pilot called Simon Carey who we all predictably nicknamed Scarey, but we also made history with a full complement of three British teams, one of them female. The departure point was from the Avon mouth, where you would normally get a sea breeze coming from the south-west, and we were praying for good weather. We had all these big tankers of hydrogen there, but only for two days so if the necessary conditions didn't come together that would have been the end of the competition. As it turned out the Saturday was perfect, crystal clear skies and winds of no more than 10 knots, so everyone could inflate comfortably during the day. Everybody we knew came down to wave us off.

Simon and I were flying a new balloon I'd bought and drew the very last place in the departure order lottery, lifting off just before midnight. We almost touched straight back down again on the podium, which would have been an embarrassing end to the race for us. We knew before the start that we would face a problem with the prevailing winds, which would have us heading out over the English Channel and across Europe, and later on if we got that far we'd almost certainly pass over Italy. With the Italian prohibition on balloons flying between an hour after sunset and an hour before sunrise, we had to ensure that we wouldn't be there at night. A Swiss team, the very first to leave, shot straight up to 14,000 feet and found a track that took them hell for leather across the continent at about 45 knots, which just brought them through Italy the following day with about fifteen minutes to spare. This was an incredibly audacious tactical gamble that paid off, but leaving ninety minutes later we never even considered that as an option.

We had to find a much slower wind speed, that wouldn't bring us to Italy before morning on the second day. Sometimes flying a balloon in a distance competition seems a bit like a three-dimensional chess game, and strategy plays a big part. Although it is described as a race it isn't really that, and many people prefer to be flying behind so they end up knowing exactly what they have to beat. The tortoise very often does end up beating the hare. Over the course of what might be three days, balloons hundreds of miles apart are obviously going to experience very different sorts of weather, and all these things have to be taken into account in your calculations.

We pottered across France and during the late afternoon when coming up to Toulouse Simon felt the call of nature. He and Jon are both wonderful pilots to fly with, but there is one very significant difference between them in that whereas Jon seems able to last a week without relieving himself Simon has to do so three times a day. In a basket about 4 by 5 feet, that rocks all over the place if you both stand up, this requires a lot of arrangement when you have all your equipment to move around, batteries and maps as well as yourselves. We had a contraption called a shit-box, which is pretty self-explanatory, into which you put a plastic bag, and whilst Simon was doing his business I'd look the other way and admire the scenery. From start to finish the whole thing must have taken nearly an hour, so it has always featured as a significant part of our trips together. I'm afraid we do tend to dispose of our bags over the side, as a sense of companionship can only extend so far.

A lot of balloons landed in the south of France as they didn't want to venture out over the Mediterranean, so that reduced us down just to the hardcore flyers, four or five of us. We had to avoid hitting Italian airspace before morning, which made a slow speed essential, and this required us to keep low. Flying over Corsica was out of the question, as the mountains would have sent us up to a higher wind speed, but we also had to avoid Sardinia as it is a part of Italy. Simon pulled off an incredible feat of flying in just managing to thread us between the two, and if you look at a map you'll see exactly how narrow that gap is. A German team were disqualified when they went further south than us, but we were safely through and reached Italy in the early morning, smack over Rome and able to see the Vatican City below. We had a fair bit of hassle with Italian ATC because of Rome's three commercial and military airports, who wanted us to fly at ridiculously specific heights, and we did have to climb high at one point to get over a bastard of a mountain, Monte Amaro I think, but by the afternoon we were safely out of Italian airspace and over the Adriatic.

We hit the coast of Croatia as it was getting dark and flew on over the Balkans through the night. By the morning we were very low on ballast, and there were only three teams still flying with the German Willie Eimers slowly trying to creep up on us. We knew we probably couldn't beat the Swiss, who had already landed long ago in Romania right on the coast of the Black Sea, but our track was taking us further south towards northern Greece and if we could keep going as far as the coast of the Aegean we might just pip them.

The Americans Richard Abruzzo and Carol Rymer Davies had taken a completely different route further south, with a longer crossing over the Adriatic to the bottom of Greece, which also might have won them the race. This was one of two options I had discussed with Luc Trullemans, but we had chosen the other one. We thought we had exclusive use of his meterological advice, but unbeknownst to us he was also advising Richard and Carol, which was a bit naughty. During the night we heard that contact had been lost with them and it was assumed they must have landed. Being a cynic and aware of all the possible ruses that pilots will try, I assumed they had probably just turned off their transponder, which isn't allowed but is something you can get away with if you pretend it was malfunctioning. It's happened before.

By the morning there was still no sign of them, and the weather was turning nasty with rain and much higher winds. With so little remaining ballast we couldn't cope with the thermals that were taking us up and down a thousand feet, so we decided we had to land. There were a lot of dense woods below us in that part of Serbia, but eventually we found some open space and managed to put down. The Swiss had beaten us, and Willie Eimers grabbed second place by just overtaking and coming down in Macedonia. He's a superb pilot, with probably 800 gas balloon flights to his name compared to my mere eight or so in total. I've probably got rather more respect for him than he has for me, since he considers me rather reckless, although he does concede me the backhanded compliment of saying that I am always a challenge to fly against as I've got no brain. But we reckoned third was an honourable position for a home team. It isn't the best of manners to grab all the presents at your own party, after all.

It took us two hours to walk out to the main road, by which time the local police who had been alerted by Gordon Bennett control were driving up and down searching for us. They looked after us fabulously well, and only about another two hours later our trusty retrieve crew of Nigel Mitchell and Bob Wilson also arrived, having followed us by car all the way from the French side of the Channel. The police entertained us in the nearest village with lots of schnapps, slivovitz probably, so we were pretty wrecked when the police commandeered a local peasant farmer's tractor and trailer and we had to set out with them to try and retrace our steps to find our balloon. The police all helped load it up, jackets off and sweating in the sun, but then had to drive us back to the police station in town. Obviously without stamps in our passports we were required to give statements about who we were and why we were there, and go through all the process of customs and immigration.

After a night in a hotel and yet more schnapps we headed back to England and Bristol, by which stage the devastating news about our American competitors was beginning to become apparent. Clearly they had been lost, and there certainly had been a big electrical storm over the Adriatic at the time, which was the main reason I hadn't chosen that route myself. The speculation was that they'd been struck by lightning, with search and rescue out, and the US military put a couple of planes into the air. In such a situation you would normally want to get down low with your life raft ready, so hopefully the storm passes above you and if you are hit you might stand a chance, but it wasn't until a couple of months later that their bodies were finally found. We'll never know exactly what did happen to them, but it certainly put a pall over what is always bleakly called the Survivors' Dinner, held that year in the Bristol Council Chambers the Saturday after our return. All thoughts were obviously with Richard and Carol, and their families who had flown over to be nearer to the search.

For the America's Challenge the next year, in October 2011, I was back in Albuquerque with Jon Mason, flying in just the night before the race with Jon arriving from Australia where he now worked. Since this had been such a happy hunting ground for us we superstitiously repeated our routine, going to eat in the same diner on Route 66 before our take-off in early evening. Once again we hoped to keep low and try to follow the same pass through the mountains as we had before, but this time the wind wouldn't take us that way and we found ourselves creeping up very slowly on the wrong side of the Rockies. Everyone else had gone high immediately, straight over the mountain range, and by the middle of the night were way out over the prairies. Our race was in danger of being a write-off almost before we started.

We hadn't used any ballast yet, and Jon then pulled off an incredible piece of flying using the cattabatic winds that slowly sucked us up and through a valley, flying low all the way, and out the other side. We knew we still needed to stay at as low a level as possible whilst easting as far as we could, as otherwise the winds would drag us north and back into the mountains. So we crept on into the morning, by which time all the other balloons were hundreds of miles away and some had even landed already. As the day wore on we started to pick off some of the stragglers, including several of those we viewed as our major competitors such as the previous year's winners. By the end of our third night we'd moved right up through the field and were now in second place. We could actually see the leading balloon ahead of us in the distance.

We followed them throughout the whole day, expecting them to land at any point, but they didn't. We'd both travelled a long way to be there, so we felt damned if we were going to stop before they did, and remained confident we must have more ballast left than they could due to how we'd reached where we were. We weren't far away from the Canadian border and it was getting on towards dusk, so we got permission ready to cross with a new transponder code. With night falling most people might have considered the sensible thing to do was land, since you want to do so in daylight and by morning we'd be up into the thick forests of Canada. This time however I'd bought my own balloon rather than borrowing one, and didn't feel constrained by the same worries about returning it in one piece. The competitive urge was so strong that I really didn't care about anything else and thought, we'll just trash it, and keep going all the way to the Arctic if necessary.

There had been heavy rain recently with flooding, and I could see lots of water beneath us. It was about 6.00 p.m. but we couldn't see the other balloon now, and more disconcertingly nor could we hear them on the radio. I asked Clive Bailey what was going on and he said they'd stopped, but he couldn't answer my other question of whether they'd actually landed. It could just be a ploy on their part, maybe they'd dropped low and were simply hovering, playing doggo, hoping to trick us into landing ourselves, showing our hand, so they knew for certain they could beat us. I called the Albuquerque control and asked if they could confirm that the other balloon had indeed landed, and they said, 'no Sir, we can't confirm that.' So, they weren't doing us any favours. Perhaps they preferred the idea of an American team winning, but more likely they didn't actually know themselves.

We were about 10 miles from the border and it was dark now as we carried on, when we finally got the confirmation we needed that the other balloon had landed. This left us a tricky choice, either of trying to land in the dark with all this water around, or push on until morning by which time we would be up into the thick woods. We'd landed in the dark before and were willing to risk that, but this time we were in a low level jet not that far above tree height that was carrying us along at 40 knots. Perhaps even lower down still it would be calmer, that was our hope. Everything was stowed for landing, with Jon ready to dole out our remaining sand and I had the trail rope out, but in the beam of our searchlight below all I could see was water. Shit! If we came down in that we would be disqualified. We had to get up again quickly and I pulled in the trail rope, and thank Christ I did as just then we barely skimmed over an electric pylon. This was certainly enough to get the adrenalin coursing through my veins.

Time to try again and this time it was just solid ploughed field that we thumped into, but there was no stopping us. The wind still dragged us along at 20 knots, bumping over the ground, the two of us crouched down in the basket for protection and desperately trying to pull the top out of the balloon. Crumbs, this was a lot more exciting, and a lot more dangerous, than any fairground ride. We were hurled around, ploughing up the mud which sprayed in around us, but by the time we finally did come to a halt we'd left a furrow two thirds of a mile long. Thank goodness for big American fields. We were both bruised and winded, but we couldn't stop laughing hysterically.

When we contacted the Albuquerque ground control they'd already called the local police to say there was an aircraft down, and they and the border patrol were out to find us. There were about six vehicles running around out searching, but we were sitting in this field in the middle of nowhere. Then, in the distance, we saw two lights approaching. It was a farmer and his girlfriend who had been following the race on the news. When they saw we had landed they got our co-ordinates from the website, worked out exactly where we were, and came to get us. They took us to the main road where the police now were, and not much more than an hour later our retrieve team arrived. The farmer helped us fetch the balloon from the field with his massive flatbed truck, we packed everything away and said goodbye and thanks to everyone, and then it was off to find the nearest hotel for a shower and dinner before starting the long drive back to Albuquerque the next morning.

The trip back is a whole lot more fun when you've won, and our reception when we returned was pretty satisfying too in a different way. I've always loved America and Americans, but their reaction to our victory was a bit churlish. They were distinctly miffed about losing to some Brits, which they didn't like one bit, no siree! But this added the America's Challenge to our names alongside the Gordon Bennett Cup. Although there are a lot more British entries to both competitions these days the only other British placing in either to date came from a young woman called Janet Folkes, who took a third place in the America's Challenge but has tragically since died of cancer.

I've certainly felt more actual sheer and unalloyed pleasure from my time spent in a balloon than anything else I have done, even if my achievements at the poles or climbing have brought their own very different rewards and feelings of satisfaction. I probably only have one more target I want to aim at in the same-sized balloon that I did the Atlantic. No one's ever done this and it sounds like fun. I'll keep you posted.

Afterword

I've had a truly wonderful life (so far!) and I consider myself incredibly fortunate in having had the opportunity to try and do all the things I wanted to attempt and achieve. I hope I've managed to explain a little about the influences that led my passions to develop in the direction they have, a constant search for adventure and new challenges, but I wouldn't pretend that things have happened in a way that followed any sort of organized plan. I'm certainly not a person, like some politicians maybe, who when young tried to sketch out their whole future career on the back of an envelope for instance. Everything that has happened to me really just seems to have been taking the logical next step that presented itself at the time. Completing the Seven Summits wasn't initially my plan, but once it was pointed out to me that it was within my grasp I pursued it with all the obsessive commitment I have. Being the first person to achieve the explorers' Grand Slam was really just the result of knowing I couldn't truly say I had proved myself until I'd made it to the North Pole. I suppose it is pretty obvious by now that having a fairly bloody-minded aspect to your personality goes with the territory, for someone like me.

Things have also happened as they did because I am not, nor have ever wanted to be, a professional at what I do, doing it for a living primarily. I am, or have become, an industrialist and businessman with a hobby in adventure, even if that hobby is an obsession that I have largely managed to make financially self-supporting. I am very lucky and grateful that so many individuals, businesspeople and companies – including my own colleagues, in allowing me so much time away – have been prepared to back me over the years, and I am also able to run expeditions for people who want their own taste of extreme adventure. I've now reached a time of life where I am slowly hoping to retire from industry and devote more time to my hobby, as there is so much I still want to do, but of course the new challenges I intend to set myself will be slightly different. I've achieved pretty much all I've wanted in mountaineering and polar expedition, and although I still climb and will certainly go back to Everest, and go to the Poles, it tends to be for shorter trips and often taking people for whom it is a new experience. I don't really see this as passing on the baton to a younger generation, but I am frankly getting a bit old for some of the longer journeys and don't quite enjoy them in the same way as I once did.

This was certainly part of the reason for my move into ballooning. None of what I've done would ever have been possible without the immense support from Claire over the years. Even though I've desperately wanted to be doing what I have I've always found it difficult to be separated from her when away, and of course that became increasingly hard after my three girls were born. I suppose it has always been a sort of balancing act, the urge to do something set against the guilt of disappearing somewhere inevitably dangerous, me worrying about them and knowing that they must be worrying about me. Over time I've felt those scales tip increasingly far in one direction, even if that isn't going to make me spend all my time at home with my feet up by the fire. The loneliness of two months away on the ice, or three months getting ready for a crack at Everest, was always very hard. Even today, with the incredible changes in communications technology, the separation of such expeditions is rather different to, say, being in America waiting to spend a few days crossing the Atlantic in a balloon, during which time you are always on the end of a simple phone. But Alicia, Camilla and Amelia are twenty-four, twenty-one and nineteen now, and perhaps don't need me in quite the same way, although it doesn't always seem like that if my credit card would come in handy.

I've discovered a new passion, for sailing, something else I can put my cold weather experience to, and I will be sailing in the Arctic and Antarctic regions, retracing some of the great sailors' trips and the journeys of the Vikings, going up Spitsbergen, to Iceland, Greenland, the Northwest Passage. I've spent a lot of time thinking about having a crack at a duration record, which really would be something, and there are still a couple of hot-air balloon duration and distance records I have my eye on. It would also be great to do a gas balloon flight with Alicia, who has her pilot's licence now, perhaps the Gordon Bennett or America's Challenge. Whatever happens, I expect to be busy.

David Hempleman-Adams

Born 10 October 1956

August 1980: Mount McKinley, Alaska, USA – highest peak in North America

August 1981: Mount Kilimanjaro, Tanzania – highest peak in Africa

March 1983: Solo and supported Geographic North Pole – *failed*

February 1984: First man to walk solo and unsupported to the Magnetic North Pole

2–21 April 1992: Led first group to Geomagnetic North Pole

October 1993: Mount Everest – South route through Nepal

August 1994: Mount Elbrus, Russia – highest peak in Europe

December 1994: Mount Vinson – highest peak in Antarctica

February 1995: Mount Aconcagua, Argentina – highest peak in South America

May 1995: Carstensz Pyramid, Papua New Guinea – highest peak in Australasia. Seven summits completed

7 November 1995–5 January 1996: First Briton to walk solo and unsupported to the Geographic South Pole

February–March 1996: Magnetic South Pole

5 March–28 April 1997: Geographic North Pole with Rune Gjeldnes unsupported – *failed*

5 March–28 April 1998: Geographic North Pole with Rune Gjeldnes supported – first person to complete the Explorers' Grand Slam

1998: First person to fly a hot-air balloon over the Andes

28 May–3 June 2000: First person to fly solo in a balloon to the North Pole

17 March–11 April 2003: First person to walk solo and unsupported to the Geomagnetic North Pole

September 2003: First person to balloon across the Atlantic in an open wicker basket. Two failed attempts September 2002 and 2003.

2004:   Breaks airship speed record

2004:   Flies Cessna light aircraft from Cape Columbia to Cape Horn

2004:   Breaks world altitude record for an airship

2004:   Breaks world distance record for an airship

October 2004:   Breaks world altitude record for a Rozier balloon. AM-05, 41,198 feet

January 2007:   Breaks AX-05 world altitude record for a conventional hot-air balloon. 32,480 feet

July 2007:   Flies the smallest gas balloon across the Atlantic

October 2008:   First British team to win the Gordon Bennett Balloon Race

21 May 2011:   Mount Everest – North route through Tibet

September 2011:   First British team to win the America's Challenge balloon race